FOOTBALL FATALITIES AND CATASTROPHIC INJURIES, 1931–2008

Football Fatalities and Catastrophic Injuries, 1931–2008

Frederick O. Mueller, Ph.D.

EXERCISE AND SPORT SCIENCE
UNIVERSITY OF NORTH CAROLINA-CHAPEL HILL

Robert C. Cantu, M.D.

EMERSON HOSPITAL-CONCORD, MASSACHUSETTS
BOSTON UNIVERSITY CLINICAL PROFESSOR OF NEUROSURGERY

CAROLINA ACADEMIC PRESS
Durham, North Carolina

Library of Congress Cataloging-in-Publication Data

Mueller, Frederick O.
 Football fatalities and catastrophic injuries, 1931-2008 / Frederick O.
Mueller, Robert C. Cantu.
    p. cm.
 Includes bibliographical references and index.
 ISBN 978-1-59460-447-8 (alk. paper)
 1. Football injuries. 2. Football injuries--Statistics. 3. Football players--
Mortality. 4. Football players--Mortality--Statistics. I. Cantu, Robert C. II.
Title.

 RC1220.F6M84 2010
 617.102763--dc22

                    2010030054

            CAROLINA ACADEMIC PRESS
                  700 Kent Street
           Durham, North Carolina 27701
             Telephone (919) 489-7486
                Fax (919) 493-5668
                 www.cap-press.com

Dedication

This book is dedicated to all of the football players who had a fatal or cata-strophic injury during their playing days. It is also dedicated to the researchers who were responsible for the many changes in the game of football that made it a much safer sport for the participants.

A special thanks to the American Football Coaches Association, the National Federation of State High School Association, and the National Collegiate Athletic Associations.

Thank you to JoAnn Mueller for reading this manuscript and making the many grammatical changes, and to Mike Oliver, Don Gleisner, Donald Cooper, and John Miller for their input into the chapter on the history of NOCSAE.

Contents

List of Images

List of Tables and Figures

Tables

Figures

Graphs

Foreword

Grant Teaff—Executive Director,
American Football Coaches Association

The book, *Football Fatalities and Catastrophic Injuries, 1931–2008*, by Frederick O. Mueller, Ph.D. and Robert C. Cantu, M.D., is a book on the history of football catastrophic injuries and the data collected by the American Football Coaches Association (AFCA) since 1931.

In 1906, the President of the United States, Theodore Roosevelt, determined that the game of American football needed to be fixed because, as the game was played at the turn of the century, catastrophic injuries were prevalent and there were few rules to govern the brutality of the sport. President Roosevelt asked prominent coaches of the day to fix the sport or he would strongly consider banning the game of football.

The coaches took the President's challenge seriously and began to create rules of play and conduct. Later, eligibility rules and academic requirements would be added as the National Collegiate Athletic Association (NCAA) was formed to enforce the new rules and regulations for the game of football.

In 1922, that same group of coaches formed an organization that they named the American Football Coaches Association. A code of ethics for coaching was laid out and in its constitution, AFCA determined "to maintain the highest possible standards in football and the profession of coaching" and to "provide a forum for the discussion and study of all matters pertaining to football and coaching."

One of the most important matters pertaining to football and coaching is the health and well-being of the student athlete. Information creates awareness and awareness creates rules, coaching techniques, and review of fundamental blocking and tackling. Therefore, data regarding catastrophic injuries in the game of football has been collected by the AFCA since 1931.

As a member of the Board, and as Executive Director, I have observed Dr. Mueller and Dr. Cantu as they have meticulously worked to secure the catastrophic injury data that has added to the desired health and well-being of our student athletes. In 1968, football had 36 fatalities. The research done by the

National Center for Catastrophic Sports Injury Research (NCCSIR), funded by the AFCA, played a major role in making the game safer, and in 1990 there were zero fatalities. In 2008, there were seven fatalities directly linked to football; all were at the high school level. The research and the data gathered on catastrophic injuries is more important now than ever, as more young men are playing the game from youth football through the professional ranks.

This book should be read by every football coach and administrator in America. There is a chapter on the history of football, and chapters with data on every decade of football beginning in 1931. Drs. Mueller and Cantu have compared the number of injuries to the rules and equipment that was used at the time. With the information provided by the yearly report and working with the NCAA, the AFCA has been a part of the implementation of numerous rule changes, spring practice and preseason legislation that provides a safer environment for workouts and games. The book clearly shows how equipment changes over the years have played a very important role in safety.

As long as there is a game of football, the work at the NCCSIR must continue to provide data that will make our great game safer.

The diligence and competence of accomplished men is shown in the details of this outstanding book on the 79 years of research that has made our game better and safer.

Football Fatalities and
Catastrophic Injuries,
1931–2008

Introduction

Ever since the first collegiate football game on November 6, 1869, the need to reduce injuries has played a major role in finding ways to improve the safety of the sport through rule and equipment changes. In that first game between Princeton University and Rutgers University (won by Rutgers, 6 to 4), there were 25 players on each side, and the teams played by any set of rules they decided on. There were no helmets, mouthpieces, or face masks. The game was more like soccer than football as we know it today. Prior to that first collegiate football game there were a number of secondary schools playing regularly on the Boston Common by 1860 (Danzig 1956).

With the death in 1896 of a University of Georgia player during a game with the University of Virginia, football was almost brought to an end in the state of Georgia. (3) When the *Chicago Tribune* newspaper reported 18 fatalities and 159 serious injuries in football during the 1905 season, there was great concern about the brutality of the game. (3) Columbia University abolished the game and did not play again until 1915. (6)

In October of the 1905 season, President Theodore Roosevelt called representatives from Harvard, Princeton, and Yale to the White House to discuss the brutality of the game. Roosevelt was an advocate of the sport, believing that it built character and that the roughness was an important part of the game. His concern in October 1905 was the intentional violence and unsportsmanlike conduct of the players. He had no intention of abolishing the game, but he wanted the dangerous elements eliminated. (5)

Not much change took place after this meeting, but a fatal head injury to a Union College player in a November 1905 game may have been the catalyst in reforming college football. In December 1905 the Chancellor of New York University brought together 13 football-playing institutions to make changes to the game. (3) They had a second meeting that same month with sixty-two football-playing institutions, and formed the Intercollegiate Athletic Association of the United States. This new committee joined together with the old rules committee, and after six meetings the game of football saw dramatic changes. Rules that were directly related to safety included personal fouls (kneeing, kicking, striking with the fist, etc.), unnecessary roughness (tripping, tackling out of bounds), tackling below the knees, and unsportsmanlike conduct (Nelson 1994). These changes to the rules can be attributed to the historic meeting called by President Roosevelt as well as the decision by the college presidents that it was time for change.

The number of football-related deaths declined in 1906 and 1907, but increased in 1908 along with a greater number of serious injuries. By 1909 there were 33 fatalities recorded that were directly related to football, but information on only 9 was credible (Nelson 1994). Another source recorded 26 deaths in 1909 (Watterson 2000). College football was again being closely looked at due to the rise in the number of fatalities. Most college presidents were in favor of football but had great concerns with the number of fatal and serious injuries.

In 1910 the Intercollegiate Athletic Association of the United States was renamed the National Collegiate Athletic Association (NCAA), which created its own football rules committee to help save the game. Some of the important rule changes in 1910 included requiring seven players on the line of scrimmage (any number could be on the line of scrimmage prior to this rule), requiring the passer to be five yards behind the line of scrimmage, dividing the game into four periods of 15 minutes each, ball must be put into play by being snapped and not kicked, and a player tackling must have one foot on the ground (eliminating the flying tackle) (Nelson 1994).

Another crisis related to injuries took place in the 1968 season when there were 36 fatalities directly related to football, the most in the history of the game (Mueller and Colgate 2007). Twenty-six were at the high school level, five at the college level, four recreational, and one professional. All of the direct fatalities in 1968 resulted from injuries to the head, neck, and spinal cord. These fatalities did not include the 12 indirect fatalities (heart attacks, heat stroke, etc.) that were also recorded. As shown in Tables I.1 and I.2, from 1966 through 1972 there were 178 direct fatalities at all levels of football and 77 indirect fatalities (Mueller and Colgate 2007). One hundred thirty-four of the 178 fatalities were at the high school level, 17 at the college level, 24 in sandlot, and three professional. Tables I.1 and I.2 also break down the injuries by year. These years were marked by the coaches teaching players to place their face into the chest of the opponent when blocking and tackling. This technique placed the brunt of the force to the head and neck of the tackler and blocker. If the player ducked his head and took the force of the blow to the top of the head, it created axial loading on the spinal cord with the result being a fracture and possible paralysis. Terms used to describe this technique were "face to the numbers," "butt tackling," and "goring."

Image I.1 Mars Hill College, North Carolina, 1914
Photo courtesy of Judy Dockery.

In addition to the fatalities, a study by Torg et al. (1979) indicated a total of 99 permanent cervical spinal cord injuries in high school and college football from 1971 to 1975. These fatalities and permanent disability injuries created a climate of lawsuits that imperiled the game of football. The lawsuits were drastically eliminating the number of sport equipment companies that were manufacturing football helmets. The number of football helmet companies, which numbered approximately 16 in 1968, dropped to two in the late 1970s. There was a major concern that if the fatalities and disability injuries did not decline, manufacturers of sport equipment would no longer find it profitable to produce football helmets. These difficult years were also associated with the fact that none of the football helmets on the market were required to meet any standard. Any individual or manufacturer could produce a football helmet and sell it to high schools, colleges, professional teams, and recreational leagues.

A major effort was made after the 1968 season to reduce the number of fatalities and disability injuries, and in 1976 a rule went into effect that prohibited initial contact with the head or face in blocking and tackling. In addition, a helmet standard by the National Operating Committee on Standards for Athletic Equipment (NOCSAE) was accepted in 1978 by the colleges and in 1980

Table I.1 Direct Football Fatalities 1966–72

Year	Sandlot	Professional	High School	College	Total
1966	4	0	20	0	24
1967	5	0	16	3	24
1968	4	1	26	5	36
1969	3	1	18	1	23
1970	3	0	23	3	29
1971	2	0	15	3	20
1972	3	1	16	2	22
Total	24	3	134	17	178

Source: Annual Survey of Football Injury Research 1931–2008.

Table I.2 Indirect Football Fatalities 1966–72

Year	Sandlot	Professional	High School	College	Total
1966	0	0	6	2	8
1967	0	0	4	1	5
1968	2	0	8	2	12
1969	3	1	8	3	15
1970	0	0	12	2	14
1971	2	1	7	2	12
1972	0	0	10	1	11
Total	7	2	55	13	77

Source: Annual Survey of Football Injury Research 1931–2008.

by the high schools. NOCSAE has been a leading force in the effort to improve athletic equipment and, as a result, reduce injuries. NOCSAE has also developed standards for baseball and softball batting helmets, baseballs and softballs, lacrosse helmets and face masks, and football face masks. In addition to the rule change and helmet standard, there was also an emphasis on coaches doing a better job of teaching the fundamentals of tackling and blocking and on better medical care of the injured athlete by physicians and athletic trainers. These changes directly reduced the number of direct football fatalities from 36 in 1968, to four in 1979, and zero in 1990. The 1990 report showed the first year in the history of data collection by the American Football Coaches Association (AFCA), the NCAA, and the National Federation of State High School Associations (NFHS) that there were no direct fatalities in all of football. (2)

More recently, football has been associated with concussions, heart-related fatalities, and heat stroke fatalities. If a player who has had a concussion returns to play prior to full recovery and receives another serious blow to the head, he may suffer second impact syndrome and possible death. Indirect fatalities related to the heart have also increased in the past 10 to 15 years and often outnumber the direct head and neck fatalities. Heat stroke deaths have been a concern since the 1950s and have numbered 39 during the past fourteen football seasons: 1995–2008 (Mueller and Colgate 2007). The highest number was eight in 1970. It is interesting that there were no heat stroke fatalities recorded from 1931 through 1954; the first case was recorded in 1955 (Mueller and Colgate 2007). The sports medicine literature states that with proper precautions, heat stroke fatalities can be eliminated. As with past crises, there are major efforts underway by researchers, athletic trainers, physicians, manufacturers, and coaches to help reduce or eliminate the injury problems associated with concussions, heart, and heat stroke-related fatalities.

The purpose of this book is to discuss catastrophic football injuries (fatalities and permanent disability) on a national level from the first organized data collection system to the present. The AFCA started catastrophic injury data collection in 1931 (*First Annual Survey of Football Fatalities*) and has continued every year since with the exception of 1942. The original survey committee was chaired by Marvin A. Stevens, M.D., of Yale University, who served from 1931 to 1942. Floyd R. Eastwood, Ph.D., from Purdue University succeeded Dr. Stevens in 1942 and served through 1964. Carl S. Blyth, Ph.D., from the University of North Carolina at Chapel Hill was appointed in 1965 and served through the 1979 football season.

In January 1980 Frederick O. Mueller, Ph.D., from the University of North Carolina at Chapel Hill was appointed by the AFCA and the NCAA to continue the data collection and research under the new title, *Annual Survey of Football Injury Research*. In 1987, a joint endeavor was initiated with the section on Sports Medicine of the American Association of Neurological Surgeons to enhance the collection of medical data. Robert C. Cantu, M.D., Chairman, Department of Surgery, and Chief, Neurosurgery Service, Emerson Hospital in Concord, Massachusetts, was selected for this position and has been responsible for the collection of medical data. The NFHS has also played a major role in data collection by being responsible for the collection of high school data. The NFHS individuals responsible for data collection began in 1965 with David C. Arnold, in 1979 with Richard D. Schindler, in 1997 with Jerry Diehl, and in 2006 with Bob Colgate.

In 1977 the NCAA initiated funding for the first *Annual Survey of Catastrophic Football Injuries*. Frederick O. Mueller, Ph.D., and Carl S. Blyth, Ph.D., at the University of North Carolina at Chapel Hill, were selected to conduct the research. The research is now conducted as part of the National Center for Catastrophic Sports Injury Research at the University of North Carolina at Chapel Hill with Frederick O. Mueller, Ph.D., Director, and Robert C. Cantu, M.D., Medical Director. The Annual Survey of Catastrophic Football Injury Research was part of a concerted effort to reduce the steady increase of football head and neck injuries taking place during the 1960s and 1970s. Catastrophic injuries were defined as football injuries that resulted in brain or spinal cord injury or skull or spine fractures. All cases involved some disability at the time of the injury and neurological recovery is either complete or incomplete (quadriparesis or quadriplegia). "Neurological status" refers to when the athlete is entered into the registry, which is usually two to three months after the injury. Football fatalities are not a part of this report.

Chapters discuss the history of football injuries by decade (1931–40, 1941–50, etc.) and critically analyze important circumstances in football that have played a role in fatality and catastrophic football injuries (equipment, rules, coaching, medical care, etc.). Additional chapters cover the history of brain and spinal injuries and how the detection and treatment have changed during the past 75 years, as well as heart-related and heat stroke fatalities. A chapter also discusses the history of NOCSAE and its effect on helmet standards and the reduction of football fatalities and catastrophic injuries.

Herb Appenzeller, Ph.D., who has been a pioneer and leader in the field of sport law and risk management since the 1960s, discusses risk management in football programs. A coach, professor, and administrator for 40 years, he has edited or authored 19 books and is recognized nationally for his work. He brings a unique and practical body of experience to the sport industry.

An important final chapter discusses recommendations for reducing football fatalities and catastrophic injuries.

References

1. Danzig A: *The History of American Football.* Prentice Hall,. Englewood Cliffs, NJ. 1956.
2. Mueller FO, Colgate B: *Annual Survey of Football Injury Research — 1931–2008.* American Football Coaches Association, National Collegiate Athletic Association, National Federation of State High School Associations. Waco, TX, Indianapolis, IN. 2007.
3. Nelson DM: *Anatomy of a Game.* University of Delaware Press. Newark, DE. 1994.

4. Torg JS, Trues R, Quedenfeld TC: The National Football Head and Neck Injury Registry. *JAMA* 241: 1477–1479, 1979.

5. Watterson JS: *College Football—History, Spectacle, Controversy*. Johns Hopkins University Press, Baltimore, MD. 2000.

6. Whittingham R: *Rites of Autumn—The Story of College Football*. Free Press, Division of Simon and Schuster. New York, NY. 2001.

Chapter 1

Fatalities and Catastrophic Injuries, 1931–1940

Chapter 1 and succeeding chapters on fatalities and catastrophic injuries, will be divided into the following three sections: 1) Fatalities and catastrophic injuries, 2) Football rules and equipment, and 3) Discussion.

Fatalities and Catastrophic Injuries, 1931–1940

Prior to 1931 football came under considerable criticism due to the great number of injuries and fatalities. The American Football Coaches Association (AFCA) thought it wise to study these accidents to answer the criticisms and to be able to rebut them. The research was carried out with the help of the National Safety Council, the National Board of Surety and Casualty Underwriters, AFCA President Marvin A. Stevens, and Professor Floyd R. Eastwood of the New York University School of Education. The results of the first preliminary study were presented to the football rules committee in February 1932. The 1931 study was conducted differently from today's research in that schools were contacted and asked to report information on all of their injuries and not only fatalities. (1) Sixty-four colleges sent in individual accident reports during each week of the season. In 1932, 157 colleges responded, accounting for 1,477 accident reports resulting in 12,632 days lost from practice and games (AFCA 1933). Each injury accounted for an average of 8.6 days lost. The colleges were located in 41 of the 49 states and districts of the United States. The knee was the part of the body most injured with 260 injuries, followed by the ankle and shoulder. Most of the injuries happened in games, but the most severe injuries (measured by time lost) took place in squad scrimmages. The most dangerous activity was tackling on the fly (tackling without feet on the ground) with 22 days lost per injury. Fractured bones accounted for the most severe injuries, followed by dazed or unconscious conditions (head and neck injuries). A comment in the report mentioned that severe head and neck injuries may have been due to not wearing helmets during practice and scrimmages. Recommendations for prevention after the 1931 season included a more thorough preseason training; better protection for the shoulder, elbow, and ankle; better protection for the head and neck; stricter interpretation of the rules by officials; and changes in night games and practices (specific changes for night games were not mentioned, but later reports mentioned poor lighting). (1)

In 1933, 117 colleges participated in the research project and a more detailed final report of the three years of data collection was presented at the AFCA national meeting in Chicago on December 26, 1933 (AFCA 1933). A few items of interest in the 1933 report mentioned improving coaching methods to help reduce injuries and fatalities. This preventive measure has been mentioned in every fatality report from 1931 through 2008. It recommended that players should not drop their knees into down-field blockers, should not sacrifice the passer or punter, and above all should not clip. Other areas mentioned were conditioning exercises in the summer and spring, proper equipment for all players, and thorough medical examinations before, during, and after the season.

The fatalities in 1931, as shown in Table 1.1, numbered 33, which included direct and indirect as they were not separated in early reports (AFCA 1932). Ten of the fatalities were at the sandlot level, 3 at the club level, 12 in the high schools, and 8 at the college level. It should be noted that in the early days of football, sandlot football was mostly played in a nonorganized fashion with no equipment and poorly maintained fields. There were no participation numbers for sandlot and club football and only high school and college incidence per 100,000 participants was available as shown in Table 1.2. In 1931 the high school incidence of injuries per 100,000 participants was 1.95 and the college incidence was 12.18. These figures were based on 616,000 high school players and 65,690 college players. (1)

As shown in Table 1.1, there were 32 fatalities in 1932 (AFCA 1933). The breakdown was sandlot (11), club (6), high school (12), and college (3). There was a major reduction at the college level from eight in 1931 to 3 in 1932. The high school numbers stayed the same and both sandlot and club saw an increase. The incidence rate per 100,000 participants stayed at 1.95 for the high schools, and the college incidence rate dropped from 12.18 in 1931 to 4.57 in 1932 (Table 1.2).

Fatalities in 1933 numbered 27, which was a reduction of 6 from 1931 (AFCA 1933). (2) College football had a reduction of one fatality from 1932, and high school football had an increase of one. Incidence rates per 100,000 participants were 2.11 for the high schools and 3.04 for the colleges. Parts of the body involved in the 1933 fatal accidents were the head and neck. At the conclusion of the 1933 report there were ten recommendations for preventing football fatalities (AFCA 1933).

Table 1.1 Football Fatalities Direct and Indirect 1931–40

Year	Sandlot	Club	High School	College	Total
1931	10	3	12	8	33
1932	11	6	12	3	32
1933	8	4	13	2	27
1934	4	4	13	4	25
1935	5	7	14	3	29
1936	12	2	15	1	30
1937	3	3	13	0	19
1938	3	3	8	2	16
1939	1	1	7	3	12
1940	2	1	7	1	11
Total	59	34	114	27	234

Table 1.2 Football Fatalities Direct and Indirect Incidence per 100,000 Participants 1931–40

Year	High School	College
1931	1.95	12.18
1932	1.95	4.57
1933	2.11	3.04
1934	2.11	6.09
1935	2.27	4.57
1936	2.43	1.52
1937	2.11	0.00
1938	1.30	3.04
1939	1.14	4.57
1940	1.14	1.52

1. Four weeks of preseason training
2. Emphasis on warm-ups before game
3. Emphasis on warm-ups before scrimmages
4. Night games abolished or better lighting available
5. Better protective equipment for knee, shoulder, and ankle
6. Better technique taught for blocking and tackling
7. Football coach should coach at least one other sport
8. Complete medical examinations
9. Physician available at all practices and games
10. Examine physical condition of all players every day

In 1934 the AFCA Annual Meeting was held December 27–28. Dr. Marvin A. Stevens was the chairman of the Committee on Football Injuries and Fatalities and he introduced Floyd R. Eastwood to make the report on the analysis of football fatalities 1931–34 (AFCA 1934). The purpose of the study was to acquire as much information as possible on every fatality in football. Reports were received from both the United and Associated Press and followed by questionnaires sent to the people that could make more in-depth comments on the fatality. More accurate information was collected in 1934 by contacting newspaper editors for actual press clippings. The questionnaire injury study was not conducted in 1934 due to lack of funding.

The 1934 report, as shown in Table 1.1, shows a total of 25 fatalities, which was the lowest number since the report had started in 1931 (AFCA 1934). The high school incidence per 100,000 participants was 2.11, and the college figure was 6.09. Major causes of death were cerebral hemorrhage, spinal cord laceration, and internal hemorrhage. Tackling was the type of activity with the greatest number of injuries, followed by blocking. From 1931 to 1934, the report indicates that head and spine injuries accounted for 67.9% of the fatalities and abdominal and internal injuries accounted for 24%. Tackling accounted for 41.9% of all fatalities, followed by blocking and being tackled with 14%.

An interesting recommendation from the 1931 to 1934 analysis states that parents of sandlot players should provide their children with helmets. It was also recommended that an association of high school coaches be formed to do for high school football what the AFCA had done for college football. A question from the audience after the report was presented asked about the use of animal manures on athletic fields for fertilization. The answer was that it would create problems for players with cuts and cause infection and possibly tetanus. Football safety has come a long way since 1934 (AFCA 1934).

Football fatalities in 1935 numbered 29 with slight increases in sandlot, club, and high school, but a decline of one at the college level (AFCA 1935). Interesting recommendations in 1935 that were not already mentioned in previous years were no scrimmages for at least seven days of preseason practice and that each coach should keep an accurate record of all injuries to be analyzed at the end of the season to determine where and how players are being injured. This accounting of all injuries would be an excellent recommendation every year.

The 1936 fatality report had a total of 30 fatalities with 12 in sandlot, 2 in club, 15 in high school, and 1 in college football (AFCA 1936). The fatalities in 1936 included, for the second time, a girl dying in sandlot football. Apparently a girl also died in sandlot football in 1931, but it was not mentioned in the report. In 1936, for the first time since 1931, the college incidence rate per

100,000 participants was lower than the high school rate: 1.52 compared to 2.43. As usual, injuries to the head caused most fatalities, and tackling was involved in over 50% of the cases. A recommendation to reduce these injuries was to teach the rolling tackle as opposed to the head-on tackle. Halfbacks and fullbacks received most of the fatal injuries. For the first time the names of states were listed with the number of football fatalities in that state. In 1936, Pennsylvania and New York were the leaders, followed by Illinois, New Jersey, and Texas. Also in 1936, it was mentioned that indirect fatalities were caused by infections from cuts and bruises. A plea was also made in the 1936 report to train "sport physicians" with clinical experience in athletic injuries (AFCA 1936).

The 1937 fatality report mentioned that since 1906 the Associated Press had kept records of football fatalities and that there had been a steady rise from 1906 to 1931 (AFCA 1937). Since 1931, there had been an observable decline. In 1937, there was a dramatic reduction of football fatalities to 19. Sandlot and club both accounted for three fatalities in 1937, high schools had 13, and for the first time since 1931 colleges were not associated with any fatalities. The incident rate for high schools was 2.11 per 100,000 participants, and for colleges the rate was 0.00. The participation rate continued to be based on 616,000 participants for high schools and 65,690 for the colleges. The 1937 report also mentioned for the first time that cause of death was too frequently reported as "cerebral hemorrhage—old concussion," which could be prevented by not allowing players to play after receiving a concussion. A recommendation was made to eliminate the practice of allowing players to continue playing after a concussion (AFCA 1937). As in past years, certain states continued to dominate the fatality picture with Pennsylvania, New York, and Illinois being the leaders. Another important recommendation stated that no school should play football unless the following are present:

1. An experienced coach
2. Good quality and well-fitted equipment
3. Good, grassed practice and game facilities
4. Medical services immediately available for practice and games
5. Doctor present on the field at all games
6. Provision for free care of all injuries (AFCA 1937)

In 1938, the report mentioned the annual preparation of the Injuries and Fatality Report and that the compiled information had been used by the Rules Committee to guide them in rule changes. As illustrated in Table 1.1, there were a total of 16 football fatalities in 1938, which was the lowest number since 1931. The incidence rate per 100,000 participants for high school and college was 1.30 and 3.04, respectively (AFCA 1938). Recommendations after the 1938 season that were not mentioned in previous years were as follows:

1. The days of "Die for Ole Siwash" are over and players should request removal from the game when injured.
2. Continued stress should be placed on the skillful execution of fundamentals.
3. Head guard construction should be improved so that better protection is provided for this area.
4. All state High School Associations should stress safety procedures in their state bulletins. Michigan has done this extensively during the past few years (AFCA 1938).

The number of fatal football injuries continued to decrease in 1939 when there was 1 sandlot, 1 club, 7 high school, and 3 college fatal injuries for a total of 12. The 1939 report on fatalities was fairly short and included a report made on the 1938 and 1939 injury research completed for six-man football (AFCA 1939). The results of this research were very similar to the injury reports for 11-man football, as were the recommendations for prevention.

The 1940 annual meeting was held December 30–31 in New York City and included fatality data not only for 1940 but also a summary of the research from 1931 to 1940. There were 11 fatalities in 1940, which was the lowest number since the research had begun in 1931. The incidence rate per 100,000 participants was very low for both the high school and college levels: 1.14 at the high school level and 1.52 at the college level (AFCA 1940). As stated earlier, it was not possible at the time to acquire accurate participation numbers for both sandlot and club football.

For the 10-year period from 1931 to 1940, there had been a continual reduction in the number of football fatalities. As illustrated in Table 1.1, there were 33 football fatalities in 1931 and this number had been reduced to 11 in 1940. For this 10-year period of time there were 234 fatal football injuries with 114 at the high school level, 59 in sandlot, 34 in club, and 27 at the college level (AFCA 1940). This improvement was related to the increased consciousness of safety on the part of parents, athletic directors, coaches, and administrators. The report also noted that with the decrease in football fatalities the press had minimized its publicity about them. A summary of the data from 1931 to 1940 is as follows:

1. Fatalities in all areas continue to decrease.
2. College fatal injuries have never been as high as in 1931 with eight. The one college fatality in 1940 represents a decrease of 87.5% in the ten-year period.

Table 1.3 Football Fatalities Direct and Indirect Cause of Death 1931–40

Cause	Sandlot	Club	High School	College	Total
Cerebral Hemorrhage	26	18	44	9	97
Spinal Cord	10	8	31	6	55
Internal Hemorrhage	9	5	15	8	37
Infection	8	3	17	2	30
Heart	0	0	1	1	2
Unknown	6	0	6	1	13
Total	59	34	114	27	234

3. The total direct fatalities has decreased 66.6% since 1931.
4. Over the ten-year period 40.2% of the fatalities occurred in October.
5. The ten-year data indicates that most fatal accidents occur during the first five minutes of a game.
6. Injuries to the head have decreased and those to the spinal column have slightly increased.
7. As shown in Table 1.3, cerebral hemorrhage was associated with the greatest number of fatalities, followed by spinal cord injuries, internal hemorrhage, infection, and heart related deaths.
8. As shown in Table 1.4, halfbacks were associated with the greatest number of fatalities.
9. Pennsylvania and New York were the states with the most fatal injuries during this ten-year period (AFCA 1940).

The 1940 report also had the following recommendations based on the data from 1931 to 1940:

1. Adequate warm-up periods before practice and games and before the start of the second half of games.
2. Three weeks or more of training before the first game.
3. Skillful execution of blocking and tackling.
4. Better equipment protection of the spine and internal organs.
5. A more thorough medical examination to include heart examination, blood pressure, tuberculin test, test for hernia, and a more thorough examination by a physician before an injured player is returned to active participation.
6. More emphasis on a fast whistle and on penalties for piling on.

Table 1.4 Football Fatalities Direct and Indirect Position Played 1931–40

Position	Sandlot	Club	High School	College	Total
Halfbacks	6	6	27	5	44
Ends	1	5	18	7	31
Tackles	2	3	13	5	23
Fullbacks	2	1	13	2	18
Guards	3	1	12	2	18
Quarterbacks	0	5	9	0	14
Centers	3	0	7	3	13
Unknown	42	13	15	3	73
Total	59	34	114	27	234

Football Rules 1931–1940: Safety and Equipment

Football safety rules and player protective equipment play major roles in helping prevent and reduce catastrophic injuries and fatalities. The following section covers the college and high school rules that involve the safety of the players, starting in 1931. The information was taken from the football rule books published by the National Collegiate Athletic Association (NCAA), and from a wonderful book written by David M. Nelson titled *The Anatomy of a Game: Football, the Rules, and the Men Who Made the Game* (1994). David Nelson was a football player at the University of Michigan, a football coach at the Universities of Maine and Delaware, and served on the NCAA football rules committee longer than Walter Camp. In his book he lists every rule change since 1876.

The high school rules, which may be different from the college rules, were taken from the National Federation of State High School Associations (NFHS) published rule books. The NFHS has been the national leadership organization for high school sports and fine arts activities since 1920. In 1931, the high schools developed their own football rules as a result of being denied representation on the NCAA Football Rules Committee and in 1932 published their first book for national distribution (NFHS Rule Books 1932–40). In the long run the separation may have been good for the high schools because the rules were made for the needs of the high school athletes. (To learn more about the NFHS visit their Web site at www.nfhs.org.)

There is no question that officiating can play a major role in the safety of the game. In 1869 there were no officials, but in 1873 that changed to 2 judges and a referee to settle disputes. The number of officials continued to increase to 4 in 1915 and in 1934 the 10 official signals were added to the NCAA rule book. As opposed to the increase in the number of officials, the number of players on each team decreased from 25 in 1869 to 11 in 1880 (NFHS Rule Book 1932–40).

Football equipment has gone through dramatic changes over the years, as have the rules that prohibited or required specific pieces of protective equipment. In 1930, a rule stated that no player shall wear equipment that, in the opinion of the officials, endangers the players. In 1931, taping of the hands was not allowed except for the protection of an injury, and then only by special permission of the umpire. In 1932 thigh guards, shin guards, and braces made of hard or unyielding substances had to be padded, and knee and elbow pads made of hard or unyielding substances were forbidden. In 1939, knee pads, elbow pads, or forearm protectors made of sole leather or other hard or unyielding substances were prohibited. It was also suggested that before his appearance on the field, the name, position or number, and type of injury of any player wearing a hand bandage be reported by the coach to the umpire for approval. Legal protection of the wrists would require no such report (NFHS Rule Book 1932–40).

A major recommendation by the NCAA in 1933 was that head protectors or helmets should be worn by all players; six years later, in 1939, the rule stated that all players must wear helmets (NFHS Rule Book 1932–40). The NFHS required helmets in 1935, four years before the NCAA did. In the early years of football, players had no head protection and many started to grow long hair for head protection. Others created different styles of leather helmets to protect their heads and ears. The origin of the leather football helmet was in the Army-Navy game of 1893 when an Annapolis shoemaker created a leather helmet for a Navy player who had been advised by a physician that he would be facing death if he took another hit to the head (Nelson 1994). In the early 1900s, the flattop soft leather helmet was one of the earliest styles and was later followed in the late 1920s by the executioner leather helmet which added a leather mask to protect the face. The executioner helmet did not last long due to it blocking the player's vision and being very hot, but it continued to be used for injured players. A big step in football helmet design was the dog-ear leather football helmet that was mostly worn during the 1920s. It offered better protection than the flattop and had two flaps to cover the ears. An earlier model of the dog-ear helmet was the beehive leather helmet that was very thin and did not offer much head protection, but was designed to protect the ears (Nelson 1994).

In 1934, shoes made of material liable to chip or fracture were forbidden and in 1939 conical cleats whose points were less than one-half inch in diameter (changed to three-eighths of an inch in 1940) or without straight sides from

Table 1.5 Football Fatalities Direct and Indirect Activity 1931–40

Activity	Frequency	Percentage
Tackling	98	41.9
Tackled	32	13.7
Blocking	27	11.5
Kicked-Kneed	15	6.4
Pile-up	10	4.3
Catching Pass	5	2.1
Blocked	1	0.4
Not Specified	46	19.7
Total	234	100.0

point to base were prohibited. Female cleats without some effective locking device were prohibited in 1940 (NFHS Rule Book 1932–40).

The use of the flying block and tackle resulted in a five-yard penalty, whether or not contact was made with the opponent, and went into effect in 1932. The flying block and tackle was made with both feet off of the ground and at the time was thought to be dangerous. Tackling and being tackled were responsible for 55.6% of all fatalities from 1931 through 1940, as shown in Table 1.5 (AFCA 1940).

Defensive players were allowed to use the palms of their hands above the shoulders of opponents to ward off or push them to get to the ball, but striking the head, face, or neck was prohibited. In 1933, the definition of clipping was broadened to include blocking by running or diving into the back of a player not carrying the ball, in addition to throwing or dropping the body across the back of the leg or legs below the knees of such a player. A rule put in place in 1940 to protect the kicker stated that protection is given the kicker only when it is reasonably obvious that he is going to kick. In 1933, no player who has made a fair catch could be tackled or thrown to the ground by an opponent. The penalty was 15 yards. (10)

Discussion

There is no doubt that the football community was concerned with the high number of fatalities and serious injuries prior to and during the 1931 season when the AFCA took it upon itself to make every effort to reduce these numbers. The AFCA knew what effects bad publicity, increasing numbers of fatalities, and serious injuries would have on the game of football and the institutions

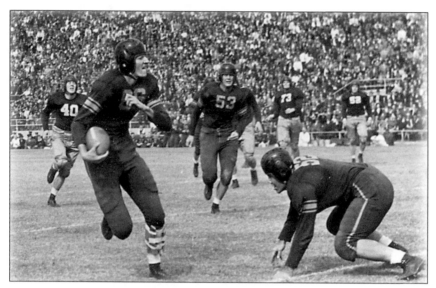

Image 1.1 All-Americans
Photo courtesy of NCAA.

that played the game, and decided that it was time to collect reliable data to an-swer critics of the game. History has shown that this was an important move by the AFCA, and over the years this data has made important contributions to the safety of the participants.

The AFCA was founded in 1922 with its top priority being the improve-ment of the game and the coaching profession, and one of its primary goals was to promote safety. The annual injury survey was begun by the association in 1931 and has provided valuable data and made a major contribution to the reduction of football fatalities. The NCAA Football Rules Committee often follows recommendations made by the Football Injury Committee. According to the constitution, the AFCA was formed to "maintain the highest possible standards in football and the profession of coaching football." In December 1921, when there were 43 coaches at an informal meeting to form the associ-ation, the AFCA had grown to over 10,000 members from all over the world. The first president of the association in 1922 was Major Charles Day from the U.S. Military Academy (West Point), where he was also the football coach. John Heisman, the legendary football coach, was the president in 1923 and 1924 and was one of only four coaches to be president for two years. Almost all of the great coaches served as president, including Bear Bryant, Darrell Royal, Eddie Robinson, and Vince Dooley. The AFCA has also had four full-

Graph 1.1 Direct Fatalities 1931–40

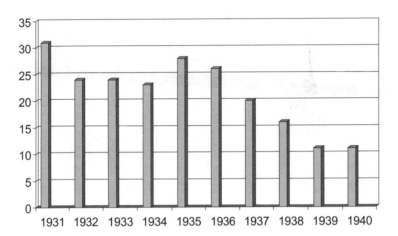

time executive directors starting with DeOrmond "Tuss" McLaughry (1960–65), William D. Murray (1966–81), Charles Y. McClendon (1982–93), and the current executive director, Grant Teaff. The AFCA is the single entity representing all levels of football and the football coaching profession. It works closely with the NCAA and was actually instrumental in the creation of NCAA football. Other groups that the AFCA works with are the National Association of Collegiate Directors of Athletics, the National Association of Intercollegiate Athletics, the National Junior College Athletic Association, the NFHS, the National Football League, the Canadian Football League, USA Football, the National Football Foundation and Hall of Fame, Pop Warner Football, and many others.

As shown by the data in Graph 1.1, the decade from 1931 to 1940 made great strides in reducing the number of football fatalities from a high of 33 in 1931 to a low of 11 in 1940—a reduction of 66%. There was also a reduction in the incidence rate per 100,000 participants from 1.95 to 1.14 at the high school level, and from 12.18 to 1.52 at the college level. There was one year, 1937, when there were zero fatalities at the college level. (6, 9)

The question that has to be asked is how this dramatic reduction took place. First has to be the wisdom of the AFCA to begin a data collection system and to evaluate the data each year to make changes in rules, equipment, coaching techniques, and other safety measures. In 1933, three important recommendations made were to teach better technique for blocking and tackling, to give complete medical examinations for the players, and to have a physician available for all practices and games (AFCA 1933). The recommendation for teaching better techniques for blocking and tackling was a direct result of the data showing that these two activities were the result of more than half of all fatalities. A recommendation was made in 1936 to teach the rolling tackle as opposed to the flying tackle (AFCA 1936). The recommendation to have a physician available for all practices and games is one that continues to exist, and there is no question that physical examinations are important. The 1936 report made a plea for the first time to train "sport physicians" with clinical experience in athletic injuries, although this did not happen for many years (AFCA 1936).

One of the most important recommendations, made in 1937, that could have played a major role in the reduction of head fatalities was that too many players were allowed to continue playing after a concussion and this practice must be eliminated. The report stated that cause of death was too frequently reported as "cerebral hemorrhage—old concussion" and that they could be prevented by not allowing players to compete after suffering a concussion (AFCA 1937). This practice continues to be a problem in today's game, and as the recommendation was relevant in 1937, it is also relevant today.

There were also important rules during this period related to the football helmet that played a role in the reduction of fatalities. In 1933 there was a recommendation that head protectors or helmets be worn by all college players, in 1935 helmets were required for high school players, and in 1939 the NCAA rule stated that all college players must wear helmets (AFCA 1933 & 1939). The helmet rules played a major role in the reduction of cerebral fatalities during the 1930s. Other rules that prohibited defensive players from using the palms of their hands in striking the head, face, or neck; the broadening of the clipping rule; and protection for the kicker were also important additions.

The 1931–40 fatality reports are an excellent example of the importance data collection plays in reducing football injuries. Along with data collection and the constant evaluation of the data, football has made tremendous strides in making the game safer for the participants. Some of the safety recommendations made 75 years ago continue to be important in protecting the lives of the players.

References

1. American Football Coaches Association: Proceedings of the Twelfth Annual Meeting of the American Football Coaches Association, December 27, 1932, New York, NY.

2. American Football Coaches Association: Proceedings of the Thirteenth Annual Meeting of the American Football Coaches Association, December 26, 1933, Chicago, IL.
3. American Football Coaches Association: Proceedings of the Fourteenth Annual Meeting of the American Football Coaches Association, December 27–28, 1934.
4. American Football Coaches Association: Proceedings of the Fifteenth Annual Meeting of the American Football Coaches Association, December 28, 1935.
5. American Football Coaches Association: Proceedings of the Sixteenth American Football Coaches Association, December 30, 1936.
6. American Football Coaches Association: Proceedings of the Seventeenth Annual Meeting of the American Football Coaches Association, December, 29, 1937.
7. American Football Coaches Association: Proceedings of the Eighteenth Annual Meeting of the American Football Coaches Association, December 27–30, 1938.
8. American Football Coaches Association: Proceedings of the Nineteenth Annual Meeting of the American Football Coaches Association, December 28–30, 1939.
9. American Football Coaches Association: Proceedings of the Twentieth Annual Meeting of the American Football Coaches Association, December 30–31, 1940, New York, NY.
10. National Federation of State High School Associations: Football Rules Books, 1932–40.
11. Nelson DM: *Anatomy of a Game.* University of Delaware Press. Newark, DE. 1994.
12. Past Time Sports: History of the Football Helmet. Richardson, TX.

Chapter 2

Fatalities and Catastrophic Injuries, 1941–1950

Introduction

For the past twenty years the Annual Survey of Football Fatalities has been produced, with the exception of the war year 1942. During these years there have been many changes and additions to the questionnaire and to the definition of a direct, indirect, and nonfootball injury. At this time it is important to point out that in Chapter 1, direct football fatalities numbered 234. The number 234 was taken directly from the 1931–40 fatality reports. When looking at the number of direct fatalities that are illustrated in the 1941 report, the data show 214 fatalities from 1931–40, as indicated in Table 2.1 (AFCA 1941). The author believes this difference is a result of the many changes that have taken place in the definition of a direct injury versus an indirect injury. As an example, direct and indirect injuries were listed together, and an infection was counted as a direct football death. Later reports also gave exact numbers of indirect fatalities for the decade 1931–40, as shown in Table 2.2. For historical accuracy, the data for direct and indirect injuries from 1931–40, as illustrated in Chapter 1, will stay at 234 and both direct and indirect injuries will be updated in Chapter 2. Having been the author of the fatality report since 1980, I have found that the numbers do change over the years when additional information becomes available. It is my intention to give historical data for each decade and to update the numbers in succeeding chapters.

Fatalities and Catastrophic Injuries, 1941–1950

As shown in Table 2.3, there were 144 direct football fatalities from 1941 through 1950, which is 70 less than the decade from 1931–40 (AFCA 1951). Sandlot football accounted for 32, professional football for 23, high school football for 84, and college football for 5. The greatest reduction was in sand-

Table 2.1 Direct Football Fatalities (Update) 1931–40

Year	Sandlot	Club	High School	College	Total
1931	10	3	10	8	31
1932	8	6	8	2	24
1933	8	4	10	2	24
1934	4	4	12	3	23
1935	4	7	14	3	28
1936	11	2	12	1	26
1937	3	4	13	0	20
1938	3	3	8	2	16
1939	1	1	6	3	11
1940	2	1	7	1	11
TOTAL	54	35	100	25	214

Table 2.2 Indirect Football Fatalities (Update) 1931–40

Year	Sandlot	Club	High School	College	Total
1931	8	0	10	0	18
1932	3	0	9	1	13
1933	7	0	9	3	19
1934	5	0	6	2	13
1935	6	0	11	2	19
1936	5	1	8	4	18
1937	3	0	6	2	11
1938	4	1	5	3	13
1939	1	1	4	1	7
1940	1	0	2	1	4
TOTAL	43	3	70	19	135

lot football from 54 to 32. College football also showed a reduction from 25 to 5. In 1941, there were a total of 14 direct fatalities with none being recorded in college football (AFCA 1941). This was the second time since 1937 that college football was not associated with any direct fatalities. The direct fatality incidence rate per 100,000 participants, as illustrated in Table 2.5, has the high school rate at 0.97 and the college rate at 0.00. These incidence rates were based on 616,000 high school and 65,690 college players (AFCA 1941). New York and Pennsylvania continued to lead the nation in the highest percentage of direct football fatalities.

In 1941, the exact position of the injured player was not obtained as well as in previous years, but the data over 11 years show more backfield players injured than linemen. Additionally, where type of activity was reported, three times as many players were fatally injured while tackling (32%) as opposed to blocking (11%) and tackled or blocked (10%). It was recommended that more emphasis be placed on the teaching of proper tackling techniques (AFCA 1941). For the first time, the 1941 report started collecting data on offensive and defensive fatalities and found that offensive fatalities were more than twice the percentage of defensive fatalities.

Also for the first time since the collection of fatality data in 1931, as shown in Tables 2.3 and 2.4, there were no fatalities either directly or indirectly related to college football in 1941. Indirect fatalities numbered only four in 1941: one at the professional level and three at the high school level. There was more of an effort in 1941 to separate direct and indirect fatalities and to eliminate fatalities that were not associated with the game.

The 1941 report recommended that there be renewed attention to pre-season teaching of fundamentals, especially tackling; continuation of the liberal substitution rules; more money, time, and research spent perfecting a more adequate head guard; and a more extensive medical evaluation (AFCA 1941).

There was no American Football Coaches Association Fatality Report in 1942 because of the Second World War. In 1943 there were a total of 11 direct fatalities, and for the first time since data collection began in 1931 there were no indirect fatalities. The 1943 report also shows another year with no direct fatalities at the college level, and for the first time no fatalities in sandlot football (AFCA 1946). Ten of the fatalities in 1943 were at the high school level and one was at the professional level.

In 1944, the number of fatalities had an increase to 17 with an additional two indirect. Sandlot had an increase from zero to five, professional football had two, high schools had a decrease from ten to nine, and the colleges accounted for an increase from zero to one (AFCA 1941, 1946).

The 1943 and 1944 reports were not as in-depth as in previous years, but the 1945 report was back on track. The 1945 report, as illustrated in Table 2.3, had the lowest number of fatalities ever reported (AFCA 1946). There were three at the sandlot level, and for the first time, none at the club or professional levels. High school football was associated with the lowest number of football fatalities ever recorded (3), and college football had its fourth year with no fatalities. In 1945 defensive football was associated with 58.3% of the total, and offensive football was associated with 15.8%. It should be noted that there was not a clear definition of defensive or offensive football, and there was also a large percentage of cases where the information was not available. Also in

Table 2.3 Direct Football Fatalities 1941–50

Year	Sandlot	Professional	High School	College	Total
1941	5	3	6	0	14
1942*	—	—	—	—	—
1943	0	1	10	0	11
1944	5	2	9	1	17
1945	3	0	3	0	6
1946	1	5	13	2	21
1947	4	4	14	1	23
1948	6	3	9	0	18
1949	7	3	9	0	19
1950	1	2	11	1	15
TOTAL	32	23	84	5	144

*No study conducted due to World War II

Table 2.4 Indirect Football Fatalities 1941–50

Year	Sandlot	Professional	High School	College	Total
1941	0	1	3	0	4
1942*	—	—	—	—	—
1943	0	0	0	0	0
1944	1	0	1	0	2
1945	2	0	1	0	3
1946	4	0	0	0	4
1947	2	1	2	1	6
1948	3	2	3	0	8
1949	3	2	1	1	7
1950	1	0	2	1	4
TOTAL	16	6	13	3	38

*No study conducted due to World War II

1945, there was a slight percentage increase in cerebral hemorrhages. For the period 1931–45, cerebral hemorrhages accounted for 44.7% of the total direct fatalities with internal injuries second (29.8%), and spinal injuries third (22.5%). Two-thirds of all fatalities were related to the head and spine.

Also in 1945, as shown in Table 2.4, there were three indirect injuries. One of the indirect fatalities was a heart attack and the other two were questionable. One was a player climbing a power pole to recover a football caught in the power lines and being electrocuted, and the second was attributed to encephalitis. From 1931 to 1945, heart attacks accounted for 16.1% of the indirect fatalities, but infections accounted for 58.0 % (AFCA 1941, 1946).

The 1946 report revealed the largest number of direct fatalities (21) since 1936, and ranked sixth in the number of direct fatalities since 1931 (AFCA 1947). Direct and indirect fatalities numbered 25—the highest number since 1938. The 1946 direct fatalities saw increases at all levels of play with the exception of sandlot that went from three to one. The average incidence of high school fatalities per 100,000 participants was the highest (2.11) in 1946 with the exception of 1935 (2.27) and 1937 (2.11). Most fatalities in 1946 occurred in games, which is consistent with previous reports. The causes of direct fatalities were skull and/or cerebral hemorrhages, internal injuries, and spinal injuries. Infections continued to be the greatest cause of indirect fatalities followed by heart attacks (AFCA 1947).

The 1946 report concluded that backfield players are more susceptible to fatal injuries, that tackling accounted for one-third of the fatalities, and that defensive football was slowly becoming more hazardous than offensive football. An interesting note in the 1946 report taken from a study by Joseph Dolan stated that spring practice injuries happened at a greater frequency among college veterans of World War II (AFCA 1947).

The 1946 report also had a table that showed the percent increase of head fatalities between 1937 and 1946 (AFCA 1947). The numbers are as follows:

Year	% of Skull and/or Cerebral Hemorrhages
1937	41.2
1938	41.5
1939	41.2
1940	41.2
1941	44.3
1942	No Study
1943	44.5
1944	44.5
1945	44.7
1946	45.7

Two of the most important recommendations from the 1946 report involved equipment. Development of new tackling and blocking dummies was recommended to insure better techniques. The strongest recommendation, in capital letters, stated the following.

APPOINT AT ONCE A QUALIFIED COMMITTEE TO SCIENTIFI-
CALLY STUDY THE CONSTRUCTION AND MATERIAL USED IN
THE PRESENT HEADGEAR. THIS STUDY COMMITTEE, IT IS
HOPED, CAN RECOMMEND A HEADGEAR THAT WILL MATE-
RIALLY REDUCE THE LARGE NUMBER OF PRESENT FATALITIES
CAUSED BY SKULL FRACTURES AND CEREBRAL HEMORRHAGE.
(AFCA 1947)

Indirect fatalities numbered four in 1946. All four of the indirect fatalities
were at the sandlot level and three were heart attacks.

In 1947, there were a total of 23 direct fatalities and 6 indirect (AFCA 1948).
This was an increase of two in the direct classification and two in the indirect
group. The direct fatalities in 1947 were more numerous than any year with the
exception of 1931, 1935, and 1936, and there were an equal number in 1932 and
1933. Approximately two-thirds of the fatalities took place in games, with the age
group 16–18 being associated with the greatest number of fatalities. Also in 1947,
an official was hit in the stomach by one of the high school players during a game
and received a ruptured spleen and fractured ribs. He died a week later in the
hospital, and it was found that he also had a case of chronic lymphatic leukemia.
The third female direct football death was recorded on November 30, 1947. She
was ten years old and fractured her skull after falling and hitting her head on a rock.

Again in 1947, tackling was associated with the greatest number of fatalities
(30.9%). The increase in tackling injuries was reflected in the increasing hazard of defensive play (36.6%) over offensive play (29.0%) associated with fatal
injuries. This change of the increasing hazard of defensive football had progressed
steadily since 1941. Cerebral injuries had also increased steadily and in 1947 accounted for 46.3% of the injuries. Spinal injuries were slightly lower. Cerebral
injuries were related to blows to the front, side, and rear of the head while
spinal injuries came from blows to the top of the head (AFCA 1948). In almost every case of head and spinal injuries, the opponent's knee was involved.

Indirect fatalities in 1947 numbered six. Five were heart attacks and one
was associated with lightning (AFCA 1948). Although there were no indirect
fatalities in 1947 that were related to infections, they continued to be the main
cause of indirect deaths during the previous 16 years.

In the discussion section of the 1947 report, it was mentioned from the very
beginning of the research that the head and spinal cord were areas that needed
special attention. In the recommendation section of the same report, it was
recommended that a joint committee of the American Football Coaches Association and the National Collegiate Athletic Association (NCAA) be responsible for obtaining funds for helmet research. It also stated that the NCAA

Image 2.1 Peter Pihos, Indiana University
Photo courtesy of NCAA.

should be responsible for starting research within 90 days and have a preliminary report ready for the 1949 meeting. A final report would be due at the
1950 meeting. It was suggested that the construction of a different football
helmet would take the best minds of the football community, including the
manufacturers. Another recommendation of the 1947 report stated that knee
pads be required for all football uniforms starting in 1948.

In 1948, there were a total of 18 direct fatalities and eight indirect (AFCA
1949). That was a reduction of five direct fatalities from 1947, and an increase
of two indirect fatalities. As had been true in the past, halfbacks and fullbacks
suffered the most fatalities, and tackling was associated with almost three times
more fatal injuries than any other activity. Almost 60% of the direct fatalities
were caused by blows to the head resulting in head or spinal cord injuries.

It was not possible to raise grant money for continued research in football
helmets, but information from the Department of Medical Aviation research
on making better helmets for pilots could be used in the future to make better football helmets. A major recommendation from the 1948 report was that
every team physician should conduct a careful study of all concussions to his
players (AFCA 1949). Information recommended was location of the hit and
the extent and severity of the injury. A second recommendation was to select
only those helmets that were well padded and included suspension of the head
inside the helmet (AFCA 1949).

The 1949 football season was associated with 19 direct fatalities and seven indirect (AFCA 1950). The direct fatalities numbered seven in sandlot, three in pro/semi-pro, nine in high school and none at the college level. It was the sixth time during the 18 years of the study that college football was not associated with any direct fatalities. The direct fatality incidence rate per 100,000 participants in 1949 was 1.46 for high schools and 0.00 for colleges (Table 2.4). It is interesting to note that during this stage of the research many of the sandlot fatalities were associated with players not wearing protective equipment. Games continued to be associated with the greatest number of direct fatalities (46.8%) in all areas except sandlot. Tackling also continued to be the activity most associated with fatalities. Cerebral hemorrhage injuries had a slight increase in 1949, and there was a slight decrease in internal and spinal cord injuries.

In 1947, the questionnaire was revised to collect data on the exact part of the head receiving the hit during an injury to the head/neck. The three-year data show hits to the top of the head causing spinal cord injuries (18.1%), back of the head (11.5%), left side of the head (8.2%), and right side of the head (6.6%) (AFCA 1948).

The 1949 report stated that equipment manufacturers had given more time to safety and coaches had increased training time on safety techniques of blocking and tackling, but there were still too many fatalities. In a bold statement, the 1949 report said that "football fatalities will not be materially decreased until equipment is built on principles derived from scientific research."

Recommendations from the 1949 report were as follows:

1. Obtain monies for safety research.
2. Require by rule knee pads as standard equipment.
3. Inspect head suspensions in all old helmets.
4. Be sure adequate absorptive materials are present in new helmets.
5. Pass no restrictive legislation against any type of headgear shells since the two prevailing types of helmets have been equally involved in football fatalities during the past three years.
6. Redesign pads for the abdomen and small of the back to better protect from internal injuries (NFHS).

Indirect fatalities in 1949 were caused by heart attacks (6) and infection (1) (AFCA 1950).

In January 1951, it was reported that during the 1950 football season there were 15 direct and four indirect fatalities (AFCA 1951). From 1949 to 1950 there was an increase of two high school direct fatalities and an increase from zero to one at the college level. There was 1 at the sandlot level, 2 in semi-pro,

Table 2.5 Direct Football Fatalities Incidence
per 100,000 Participants 1941–50

Year	High School	College
1941	0.97	0.00
1942*	—	—
1943	1.62	0.00
1944	1.46	1.52
1945	0.48	0.00
1946	2.11	3.04
1947	2.27	1.52
1948	1.46	0.00
1949	1.46	0.00
1950	1.77	1.52

*No study conducted due to World War II

11 in high school, and one at the college level. For the first time of the study there were fatalities in South Carolina (2), and in Pennsylvania, which had the highest percentage of fatalities during the preceeding nineteen years, there were none (AFCA 1951).

The position of halfback continued to be the most hazardous, accounting for 35.2% of all fatalities, followed by the fullback and quarterback. The guard position was the least hazardous. Defensive football was associated with the most fatalities (35.2%) and in 1950, eight of the fatalities occurred on defense. There had been a steady increase of defensive fatalities since the 1941 report. Also in 1950, blows to the head accounted for 69.9% of the fatalities (AFCA 1951).

Indirect fatalities in 1950 were associated with heart attacks (1), infections (2), and one unspecified. During the first 19 years of the study 51.7% of the indirect fatalities were associated with infections and 24.3% with heart attacks.

Discussion in the 1950 report centered on the increased number of head-related fatalities and the fact that the helmet had been redesigned, but fatalities were still occurring in the newly designed helmets. Fatalities in the newer helmet were more in proportion to the total than those in 1949 (AFCA 1951). From studies at the University of Southern California by Dr. Lombard, it was clear that the knee was a lethal body part causing injuries to the head, helmets were not providing adequate protection, and the suspension system of the helmet must be inspected before play to prevent the head from making contact with the helmet shell during contact (AFCA 1951). The report stated that head injuries can only be reduced by scientifically designed helmets, and that re-

Table 2.6 Direct Football Fatalities Cause of Death 1941–50

Cause	Sandlot	Professional	High School	College	Total
Cerebral Hemorrhage	22	9	40	3	74
Spinal Cord	0	7	15	2	24
Internal Abdominal	10	6	29	0	45
Unknown	0	1	0	0	1
TOTAL	32	23	84	5	144

Table 2.7 Indirect Football Fatalities Cause of Death 1941–50

Cause	Frequency	Percentage
Infantile Paralysis	1	2.6
Heart Attack	23	60.5
Infection	6	15.8
Electrocuted by Pad or Wire	1	2.6
Lightning	1	2.6
Unknown	6	15.8
TOTAL	38	99.9

search must be paid for by those most interested in football. This statement has been repeated since 1943 and the data verify the need. The recommendations in 1950 were the same as reported in the 1949 report.

As shown in Table 2.6, the football fatalities in the decade 1941–50 were caused by cerebral hemorrhages (74), spinal cord injuries (24), internal/abdominal (45), and the cause of one was unknown.

Table 2.7 shows that indirect fatalities from 1941 through 1950 were caused by heart attacks (23), infections (6), lightning (1), electrocution (1), infantile paralysis (1), and the cause of six were unknown.

For the years 1941–50, halfbacks were associated with the most fatalities followed by ends, with guards having the lowest number (Table 2.8). The data did not indicate whether the halfbacks were playing offensive or defensive football at the time of the injury, but Table 2.9 shows that tackling was the activity associated with the greatest number of fatalities. More than half of the activities associated with fatalities were listed as unknown.

The 20-year data from 1931 through 1950 show a total of 359 direct fatalities and 172 indirect (AFCA 1951). The direct fatalities had a distribution of 86 in sandlot play, 58 at pro and semi-pro level, 184 at the high school level,

Table 2.8 Direct Football Fatalities Position Played 1941–50

Position	Frequency	Percentage
Halfback	28	19.4
End	12	8.3
Backfield	9	6.3
Center	9	6.3
Fullback	8	5.5
Tackle	7	4.9
Quarterback	5	3.5
Guard	3	2.1
Unknown	63	43.7
TOTAL	144	100.0

Table 2.9 Direct Football Fatalities Activity 1941–50

Activity	Frequency	Percentage
Tackling	15	10.4
Catching Pass	13	9.0
Blocked	13	9.0
Tackled	11	7.6
Blocking	8	5.5
Under pile-up	7	4.9
Unknown	77	53.5
TOTAL	144	100.0

30 at the college level, and one being an official. The average incidence per 100,000 participants for the 20 years was 1.49 for the high schools and 2.28 for the colleges. Pennsylvania and New York led the states in the number of fatalities. Halfbacks were the position most injured and tackling was the activity that was related to the greatest number of injuries. Infections led the list of indirect fatalities followed by heart attacks.

Football Rules 1941–1950: Safety and Equipment

As stated in the previous chapter, football safety rules and player protective equipment play major roles in helping to prevent and reduce catastrophic injuries and fatalities. The following section will cover the college and high school rules that involve the safety of players from 1941 through 1950. The information was taken from the rule books published by the NCAA and the National Federation of State High School Associations (NFHS), and from the book written by David M. Nelson titled, *The Anatomy of a Game: Football, the Rules, and the Men Who Made the Game.*

One of the rule changes in the 1940s that affected the safety of the game was the 1941 rule that permitted players to substitute at any time, which made two-platoon football possible. Two-platoon football was good in that it gave players time to rest on the sidelines, but it could also create problems if one team did not have enough players for two-platoon football. Also, a fair catch could be made on a kickoff, free kick, and a return kick, and any player could signal for a fair catch by raising and waving one hand above the head and catching the ball before it hit the ground. However, waving the hand created problems for both players and officials and in 1948 was changed to one hand over the head, eliminating hand waving. A 1949 rule stated that no player shall block or tackle a fair catcher, which was a definite safety factor. In 1950 the fair catch was totally eliminated, which created additional problems related to safety.

In 1945 the wording "running into the kicker" was deleted, the referee was able to declare a timeout when necessary for repair or replacement of equipment, and forward passes were permitted anywhere behind the neutral zone.

In 1946 the number of timeouts was changed from three to four, and excess timeouts could only be called for injuries. The addition of another time out was an asset to safety, especially the rule that allowed excess timeouts for injuries.

In 1947 striking with the forearm on any part of the opponent's body was prohibited, which was another rule that helped make the game safer. One of the few rules in this decade related to equipment permitted a one-inch kicking tee for kickoffs in 1948. An equipment rule in 1949, which was directly related to safety, stated that no one wearing illegal equipment was permitted to play, and shoe cleats made of metal, other than non chip aluminum alloy, were prohibited. Also, shoe cleats with conical sides and the free end not parallel with its base were also prohibited. In addition, in 1949 there was a rule prohibiting clipping during a free kick down. During a scrimmage down there was to be no clipping on middle linemen of the offensive formation outside a rectangular area and extending four yards laterally in each direction and three yards longitudinally in each direction. A rule stated that no official shall declare clipping unless he sees the initial contact.

A rule in 1950 gave equal protection to both the kicker and holder of place-kicks, and the flying block and flying tackle prohibitions were deleted. A blocking rule in 1950 stated that in performing a chest or shoulder block and using the hand or forearm to supplement the block, the hand must be in contact with the blocker's body and must be below the shoulders of the opponent during the entire block. This rule eliminated head contact by the blocker. Also in 1950 a team could replace an injured player only during injury timeouts, but the opponent could substitute any number of players.

The 1948 rules committee failed to bring the NCAA and the NFHS rules into one common code, but the original 13 rules were re-codified into a set of ten for both groups. The rule book of 1949 covered thirty-seven major changes to the rules and was considered one of the major contributions to football rule writing. A major change in 1949 was the clipping rule that eliminated contact above the waist, which could have caused future injuries.

It is important to point out that the rule committees were always interested in making the game safer for the participants, and when certain rules did not accomplish that goal, they were changed in later years.

Discussion

There is no doubt that the game of football was safer for the decade of 1941–50 when compared to the decade of 1931–40 (AFCA 1951). The original data for 1931–40 had a total of 234 direct fatalities, with the updated numbers showing 214 direct fatalities for the same years (AFCA 1941). In both cases the number of direct fatalities from 1941 to 1950 was lower than the previous decade. The decade from 1941–50 had 90 fewer fatalities than the original 1931–40 data, and 70 fewer than the updated data (AFCA 1951). Comparing the updated numbers in 1931–40 to the 1941–50 data, sandlot football had 22 fewer fatalities, professional had 12 fewer, high school had 16 fewer, and college had 20 fewer. It was obvious from these numbers that safety played a major role in the work of the rules committee and was a concern to everyone associated with the game.

The incidence rate per 100,000 participants also showed a decline between the two decades mentioned in the previous paragraph. For the decade 1931–40, the incidence rate for the high schools was 1.62 compared to 1941–50 when it was 1.36 (AFCA 1951). For colleges, the 1931–40 incidence rate was 3.80 and for the decade 1941–50 it was 0.76. The incident rate per 100,000 participants was based on 616,000 high school players and 65,690 college players each year.

In 1931–40, there was a total of 97 cerebral hemorrhage fatalities, 55 spinal cord fatalities, and 37 internal fatalities. In 1941–50, direct football fatalities were caused by 74 cerebral hemorrhages, 24 spinal cord injuries, and 24 internal injuries. Along with the reduction of fatalities in the decade 1941–50, there was also a decrease in the number of head and neck fatalities. Halfbacks were

Graph 2.1 Direct Fatalities 1941–50

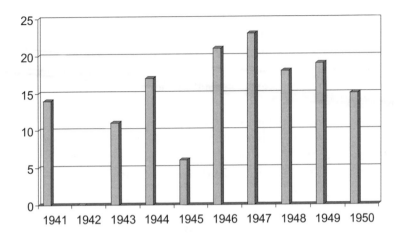

related to the greatest number of fatalities in both decades, but as stated earlier it was not clear if the writers included both offensive and defensive halfbacks. There were fewer tackling fatalities from 1941 to 1950, but tackling continued to lead the list of activities most associated with fatalities. A major concern was that the knee of the tackled player was usually involved in the injury by hitting the head of the tackler, and there was a continued recommendation to mandate knee padding in the uniform (AFCA 1951).

Indirect injuries accounted for 135 fatalities from 1931 through 1940, and only 38 in the decade of 1941–50. Infections and heart attacks continued to be the main cause of indirect fatalities (AFCA 1951).

As the decade from 1941–50 came to an end, there was continued concern about the football helmet and that any future reduction of head injuries could only be achieved by a scientifically designed helmet. It was recommended that research is needed as to the best materials used in the construction of the helmet shell, and what type of suspension, if any, is needed. Chapter 3 will report on the progress made in these areas of concern.

References

1. American Football Coaches Association: Proceedings of the Twenty-First Annual Meeting of the American Football Coaches Association, December 30–31, 1941, Detroit, MI.

2. American Football Coaches Association: Proceedings of the Twenty-Third Annual Meeting of the American Football Coaches Association, January 9–10, 1946, Saint Louis, MO.
3. American Football Coaches Association: Proceedings of the Twenty-Fourth Annual Meeting of the American Football Coaches Association, January 6–7, 1947, New York, NY.
4. American Football Coaches Association: Proceedings of the Twenty-Fifth Annual Meeting of the American Football Coaches Association, January 8–9, 1948, New York, NY.
5. American Football Coaches Association: Proceedings of the Twenty-Sixth Annual Meeting of the American Football Coaches Association, January 6–7, 1949, San Francisco, CA.
6. American Football Coaches Association: Proceedings of the Twenty-Seventh Annual Meeting of the American Football Coaches Association, January 12–13, 1950, New York, NY.
7. American Football Coaches Association: Proceedings of the Twenty-Eighth Annual Meeting of the American Football Coaches Association, January 11–12, 1951, Dallas, TX.
8. National Federation of State High School Associations: Football Rules Books, 1941–1950.
9. Nelson DM: *Anatomy of a Game.* University of Delaware Press, DE. 1994.

Chapter 3

Fatalities and Catastrophic Injuries, 1951–1960

Introduction

For 20 years since 1931, with the exception of 1942 during World War II, the Annual Survey of Football Fatalities was produced (AFCA 1952). During these years there were many changes and additions to the questionnaire and to the definition of a direct, indirect, and nonfootball injury. The numbers from 1941–50 were consistent and therefore there were no updates for those years (AFCA 1952). The decade of the 1950s also saw the continued reduction of direct fatalities that started in the previous decade.

Fatalities and Catastrophic Injuries, 1951–1960

As illustrated in Table 3.1, there were 142 direct football deaths in the decade from 1951–60 (AFCA 1961). The 142 fatalities included 30 in sandlot, 11 in professional, 89 in high school, and 12 in college. When comparing this total to the 1941–50 totals, there were 2 fewer direct fatalities from 1951–60 (AFCA 1952). When comparing levels of play, the 1951–60 totals show 2 fewer at the sandlot level, 12 fewer at the professional level, 5 more at the high school level, and 7 more at the college level. There were three years at the college level—1952, 1957, and 1958—when there were no direct fatalities. When comparing direct fatalities during the 1951–60 decade with the 1931–40 updated numbers, there were 72 fewer direct fatalities from 1951–60 (AFCA 1961).

Indirect fatalities in the decade 1951–60 totaled 55 (Table 3.2). Sandlot accounted for 13, professional for 3, high school for 31, and college for 8. When compared to the previous decade (1941–50), there were 17 more indirect fatalities in 1951–60. The increase in the indirect fatalities was mainly at the high school level (+18) and the college level (+5).

Table 3.1 Football Direct Fatalities 1951–60

Year	Sandlot	Professional	High School	College	Total
1951	3	2	6	1	12
1952	1	0	5	0	6
1953	3	2	6	2	13
1954	3	2	12	2	19
1955	2	0	6	2	10
1956	3	1	12	1	17
1957	2	1	13	0	16
1958	6	0	11	0	17
1959	6	2	7	3	18
1960	1	1	11	1	14
TOTAL	30	11	89	12	142

Table 3.3 shows the incidence per 100,000 participants for direct fatalities based on 616,000 high school players and 65,690 college players for the years 1951–60. Over the 10-year period the average incidence rate for the high schools was 1.44 per 100,000 participants, and for the colleges the incidence rate was 1.82 (AFCA 1961).

During the 20-year period from 1931–50, there were 358 direct football fatalities for an average of 17.9 per year, and in eleven of those years, direct fatalities were above average. In 1951, there were 12 direct fatalities, 5.9 below average. Three fatalities were at the sandlot level, two professional, six high

Table 3.2 Football Indirect Fatalities 1951–60

Year	Sandlot	Professional	High School	College	Total
1951	3	1	3	1	8
1952	1	0	2	1	4
1953	2	0	4	0	6
1954	3	1	2	0	6
1955	1	0	3	0	4
1956	0	0	4	1	5
1957	0	0	3	1	4
1958	0	0	2	1	3
1959	3	1	6	1	11
1960	0	0	2	2	4
TOTAL	13	3	31	8	55

Table 3.3 Football Direct Fatalities Incidence
per 100,000 Participants 1951–60

Year	High School	College
1951	0.97	1.52
1952	0.81	0.00
1953	0.97	3.04
1954	1.94	3.04
1955	0.97	3.04
1956	1.94	1.52
1957	2.11	0.00
1958	1.78	0.00
1959	1.13	4.56
1960	1.78	1.52

Based on 616,000 high school players and 65,690 college players

school, and one college. The incidence rate per 100,000 participants was 0.97 at the high school level and 1.52 at the college level (AFCA 1952).

It is interesting that the 1951 report stated the following: "There seems to be little reason for making new recommendations, as those submitted in 1950 were only infrequently, if ever, put into practice" (AFCA 1952). The 1950 recommendations were as follows:

1. American Football Coaches Association should initiate action on the imperative and impartial research necessary on the football helmet. The day is past for only the acceptance of this report—implementation is the next step.
2. Adequate warm-up should be provided before any player enters the game, including en masse substitutions.
3. Teaching of tackling that emphasizes elimination of contact between the player's head and his opponent's knee or thigh.
4. Knee pads or padding of the knees of pants should be required by rule as standard equipment.
5. Inspect head suspensions in all old headgear. Discard helmets which cannot keep the head from contact with the crown of the helmet. Check and repair suspensions before every game and practice.
6. Be sure that adequate absorptive materials are present in newly purchased helmets.

Image 3.1 Era of No Face Masks
Photo courtesy of the North Carolina Coaches Association.

7. Pass no restrictive legislation, at present, against any type of the present headgear shells. The two prevailing types have been equally involved in fatalities during the last three years (AFCA 1952).

Six direct football fatalities were reported in 1952 by Dr. Floyd Eastwood at the Twentieth Annual Meeting of the AFCA. As shown in Table 3.1, five were at the high school level and one was in sandlot football. There were none in professional or college football. Six is the lowest number of direct fatalities since 1931, with the exception of 1945 when there were also six. Football also accounted for four indirect fatalities: two high school, one college, and one sandlot (AFCA 1953).

In the discussion section of the 1952 report it was stated that there had not been a reduction of fatalities related to the free substitution rule, and that the mass substitutions are bringing about an increase in the fatality rate during the first five minutes of entering a game (AFCA 1953).

Recommendations made from the 1952 report are as follows:

Image 3.2 c. 1952
Photo courtesy of the North Carolina Coaches Association.

1.   The AFCA Board of Directors should initiate, with the NCAA, an impartial research project on materials and construction of the football helmet. An approximate cost of $12,000 was given for this research.
2.   A caution that in 1945 there were only 6 direct fatalities, but in 1946 the number increased to 21. The year 1952 may be the calm before the storm.
3.   Tackling and blocking dummies should be constructed to simulate game situations.
4.   Inspect head suspensions of all helmets before every game. Discard helmets where the head suspension cannot keep the head from contact with the crown of the helmet when the head sustains a blow.
5.   Find a technique that will keep the players warmed up between offensive and defensive mass substitutions (AFCA 1953).

In 1953 there were nineteen football fatalities. Thirteen were direct fatalities and six indirect. Sandlot accounted for three direct and two indirect, professional football accounted for two direct, high schools had six direct and four indirect, and colleges had two direct. During the past year the report noted that new equipment was still being worn in most fatal situations, which may indicate that equipment research had not made much progress. Recommendations for 1953 were as follows:

1. Board of Trustees should again consider the possibility of a football material research study during 1954.
2. If the history of fatalities is correct, there may be a rise in the number of football fatalities in 1954. Coaches can help reduce this possibility by paying more attention to fundamentals, scheduling at least three weeks of preseason training, and never scrimmaging until six days of fundamentals have been completed.
3. There has been more piling on and roughing the kicker and passer this year. This situation should be reversed by coaches and referees.
4. Vigorous warm-up should precede the first and third periods.
5. No high school or college touch football should be permitted for players without a thorough physical examination.
6. More attention should be given to adequate physical examinations for football candidates. The decline of indirect fatalities has not met levels one would expect with complete and adequate physical examinations (AFCA 1954).

As predicted in previous reports, the number of direct fatalities in 1954 rose to 19, which was a 6.7% increase over the average for the last 23 years. In addition, there were also 6 indirect fatalities in 1954. The 1954 report makes the point that the National Safety Council statistics state that football is safer than swimming, hunting, and driving a car for the age group 15 to 24 (AFCA 1955).

In 1954, as in the past 22 reports, the majority of fatalities occurred during games (AFCA 1955). Data collected since 1947 show that death was most frequently caused by blows directly on top of the head resulting in spine injuries, or by a blow to the back of the head. The greatest number of fatalities continued to take place during the first five minutes of a practice, game, or scrimmage. Inspections of helmets worn by fatally injured players revealed that the head was allowed to make direct contact with the shell. Heart related fatalities increased in 1954 over the number in 1953, but infections continued to be the largest cause of indirect fatalities. Recommendations from the 1954 report are as follows:

1. A physical examination is required before participation and a mid-season physical examination.
2. No player with a history of heart abnormalities should be allowed to play.
3. Every concussion should be X-rayed immediately and studied with an encephalogram.

4. Players should be barred from participation and contact sports if they have suffered a serious concussion.
5. No institution should be permitted to play a football game without a physician on the bench.
6. Continued and increasing emphasis should be placed on tackling and blocking practice throughout the season (AFCA 1955).

In his opening remarks to the AFCA annual meeting in 1956, Dr. Floyd Eastwood stated that over the last 25 years, fatalities to the head and spine had increased and there had been a decrease in abdominal and internal injuries. He asked if this may have been due to lack of conditioning to other parts of the body and most time being spent on the legs (AFCA 1956).

The 1955 AFCA report showed a total of 10 direct and four indirect fatalities. Six of the direct injuries took place at the high school level, one in college, and two in sandlot. The report stated that during the preceding 24 years, the state of Pennsylvania accounted for 20 high school direct fatalities and Texas for 17. Recommendations from the 1955 report include a couple of new recommendations that had not been mentioned in past reports. Those new recommendations are as follows:

1. Increased attention should be paid to strengthening the muscles of the neck and shoulders.
2. Study concussions as to location of blow, part of opponent's body causing concussion, and type of activity injured player was engaged (AFCA 1955).

The 1956 football season accounted for 17 direct football fatalities (AFCA 1956). Twelve of the 17 fatalities were associated with high school football, 3 with sandlot, 1 with professional, and 1 with college. One of the high school fatalities was in a touch football game. In addition to the direct fatalities, there were also four high school and one touch football indirect fatalities. In those early years of data collection, touch football fatalities were counted with tackle football numbers, but in later years were not included in reports. There were seven more direct fatalities in 1956 when compared to the 1955 total. The incidence rate per 100,000 participants in 1956 was 1.94 at the high school level and 1.52 at the college level (AFCA 1956).

Recommendations for 1956 were very much the same as in 1955. The 1956 report did mention that evidence had been accumulating since 1942 that the best existing helmets used in high school and college football were meant only to protect for low velocity impacts. High velocity impacts were resulting in fatal injuries, and standards of construction could be established and fatalities reduced. Advanced research was recommended to be initiated immediately under the direction of the AFCA (1956). The *Twenty-Sixth Annual Survey of Football Fatalities 1931–57* shows 16 direct fatalities in 1957 (1 fewer than in 1956), and 4 indirect (AFCA 1958). It is interesting to note that the one college indirect fatality was listed as a possible aneurysm, but the case study showed that the year before, while in high school, the player suffered several concussions and one serious concussion that involved 20 minutes of unconsciousness. The player complained of dizziness while participating in drills in the fall of the following year, collapsed, went into a coma, and later died. Because they did not see the blow that may have caused the injury, the injury was ruled indirect. Today, the death would most likely have been ruled direct due to second impact syndrome.

The discussion section of the report emphasized that football fatalities in the age group 15–24 during August through December, were outnumbered 236 to 1 when compared to motor vehicle deaths, and 337 to 1 compared to drowning deaths (AFCA 1958). The purpose of the above data was to illustrate that football is not as dangerous as other activities football players may participate in. Recommendations from the 1957 report are as follows:

1. A 5–10 minute warm-up before football contact activity.
2. More emphasis on development exercises for the shoulder and neck muscles.
3. At least six days of fundamentals before starting the first squad scrimmage of the season.
4. At least three weeks of pre-season before the first game.
5. Spring practice for those not participating in other spring sports with no scrimmages until the last week of fundamentals. This is a great time to improve blocking, tackling, and ball handling skills.
6. More complete medical examinations with special attention to previous injuries.
7. Qualified sport physicians on the bench at all games and immediately available during practices.
8. Football helmets that can stand high velocity blows from an opponent's knee and thigh. It was noted that there had been a 4.5% increase in the total number of fatalities caused by blows to the head since 1947, and it is evident that helmet construction had not kept pace with the speed of the game in 1957 (AFCA 1958).

As illustrated in Table 3.1, there were 17 direct football fatalities in 1958 (AFCA 1959). Eleven occurred in high school football and six in sandlot. There were none at the professional or college levels. During the preceding 27 years, direct fatalities averaged 16.7 per year. Also, in 1958 there were three indirect fatalities: two in high school football and one in college. The 1958 report noted that the increase in direct fatalities was due in large measure to the six fatalities in sandlot football, a completely unsupervised area. Sandlot football accounted for over one-fifth (23.3%) of the direct fatalities from 1931–58. High school accounted for 54.6%, professional for 14.1%, and college for 7.9%. Recommendations for 1958 are as follows:

1. Increased attention to development of the muscles of the neck, back, chest, and shoulder.
2. More attention to the fundamentals of tackling and blocking.
3. More organized and directed football for sandlot groups.
4. More extensive warm-up activities for both game and practices.
5. Helmets that will further protect the front, sides, top, and back of the head.
6. Regular inspection of the player's uniform for helmet suspension that will not allow the head to come in contact with the helmet shell when struck, and placement of pads to properly protect the internal organs (kidneys, liver, and spleen) (AFCA 1959).

The 1959 fatality report had a total of 18 direct and 11 indirect fatalities (AFCA 1960). High school football was associated with seven direct fatalities and six indirect. College football had three direct and one indirect, pro and semi-pro had two direct and one indirect, and sandlot had six direct and three indirect. The incidence rate per 100,000 participants was 1.13 in high school football and 4.56 for colleges. This was an increase for the college level since they had no direct fatalities in 1958 (AFCA 1960).

The 1959 football season was unusual in that it had a crushed larynx as a fatal injury, two spectators were fatally injured at the site of a game (a female death caused by a falling goal post and a female broken neck when she was knocked over by a pass receiver in a sandlot game), and there were four indirect deaths due to heat stroke. There had been only one heat stroke death over the previous 27 years (AFCA 1960).

Recommendations from the 1959 report are as follows (first time recommendations concerning football practice in the heat):

1. Vigorous practice to be abandoned when the shaded dry bulb temperature exceeds 85 degrees Fahrenheit.
2. Whenever the temperature exceeds 80 degrees Fahrenheit on the playing field, alternate 30 minute periods of strenuous activity with equal periods of rest.

3. Light uniforms such as tee-shirts and shorts for first week of practice.
4. Adequate intake of salt and water throughout practice whenever sweating occurs. Two teaspoons of table salt to one gallon of water is a recommended replacement for fluid loss.
5. Increase the organized leagues supervised by recreation agencies in "Flag Football" for sandlot groups.
6. Study the possibility of using rubber or plastic goal posts.
7. Study the possible hazards of the present nose guard (related to being hit on the face guard, snapping the head back, and causing a neck injury).
8. The establishment of a standardized medical examination for football participation by the Sports Injury Committee of the American Medical Association (AFCA 1960).

The 1960 report saw a drop in direct fatalities from 18 in 1959 to 14 in 1960 (Table 3.1). Indirect fatalities also saw a reduction from 11 in 1959 to four in 1960. The direct fatality incidence rate per 100,000 participants for 1960 was 1.78 for the high schools and 1.52 for the colleges. The average incidence rate for the previous 29 years was 1.54 at the high school level and 2.28 at the college level (AFCA 1961).

In 1960 heat stroke fatalities were involved in three indirect deaths, with two being in college football and one in high school football (AFCA 1961). The report stated that many doctors were recommending reduced activity during hot and humid weather, and adequate liquid intake in some form, such as salty bouillon before and during practice, scrimmage, and game situations. The report also stated that the Wisconsin Interscholastic High School Association would not permit participation in contact sports after a player suffers a concussion (AFCA 1961). It also stated that professional football had its first direct fatality[1] in 1960, and it was assumed that the increased skill of the professional players was the major reason for the nonfatal record (AFCA 1061).

Recommendations from the 1960 report are as follows:

1. Continued attention to procedures which will maintain an adequate salt balance during practice and games.
2. Increased emphasis on a complete and thorough medical examination, including an encephalograph test for all players before the season and after each concussion.
3. Continued research on improving helmets.

---

1. The writer assumes that previous listed professional fatalities were semi-pro or other.

Table 3.4 Direct Football Fatalities Cause of Death 1951–60

Cause	Sandlot	Professional	High School	College	Total
Head Injury	14	4	61	8	87
Spinal Injury	1	3	12	4	20
Internal Abdominal	4	1	14	0	19
Not Specified	11	3	2	0	16
TOTAL	30	11	89	12	142

4. Inclusion of weightlifting and tumbling in the conditioning procedures, especially at the beginning of the season (AFCA 1961).

Table 3.4 illustrates the total number of direct fatalities (142) for the decade
1951–60, and the cause of death for each level of play. Head injuries topped
the list at 61.3%, followed by spinal injuries at 14.1%, and internal injuries at
13.4%. When compared to the 1931–40 decade there was a reduction (updated Table) from 214 to 142. Sandlot went from 54 to 30, professional went
from 35 to 11, high school went from 100 to 89, and college went from 25 to
12. When compared to the 1941–50 decade there was a reduction of only two
direct fatalities. It should be noted that the direct and indirect fatality data in
the decade 1931–40 were not separated (AFCA 1961).

Indirect fatalities numbered 55 for the decade 1951–60, and as shown in
Table 3.5, heart related deaths were associated with 22 deaths, or 40% of the
total. Heat stroke fatalities were associated with eight deaths. The first heat
stroke death since 1931 was recorded in 1955. Indirect fatalities in the decade
1951–60 totaled 55, which was an increase of 17 from the decade 1941–50.

Table 3.5 Indirect Football Fatalities Cause of Death 1951–60

Cause	Frequency	Percentage
Heart Attack	22	40.0
Heat Stroke	8	14.5
Aneurysm	8	14.5
Embolism	3	5.5
Lightning	2	3.6
Infection	1	1.8
Other	3	5.5
Not Specified	8	14.5
TOTAL	55	100.0

Table 3.6 Direct Football Fatalities Position Played 1951–60

Position	Frequency	Percentage
Halfback	27	19.0
End	15	10.6
Fullback	11	7.7
Quarterback	7	4.9
Guard	7	4.9
Tackle	6	4.2
Center	5	3.5
Backfield	1	0.8
Not Specified	63	44.4
TOTAL	142	100.0

The direct and indirect fatalities in the decade 1931–40 were not separated so it was not possible to get an accurate number.

Halfbacks had the most fatalities, as illustrated in Table 3.6, followed by ends and fullbacks. Ends were not separated by tight ends or wide receivers so it was not possible to distinguish between the two. Sixty-three, or 44.4% of the fatalities were not specified by position, making this data not very reliable.

As would be expected, tackling, being tackled, and blocking were associated with the greatest number of fatalities (63.4%) (Table 3.7). Many of the safety recommendations during the 29 years of data collection emphasized teaching the proper fundamentals of tackling and blocking (AFCA 1961).

Table 3.8 shows that offensive and defensive football, as expected, was associated with the majority of football fatalities, with defensive football having approximately 4% more. This number coincides with tackling being associ-

Table 3.7 Direct Football Fatalities Activity 1951–60

Activity	Frequency	Percentage
Tackling	53	37.3
Tackled	22	15.5
Blocking	15	10.6
Catching Pass	6	4.2
Blocked	4	2.8
Under Pile up	4	2.8
Not Specified	38	26.8
TOTAL	142	100.0

Table 3.8 Direct Football Fatalities Offensive vs. Defensive 1951–60

Activity	Frequency	Percentage
Offensive	42	29.6
Defensive	48	33.8
Fundamentals	13	9.1
Not Specified	39	27.5
TOTAL	142	100.0

ated with the most fatal injuries. Since 1947, the head, face, and spine were associated with 80.8% of the fatal injuries. Contact with the top of the head resulted in the majority of spinal injuries (AFCA 1961).

Early reports gathered the names of states associated with football fatalities and over a 29 year period, the following states were associated with the greatest number of fatal injuries:

Sandlot	Pennsylvania (20) and New York (13)
Semi-Pro	New Jersey (12) and New York (11)
High School	Texas (26) and Pennsylvania (23)
College	California (5)

Football Rules 1951–1960: Safety and Equipment

As stated in previous chapters, football safety rules and player protective equipment play major roles in helping to prevent and reduce catastrophic injuries and fatalities. The following will cover the college and high school rules that involve the safety of players from 1951–60. The information was taken from the rule books published by the National Collegiate Athletic Association (NCAA) and the National Federation of State High School Associations (NFHS), and from the book written by David M. Nelson titled, *The Anatomy of a Game: Football, the Rules, and the Men Who Made the Game* (1994).

Equipment changes related to safety during the decade 1951–60 concerned the football cleat and the facemask. The first, in 1951, stated that any circular or ring cleat be prohibited unless it had rounded edges and a wall at least 3/16 of an inch thick. Also in 1951, any face mask was prohibited unless it was made of nonbreakable, molded plastic with rounded edges or of a rubber-covered wire. The second rule change related to the cleats was in 1955 when the term "non-chip aluminum alloy" was removed from the shoe cleat rule, and any cleat made of any material liable to chip or fracture was prohibited. In addition, cleats with concave sides and those that were conical with flat, free ends that

Image 3.3 Art Luppino, Arizona State University
Photo courtesy of NCAA.

were not parallel with their base, or those that were less than 3/8 of an inch in diameter or with rounded free ends having arcs less than 7/16 of an inch in diameter, were prohibited. Another equipment change that took place involved the goalposts being widened from 18 ft. 6 ins. to 23 ft. 4 ins. In 1959, the goalpost width was again changed to an inside measurement of 23 ft. 4 ins. and an outside measurement of 24 ft.

The fair catch rule had gone through a number of changes and was actually eliminated in 1950. In 1951 the fair catch was reinstated and changes to the definition were as follows: 1) the free kick option after a fair catch was eliminated, 2) a player making a fair catch signal was allowed two steps to regain his balance after making the catch, and 3) an invalid fair catch signal carried a penalty of fifteen yards. Again, in the 1953 rules it was stated that the fair catch signal must be obvious, and in 1955, the requirement for waving the hand was eliminated. Another rule in 1955 that may have affected safety stated that the ball was not dead when a player was ostensibly holding for a kick and he may kick, pass, or advance the ball.

In 1958, the free time outs for each team during a half were reduced to four, and in 1959 the number of free time outs allowed each half was changed from four to five.

Substitution rules were going through many changes prior to the 1951–60 decade, and in 1953, two-platoon football was abolished and players were al-

Image 3.4 Billy Cannon, Louisiana State University
Photo courtesy of NCAA.

lowed to enter the game only once in each quarter. In 1959, one player was permitted to substitute when the clock was stopped, and in 1960, one substitute for each team could enter any time between successive downs.

Blocking rules also saw some changes in this decade. In 1958 in offensive blocking, the opponent may make contact with only one hand or arm at a time, but in 1959 the one-arm blocking rule was rescinded. In 1952, clipping was redefined as blocking any opponent other than the runner from behind. Clipping was again redefined in 1956 as running or diving into the back, or throwing or dropping the body across the back of the legs of an opponent not carrying the ball. Also in 1952, there was a mandatory disqualification for striking with the forearm, elbow, or locked hands, and for flagrantly rough play or unsportsmanlike conduct. Piling on was defined as piling on, falling on, or throwing oneself on the body of an opponent after the ball becomes dead. In 1957 the rules stated that no player shall grab the facemask of an opponent. The penalty for grabbing the facemask was 15 yards, and flagrant offenders were disqualified.

Discussion

As shown in earlier chapters, there was a great reduction of direct football fatalities from the decade 1931–40 to the decade 1941–50. There was also a

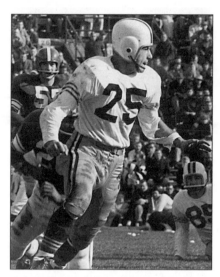

Image 3.5 Earl Morrall, Michigan State University
Photo courtesy of NCAA.

reduction of direct fatalities in 1941–50 when compared to 1951–60, but the reduction was only by two. Graph 3.1 shows the increase in direct fatalities in 1954, a decrease in 1955, another increase in 1956, and then holding steady for the remainder of the decade. When looking at indirect fatalities, there was

Graph 3.1 Direct Fatalities 1951–60

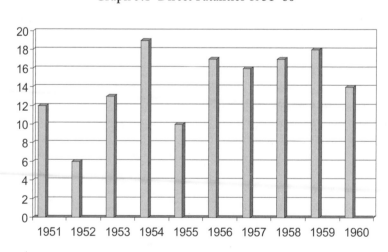

an increase from 1941–50 when there were 38 indirect fatalities, to 1951–60 when there were 55 indirect fatal injuries. In the decade 1941–50, the indirect fatalities were listed mainly as heart related deaths (60.5%) and death due to infection (15.8%). In the decade 1951–60, a majority of the indirect fatalities were related to the heart (40%), infection related deaths were reduced to 1.8%, and for the first time, indirect fatalities included heat stroke (eight deaths for 14.5%).

From 1931 to 1940, there was a total of 97 cerebral hemorrhage fatalities, 55 spinal injuries, and 37 internal injuries that were listed as direct deaths. In the decade 1941–50 cerebral hemorrhage fatalities were reduced by 23 to 74. Spinal fatal injuries were also reduced by 31 from 55 to 24, a reduction of 31. There was an increase in internal fatal injuries from 37 in 1931–40 to 45 in 1941–50, an increase of 8. In the decade 1951–60 the numbers continued to change for direct fatalities. Cerebral hemorrhage deaths increased to 87, an increase of 13 from the previous decade. Almost every year during the decade 1951–60, the report included recommendations to initiate helmet research in order to help make the game safer and to reduce the number of direct cerebral hemorrhage deaths. As of 1960, this research had not taken place. Spinal injuries during this decade continued to decrease with a reduction of 4 over the previous decade and a reduction of 35 from 1931–40. The data collection in 1951–60 reported that most of the cervical vertebrae injuries happened when there was contact with the top of the helmet. There was a major reduction of internal injuries during the decade 1951–60 to a total of 19, the lowest number recorded to date.

The average incidence rate per 100,000 participants for high school football players for the three decades mentioned above stayed fairly steady, starting at 1.62, decreasing to 1.36, and rising slightly to 1.44. College average incidence rates per 100,000 participants during the same decades started at 3.80, then a dramatic decrease to 0.91, followed by an increase to 1.82.

The halfback position continued to be associated with the greatest number of fatalities in the decade 1951–60 (19%), but the data did not distinguish between offensive and defensive backs. The data did state that defensive players were associated with 33.8% of the fatalities, offensive players with 29.6%, and 27% not specified. In all three decades, tackling was associated with the greatest number of fatal injuries followed by being tackled, and blocking. The problem with these numbers was that a majority of the fatalities recorded did not specify the activity in which the participant was involved.

As the decade from 1951 to 1960 came to an end, there was continued concern about the football helmet and its ability to protect participants. It was recommended, as it was in the previous decade, that research was needed to

Image 3.6 Walt Kowalczyk, Michigan State University
Photo courtesy of NCAA.

find best materials for construction of the helmet shell and to determine what type of suspension, if any, was needed. Chapter 4 (1961–70) continues to report on the history of football fatalities and the progress, if any, made in these areas of concern.

References[*]

1. American Football Coaches Association: Proceedings of the Twenty-Ninth Annual Meeting of the American Football Coaches Association, January, 10, 1952, Cincinnati, OH.
2. American Football Coaches Association: Proceedings of the Thirtieth Annual Meting of the American Football Coaches Association, January 7–9, 1953, Washington, D.C.

---

[*] American Football Coaches Association proceedings numbers started to change during this decade. The author does not know the reason for the changes, except for the fact that the proceeding numbers are now equal to the number of years of the original study in 1931.

3. American Football Coaches Association: Proceedings of the Thirty-First Annual Meeting of the American Football Coaches Association, January 6–8, 1954, Cincinnati, OH.
4. American Football Coaches Association: Proceedings of the Thirty-Second Annual Meeting of the American Football Coaches Association, January 5, 1955, New York, NY.
5. American Football Coaches Association: Proceedings of the Thirty-Third Annual Meeting of the American Football Coaches Association, January 9–11, 1956, Los Angeles, CA.
6. American Football Coaches Association: Proceedings of the Thirty-Fourth Annual Meeting of the American Football Coaches Association, January 9–11, 1957, Saint Louis, MO.
7. American Football Coaches Association: Proceedings of the Thirty-Fifth Annual Meeting of the American Football Coaches Association, January 6–8, 1958, Philadelphia, PA.
8. American Football Coaches Association: Proceedings of the Thirty-Sixth Annual Meeting of the American Football Coaches Association, January 8, 1959, Cincinnati, OH.
9. American Football Coaches Association: Proceedings of the Thirty-Seventh Annual Meeting of the American Football Coaches Association, January 5, 1960, New York, NY.
10. American Football Coaches Association: Proceedings of the Thirty-Eighth Annual Meeting of the American Football Coaches Association, January, 1961, Pittsburgh, PA.
11. National Federation of State High School Associations: *Football Rules Books*, 1951–1960.
12. Nelson DM 1994. *The Anatomy of a Game: Football, the Rules, and the Men Who Made the Game.* University Press, DE.

Chapter 4

Fatalities and Catastrophic Injuries, 1961–1970

Introduction

For the past 40 years, the Annual Survey of Football Fatalities has been produced with the exception of 1942 during World War II. In these years there have been many changes and additions to the questionnaire and to the definition of a direct, indirect, and nonfootball injury. There have been changes to some of the data in earlier chapters, but the data from 1961–70 remained consistent. Some of the earlier changes were due to new or revised information received after the publication date. As stated in previous chapters, it is the intention of the authors to give historical data for each decade and to update the data in succeeding chapters.

The 1960s were known for the changes in blocking and tackling techniques, with the initial contact being with the face and head. These changes led to a dramatic increase in direct fatalities—the greatest number since the beginning of research in 1931.

Fatalities and Catastrophic Injuries, 1961–1970

As shown in Table 4.1, there were 244 direct football fatalities from 1961 through 1970 (AFCA 1971). Sandlot football accounted for 37, professional football for 5, high school football for 178, and college football for 24. The total number of direct fatalities in the decade 1961–70 was higher than the three previous decades: 102 greater than in 1951–60, 100 more than in 1941–50, and 30 more than the updated numbers for 1931–40. The greatest increase was at the high school level with 89 fatalities over the previous decade. College football fatalities during this same time also doubled from 12 to 24. Sandlot football increased by seven, and professional football saw a reduction of six fatal injuries. Indirect fatalities also showed an increase of 70 fatalities in

Table 4.1 Direct Football Fatalities 1961–70

Year	Sandlot	Professional	High School	College	Total
1961	3	0	10	6	19
1962	6	1	12	0	19
1963	1	1	12	2	16
1964	4	1	21	3	29
1965	4	0	20	1	25
1966	4	0	20	0	24
1967	5	0	16	3	24
1968	4	1	26	5	36
1969	3	1	18	1	23
1970	3	0	23	3	29
TOTAL	37	5	178	24	244

1961–70 over 1951–60, and an increase of 87 over 1941–50. With updated numbers, there was a reduction of 10 indirect fatalities in 1961–70 when compared to the numbers in 1931–40.

During the 1961 football season there were 19 direct football fatalities with 3 at the sandlot level, 10 at the high school level, and 6 at the college level. In addition, there were 16 indirect fatalities with 4 at the sandlot level, 1 at the professional level, 11 at the high school level, and 0 at the college level. The direct incidence rate per 100,000 participants in 1961 was 1.62 for high schools and 9.13 for colleges. These numbers were based on 616,000 high school players and 65,690 college players.

Cerebral injuries were related to the highest number of fatalities in 1961 with 13, followed by three spinal injuries, and three internal injuries. As in most previous years, tackling was the activity associated with the most fatalities (AFCA 1970), followed by blocking, being blocked, and being tackled. Overall in the past decades, defensive football had produced the most fatalities, but in 1961, offensive football was associated with six, defensive football had four, and fundamentals had seven. Halfbacks and backfield participants continued to be associated with the greatest number of fatal injuries.

The 1961 report stated that more attention was given to follow-up questionnaires and press clippings, which resulted in more accurate information. Recommendations from the 1961 report included the following:

1. Continued attention to maintaining an adequate salt balance during practice and game situations. There were three heat stroke deaths in 1961.

Image 4.1 Brian Dowling, Yale University
Photo courtesy of NCAA.

2. Physical examinations should be required of all participants before the first practice, which include special attention to weight, blood pressure, heart, lungs, abdomen (for liver or spleen), hernia, vascular or bony abnormalities. It was stated that during the preceding 11 years, 22% of the heart-related fatalities could have been diagnosed by an electrocardiogram.

3. Efforts should be coordinated between several research projects on helmet construction.

4. Rules should be established on acceptable kinds of face-nose guards.

5. A renewed and much increased emphasis should be placed on body conditioning during the preseason.

6. Officials need to use the "quick whistle" more often to minimize the hazardous situation of piling-on.

7. Officials need to be more consistent in calling defensive blocking related to the face block, i.e. grasping the face mask or using the arm and/or elbow against the face mask.

8. Teach every player the necessity of keeping the head up at all times while blocking, tackling or carrying the ball.

9. A 60-second warm-up before entering the game or scrimmage.

The 1962 fatality report shows a total of 19 direct fatalities with increases of three at the sandlot level, one at the professional level, and two at the high school level (Table 4.1). There were none at the college level, which was a reduction of six compared to the 1961 report. The direct fatality incidence rate per 100,000 participants was 1.94 for the high schools and 0.00 for the college level. The incidence rate was based on 616,000 high school players and 65,690 college players. Indirect fatalities in 1962 showed a decrease of 11 when compared to 1961.

Cerebral injuries continued to be associated with the most fatalities followed by spinal injuries and internal injuries. As was true in the 1961 report, tackling was the activity most often associated with fatalities in the 1962 report. Defensive football in 1962 was also responsible for the most fatalities followed by fundamental play and offensive football.

The Thirty-First Annual Survey of Football Fatalities had a number of recommendations in the discussion section of the report and the author stated that the game of football is much faster, demands more motor skills, greater conditioning, and is more widely participated in than a decade ago. He went on to state that safety controls have not kept up with the game and that only strict attention paid to a list of controls will reduce the potential hazards of the activity (AFCA 1963). These controls were listed as follows:

A. Administrative
  1. Medical
    a. Complete medical examination of players by a team physician.
    b. A physician in attendance should be mandatory at every game and available at every practice.
    c. An adequately prepared faculty trainer present at all games and practices.
    d. Disqualify from contact sports all players who have had a serious concussion.
  2. Schedule
    a. Senior-high school and junior high school competition regulated by a comparable age-height-weight system.
    b. Longer period for preseason training (at least three weeks, perhaps four).
    c. A shorter competitive schedule for junior and senior high schools.
    d. Ten to 20 days for spring practice in junior and senior high schools and colleges. Time devoted to the teaching of fundamentals.
  3. Game rules and prerequisites for touch football. Flag football should be required in intramurals and physical education classes.
B. Program Controls

1. Attention should be given to the suggestions given by the Mechlenburg County Medical Society of North Carolina.
   a. Vigorous practice abandoned when the shaded dry bulb temperature exceeds 85°F.
   b. When the temperature on the playing field exceeds 80°F, alternate 30 minutes of strenuous activity with equal periods of rest.
   c. Light uniforms such as T-shirts and shorts for first week.
   d. Adequate intake of salt and water throughout practice whenever visible sweating occurs (two teaspoons of table salt to one gallon of water is a recommended replacement for fluid loss). Liquid should be ingested in amounts of at least one quart per hour during profuse sweating. There were 5 heat stroke deaths in 1962 and only 10 in the previous 30 years.
2. Specific conditioning activities should be increased for strengthening the neck, upper arm, shoulder girdle, and legs.
3. Increased emphasis should be placed on head-up tackling and blocking.
4. Less vicious face blocks and abdominal blocks.

C. Equipment Controls
   1. Helmets need to be better constructed based on a safety zone rather than on the comfort zone.
   2. Collection and use of research on the head's "tolerance zone" which is necessary for safe helmet construction.
   3. Require that knee pads be made of slow recovery rubber
   4. First session at the beginning of the season devoted to how to select better fitting equipment and how to wear this equipment.

D. Game Controls
   1. Better calling by officials in cases of twisting the face guard, piling-on, and vicious blocks which may cause neck torsion.
   2. At least a 60-second warm-up before players enter a game, as well as a 5-minute warm-up before entering the third quarter.
   3. Officials should be taught to strictly rule infractions in "Flag Football" in recreational and intramural contests.

During the 1963 football season there were 16 fatalities, which is 3 fewer than in 1961 and 1962 (Table 4.1). High school football was associated with 12, college with 2, and both sandlot and professional with 1 each. The incident rate per 100,000 participants was 1.94 at the high school level and 3.04 at the college level (Table 4.3). There were also eight indirect fatalities, which was one fewer than in 1962 and eight fewer than in 1961 (Table 4.2). For the first

Table 4.2 Indirect Football Fatalities 1961–70

Year	Sandlot	Professional	High School	College	Total
1961	4	1	11	0	16
1962	0	1	4	2	7
1963	2	0	4	2	8
1964	3	0	12	1	16
1965	4	1	14	5	24
1966	0	0	6	2	8
1967	0	0	4	1	5
1968	2	0	8	2	12
1969	3	1	8	3	15
1970	0	0	12	2	14
TOTAL	18	4	83	20	125

time in the past 32 years, sickle cell anemia was the cause of 2 indirect deaths. There were no heat stroke deaths in 1963. Tackling and being tackled were associated with the greatest number of fatal injuries, and the head was the body part most injured. Head injuries were followed by spinal and internal injuries.

Recommendations from the 1963 report again emphasized the imperativeness of a complete medical examination of each player by a team physician, planning practices in hot and humid weather, and continued research on helmet construction. For the first time, it was recommended that trainers, coaches, and doctors needed to know mouth to mouth resuscitation. Another interesting recommendation was that during practices in the heat, salt intake should be increased by ingesting tablets or salty bouillon (salt tablets are prohibited in present day football).

The 1964 fatality report shows a dramatic increase in the total number of direct football fatalities, and the greatest one year total since the first year of the research in 1931. There were 29 fatalities in 1964 with the highest number ever at the high school level with 21. That is an increase of nine high school fatalities over 1963. There were also four fatalities in 1964 at the sandlot level, one at the professional level, and three at the college level (Table 4.1). During the past 34 years, fatalities directly due to football had averaged 17.60 per year. In 1964 the direct fatality incidence rate per 100,000 participants was 2.23 at the high school level and 4.56 at the college level. Incidence rates were based on 616,000 high school players and 65,690 college players. There was also a dramatic increase of indirect fatalities in 1964 to 16, which was an increase of 8 from the 1963 number. The high schools tripled their number of indirect fatalities in 1964 when compared to the four in 1963.

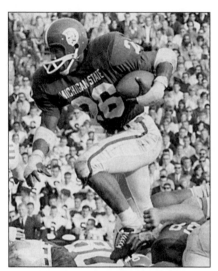

Image 4.2 Clinton Jones, Michigan State University
Photo courtesy of NCAA.

Head/brain injuries were associated with the greatest number of fatalities with 20, followed by 3 spinal injuries, 3 internal injuries, and 3 injuries where the body part was not specified. As in the past, the activities most associated with fatalities were tackling, being tackled, and blocking. Ten of the 29 fatal injuries took place with the participant playing on the defensive side of the ball, 5 were on offense, 6 were participating in fundamental play, and 8 were not specified.

In the discussion section of the 1964 report, the author states that due to the sudden increase in fatalities, football requires additional analysis by physicians, team coaches in charge of planning conditioning programs and practices, rules committees dedicated to safer football, equipment manufacturers who are constantly trying to improve equipment (especially the helmet), officials who should call all infractions of the rules more vigorously, and school authorities who should permit football only when all of the present known safety guards are present. Other factors mentioned were substitution rules, presence or absence of physicians on the field during all games, and the results of insufficient conditioning before full contact. The report continued to point out that the fatality incidence rates per 100,000 football participants from August to January was less than the 100,000 exposures when compared with the leading causes of death in the same age group and during the same months.

Recommendations in the 1964 report were very similar to earlier reports and included the following:

1. Enrich contacts with press associations and individual sports editors so they could see the multiple variables that establish the possibility for football fatalities.
2. Request a rule be created where it does not exist that requires a physician in attendance at all levels of play.
3. Increase the amount of time spent on contact and noncontact fundamentals, with a minimum of three weeks before the first scheduled game.
4. Enforce a minimum player warm-up of 60–120 seconds before entering a game.
5. Develop increased safety procedures to meet the "quick opening" plays used extensively in today's football.
6. Conduct another nationwide injury study of high school and college injuries.
7. Conduct extensive research on establishing a more efficient head guard and the effect of the nose guard on head and neck injuries. Facts, not opinions, are necessary.
8. Establish a physical examination minimum for all high school and college players (AFCA 1965).

The 1965 football season saw a slight decline in direct football fatalities from 29 in 1964 to 25 (Table 4.1). Even with the slight reduction, 25 was the highest number since 1936 (not counting the 29 in 1964) when there were 28 fatalities. The fatality incidence rate per 100,000 participants was 2.00 at the high school level and 1.33 at the college level. Participation numbers were higher in 1965 with 1,000,000 high school players and 75,000 college players (Table 4.3). There was an increase of 8 indirect fatalities in 1965 over the previous year for a total of 24 (Table 4.2). Eleven of the indirect fatalities were heart-related and six were heat stroke deaths. Tackling and being tackled accounted for 19 of the direct fatal injuries in 1965, while head and neck injuries accounted for 24 of the 25 direct fatalities. Defensive football play continued to account for most of the fatalities. This would seem obvious since most of the direct fatalities took place while tackling.

Discussion and recommendations for the 1965 report stated that 96% of the fatal injuries in 1965 were head and neck injuries, and they must be reduced. It also stated that the practice of spearing, driving the head directly into the chest, stomach, and kidney areas of the opponent while tackling or blocking, be condemned by all responsible persons truly interested in the game of football and the welfare of the participants. When the human head is used as

Image 4.3 Sample of Head Down Tackling
Photo courtesy of the North Carolina Coaches Association.

a battering ram there is danger of hyperflexion, hyperextension, or compression of the cervical vertebra, as well as the possibility of concussion. None of the fatality reports in 1965 stated that the equipment contributed to the injury, but there should be continued research for safer and improved equipment. The 1965 report also mentioned the importance of conditioning exercises to strengthen the neck muscles so participants would be able to hold their heads firmly erect when making contact (AFCA 1966).

A major concern mentioned in the 1965 report was the number of heat stroke fatalities in 1964 and 1965 (10 total). From 1931 through 1963, there had been a total of 15 heat stroke fatalities, and 10 in two years was not acceptable. The report stated that this dramatic increase in heat-related deaths needed immediate attention. Suggestions for reducing heat stroke deaths were as follows:

1. Hold sensible practice sessions in early morning or late afternoon during hot months.
2. Acclimatize athletes to hot weather with carefully graduated practice sessions.
3. Provide rest periods of 30–45 minutes after workouts of one hour.
4. Ingest extra water and salt in recommended amounts.
5. Watch athletes for signs of trouble (fatigue, lethargy, inattention, stupor, awkwardness, etc.), especially in the determined athlete who may not report discomfort.

Table 4.3 Direct Football Fatalities Incidence
per 100,000 Participants 1961–70

Year	High School	College
1961	1.62	9.13
1962	1.94	0.00
1963	1.94	3.04
1964	2.23	4.56
1965	2.00	1.33
1966	2.00	0.00
1967	1.60	4.00
1968	2.60	6.66
1969	1.64	1.33
1970	1.92	4.00

6. Remember that the temperature and humidity, not the sun, are the important factors and that heat stroke, and heat exhaustion can occur in the shade.

The Thirty-Fifth Annual Survey of Football Fatalities 1931–66 shows 24 direct football fatalities in 1966, 1 fewer than in 1965 (Table 4.1). The fatal injury incidence rate per 100,000 participants was 2.00 at the high school level and 0.00 at the college level (Table 4.3). The last time there were no fatalities at the college level was in 1962, and prior to that was in 1957 and 1958. During the preceding 36 years, direct football fatalities averaged 18.09 per year. Indirect fatalities had a reduction of 16 fatalities from 1965 to 1966 (Table 4.3).

Tackling accounted for eight fatalities in 1966, being tackled for seven, blocking for three, and piling-on for one. Head fatalities continued to be a problem with 18, followed by 5 spinal injuries. Defensive football play was associated with nine fatal injuries, offensive football had seven, and six took place working on fundamentals. With the major reduction in indirect fatalities, there was one heat stroke death and five heart-related deaths.

The recommendations from the 1966 fatality report were very similar to the 1965 report with one exception. This exception was the addition of the word "goring" to the word "spearing" when recommending that these techniques be eliminated from the game of football. This is the first time the authors had seen the word "goring." The recommendation went on to say that these techniques are extremely dangerous to the ball carrier, and more frequently however, it is the tackler who is the more severely and seriously injured.

In the 1967 AFCA football fatality report, there were 24 direct fatalities. This was the same number as in 1966 and approximately six more than the average for the past 36 years (Table 4.1). The direct fatality incidence rate per 100,000 participants was 1.60 at the high school level and 4.00 at the college level (Table 4.2). Indirect fatalities numbered 5 in 1967, which was 3 fewer than in 1966 and 19 fewer than in 1965 (Table 4.3).

Tackling and being tackled accounted for approximately half of the direct fatalities, and head injuries numbered 19, followed by spinal injuries with 3. Offensive and defensive player fatalities were almost equal with nine on offensive and eight defensive incidents. Indirect fatalities continued to show a dramatic decline when compared to the 1965 report. The five indirect fatalities in 1967 included two heat-related and one heart-related, which were the main causes of indirect fatalities during the 1960s.

Since 1960, most of the direct fatalities had been caused by injuries to the head and neck. In 1967, 22 of the 24 fatalities were caused this way. The 1967 report stated that the helmet was designed as a protective device and should not be used as a weapon. It was again pointed out that the techniques of spearing and goring had to be eliminated if the number of head and neck injuries were to be eliminated. The report also emphasized the importance of taking proper precautions while practicing in the heat and humidity since there were two additional heat stroke deaths in 1967. Most of the other recommendations were the same as in the 1966 report.

The Thirty-Seventh Annual Survey of Football Fatalities 1931–68 was historic in that there were 36 direct fatal injuries in 1968, the greatest number since the study was initiated (Table 4.1). The next highest number of direct fatalities was in 1931 when there were 31. Tackling and being tackled accounted for half of the fatalities, with the head and neck injuries associated with all 36 fatalities. Head injuries numbered 30 and neck injuries numbered 6. Twenty-six of the fatalities were at the high school level, five were at the college level, four were at the sandlot level, and one was at the professional level. Defensive football accounted for 14 fatal injuries and offensive football also accounted for 14. The direct incidence rate per 100,000 participants was 2.60 at the high school level, which was the highest high school rate since the study began in 1931. The college direct rate was 6.66, which is the third highest rate since the start of the study. The college rate was 9.23 in 1961 and 12.17 in 1931. The 1968 rate per 100,000 participants was based on 1,000,000 high school and 75,000 college participants (Table 4.3).

There was also an increase in indirect fatalities in 1968 with a total of 12, which is an increase of seven over the 1967 total (Table 4.2). A major concern was the five heat stroke deaths in 1968.

There were no changes to the recommendations in the 1968 report, but there was general concern by coaches, administrators, physicians, and others responsible for the safety of football players that 36 fatalities in one year could not be tolerated, and that heat stroke fatalities had to be eliminated.

After the historic report in 1968, which showed 36 direct football fatalities, the 1969 report illustrated a reduction of 13 fatalities to 23 (Table 4.1). Twenty-three is still higher that the 38-year average of approximately 18, but not as high as 36. The 1969 data continued to demonstrate that head and neck injuries were the major cause of football fatalities with 17 head and 2 neck fatalities. Internal injuries numbered four. As would be expected, tackling and being tackled were the two activities that were responsible for a majority of the fatalities. In 1969, these activities accounted for 17 of the 23 deaths. The direct incidence rate per 100,000 participants was 1.64 at the high school level and 1.33 at the college level (Table 4.3). In 1969, defensive football was associated with 13 fatalities and offensive football accounted for 7. In addition to the 23 direct fatalities, there were also 15 indirect fatalities (Table 4.2). Heat stroke was again responsible for five of the indirect fatalities and heart-related fatalities accounted for four. A variety of causes was responsible for the remainder.

The 10 recommendations for injury prevention that were listed in the past three reports were listed again, but special emphasis was again placed on eliminating injuries to the head and neck. Emphasis was also given to heat stroke fatalities when the report stated that all coaches, trainers, and physicians should continue their efforts toward eliminating athletic fatalities which result from physical activity in hot weather. In the years from 1961 to 1969, there had been 29 heat stroke deaths.

The 1970 football season continued the trend of high numbers of direct football fatalities with 29 (Table 4.1). That was 6 more than the 1969 season, 7 less than the historic 1968 season, and equal to the 29 recorded in 1964. Head and spine fatalities were the most injured body parts with 18 and 8, respectively. Tackling and being tackled continued to be the activity that produced the greatest number of direct fatalities. Offensive and defensive play were both involved in similar numbers of fatalities, but there were 10 fatalities in which the type of play was not specified. The direct fatality incidence rate per 100,000 participants was 1.92 for high schools, and 4.00 for colleges (Table 4.3).

Indirect fatalities numbered 14 in 1970, a decrease of one from 1969 (Table 4.2). There were eight heat stroke fatalities in 1970, which was the highest number recorded since the first heat stroke death in 1955. Prior to 1955, there was no record of heat stroke deaths in football. For the first time in many years there were no heart-related indirect deaths.

Recommendations from the 1970 report stated that the practice of spearing should be condemned by all responsible persons truly interested in the game of football and the rules prohibiting spearing should be enforced. Enforcement of the rules prohibiting spearing, along with properly fitted helmets and excellent physical condition are factors which help reduce fatalities and serious head and neck injuries resulting from participation in football. As in past reports, a recommendation was made that all coaches, trainers, and physicians should continue their efforts toward eliminating athletic fatalities which result from physical activity in hot weather. Recommendations to achieve this goal were listed and were identical to earlier reports.

As illustrated in Table 4.4, cerebral hemorrhages were the leading cause of football direct fatalities in the decade 1961–70. Cerebral hemorrhages accounted for 179, or 73.4% of the total number of 244 fatalities. Spinal injuries followed with 40 (16.4%) and internal/abdominal injuries were third with 19 (7.8%). High school football accounted for the greatest number with 178, or 72.9% of the total number of fatalities. It should be pointed out that high school football also had the greatest number of participants. It was interesting that sandlot football was associated with more direct fatalities than college football.

Table 4.4 Direct Football Injuries Cause of Death 1961–70

Cause	Sandlot	Professional	High School	College	Total
Cerebral Hemorrhage	27	3	137	12	179
Spinal Cord	2	1	28	9	40
Internal Abdominal	5	1	10	3	19
Unknown	1	0	3	2	6
TOTAL	35	5	178	26	244

Table 4.5 Indirect Football Fatalities Cause of Death 1961–70

Cause	Frequency	Percentage
Heart Attack	46	36.8
Heat Stroke	37	29.6
Aneurysm	5	4.0
Infection	2	1.6
Other	35	28.0
TOTAL	125	100.0

Table 4.6 Direct Football Fatalities Activity 1961–70

Activity	Frequency	Percentage
Tackling	77	31.6
Tackled	52	21.3
Blocking	23	9.4
Collision	14	5.7
Pile–up	8	3.3
Blocked	8	3.3
Catching Pass	1	0.4
Not Specified	61	25.0
TOTAL	**244**	**100.0**

As shown in Table 4.5, indirect fatalities numbered 125 for all of the 1960s. Heart-related deaths were the leading cause with 46 (36.8%), and were followed closely by heat stroke deaths with 37 (29.6%). Infections were the leading cause of indirect deaths during the 1930s, but there were only two infection-related deaths in the 1960s. Indirect deaths increased from 38 in 1941–50 to 125 in the 1960s.

Over half of the direct football fatalities from 1961–70 were caused by tackling and being tackled (Table 4.6). In the previous decade, over half of the activity-related deaths were listed as nonspecified, and in the current decade one-quarter of the activity-related fatalities were listed this way. The data also shows that tackling and being tackled increased dramatically from previous decades. Table 4.7 also indicates that tackling fatalities were on the rise with defensive players, accounting for the greatest number of fatalities with 90, or 36.9%. Almost one-quarter of the injuries in Table 4.7 were listed as nonspecified. Information from previous decades had the number of fatalities related to position played, but for some unknown reason the data was not available in the 1960s.

Table 4.7 Direct Football Fatalities Offensive vs. Defensive 1961–70

Activity	Frequency	Percentage
Offensive	64	26.2
Defensive	90	36.9
Fundamentals	36	14.8
Not Specified	54	22.1
TOTAL	**244**	**100.0**

Football Rules 1961–1970: Safety and Equipment

As stated in previous chapters, football safety rules and player protective equipment had major roles in helping to prevent and reduce catastrophic injuries and fatalities. The following section covers college and high school rules that involve the safety of players from 1961 to 1970. The information was taken from rule books published by the National Collegiate Athletic Association (NCAA) and the National Federation of State High School Associations (NFHS), and from David M. Nelson's book, *The Anatomy of a Game: Football, the Rules, and the Men Who Made the Game*.

In 1962, the college rule book recommended that all players wear properly fitted mouth protectors, which was the first step in making the mouthpiece mandatory. An interesting note here is that in the same year at the NCAA Football Rules Committee meeting, the representative of the American Football Coaches Association (AFCA) recommended to the rules committee that the facemask be removed from helmets. There seemed to be a contradiction between the recommendation for mouth protectors and the removal of the facemask from helmets, which was blamed by some for the increase in injuries the previous year. There was no action on the removal of the facemask by the rules committee, but officials were given a mandate to crack down on piling on the ball carrier and clipping. Officials were also instructed to crack down on defensive heckling, by word or deed, which was intended to distract signal-calling by the offensive team. Also in 1962, the NCAA created a new position of Secretary-Rules Editor of the NCAA Football Rules Committee. David M. Nelson was appointed to the position without reappointment restrictions. The NCAA Football Rules Committee in 1962 formed a Subcommittee on Injuries and Equipment and their first report made four recommendations: 1) purchase only the best protective equipment, 2) devote more time to physical conditioning of the neck and knees, 3) emphasize consistent officiating throughout the country, and 4) eliminate coaching techniques that encourage foul play (Nelson 1994).

An important rule in 1963 made it illegal for an offensive player, who was outside the clipping area and in motion toward the ball, to clip in the clipping area. As close as possible to unlimited substitution, the committee approved unlimited substitution when the clock was stopped except on fourth down and the down when the ball changes hands. At these times, each team was limited to two substitutions whether or not the clock was running. Also during this time, the executive director of the AFCA sent a letter to the membership stating that the coach was responsible for eliminating brutality in football and that training methods aimed at injuring the opponent should be eliminated. The Rules

Image 4.4 Jim Grabowski, University of Illinois
Photo courtesy of NCAA.

Committee placed in the interpretations book the following: "A deliberate malicious act in which the head and helmet are used to strike an opponent's head, neck, or face is a personal foul." This was added to the rule book in 1964 (AFCA 1964 and Nelson 1994).

In 1964, a player giving a fair catch signal was prohibited from advancing the ball if it touched the ground or another player. There was another change to the substitution rule that stated that there was unlimited substitution while the clock was stopped, and a limit of two substitutions while the clock was running.

In 1965, a rule was initiated that stated no player may deliberately and maliciously use his helmet or head to unnecessarily butt or ram an opponent. It was a 15-yard penalty and flagrant offenders were disqualified. After many years of different and complicated rules, unlimited substitution was permitted in 1965. The rule changes in 1966 had little effect on the game and safety measures.

In 1967, it was recommended to the NCAA Football Rules Committee and the NFHS that they join forces as soon as possible to produce a joint code of football rules. It was during these years that litigation involving football injuries was on the rise and the Rules Committee realized that immediate action was needed to make the game safer and that the playing rules had to be defensible in a court of law. The Equipment and Injuries Committee recommended the establishment of minimum standards for football helmets by an organization capable of undertaking the project. They also recommended a committee be formed to collect and organize materials concerning injuries to the head, neck, and spine in football. Richard Schneider, M.D. was invited to lecture on the subject of head and spine injuries, and he reported 225 neurosurgical injuries and fatalities between 1959 and 1964. He concluded from his research that wearing the face mask was dangerous (AFCA 1967). This report threatened to eliminate the face mask on football helmets. Also in 1967, sole leather or other hard or unyielding substances were prohibited in thigh guards, knee and other braces unless they were covered on both sides and overlapped on all edges with at least one-quarter inch of closed cell, slow recovery foam padding, or an alternate material.

The 1968 rules again mentioned the clipping rule and made it mandatory that a player positioned five yards or more outside the legal clipping area be prohibited from clipping. The fair catch rule continued to receive attention, and in 1968, it was stated that a player of the receiving team who signals for a fair catch and does not touch the ball shall not block an opponent during that down. Face masks were still in use and a new rule stated that metal facemasks covered with surfaces as resilient as rubber would be permitted.

In 1969, the thickness of padding for thigh guards, shin guards, knee and other braces changed from one-quarter inch to one-half inch. Surfaces designed to prevent chipping, and which show no sign of producing burrs or abrasions that would endanger the players, were made legal. Legislation was passed by the NCAA convention requiring the first three days of fall football practice to be conducted without pads. The athletic trainers continued to speak out about excessive spearing and the danger to both the player doing the spear and the player being speared. They stated that the best prevention was educating coaches not to teach the technique of spearing. Also a kicker was defined as any player who punts, dropkicks, or placekicks and he remains the kicker until he has had reasonable time to regain his balance. The rules covering the kick coverage were expanded to require players on the kicking team to remain two yards from the kick receiver.

A major rule in 1970 defined spearing as the deliberate and malicious use of the head and helmet in an attempt to punish a runner after his momentum has stopped. This rule was in response to the 36 fatalities in 1968 which were all head and neck injuries. In response to the number of knee injuries, shoe cleats more than half an inch long were prohibited. During the previous 3 years, the NFHS and the NCAA joint rules committee meetings resulted in a total of 16 High School Federation rules changed to NCAA rules.

Graph 4.1 Direct Fatalities 1961–70

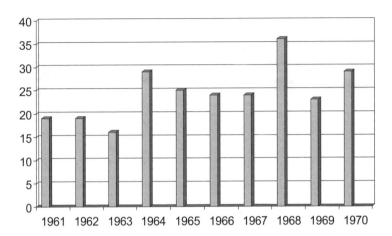

Discussion

As shown in Graph 4.1, the years from 1961 to 1970 were dramatic in that the number of direct fatalities reached an all time high of 244, with a single year high of 36 in 1968. The greatest increase was at the high school level with 89 above the previous decade. Indirect fatalities also increased to a total of 125, an increase of 70 over the previous decade.

When looking at direct football deaths from 1961 to 1970, the leading cause of death was cerebral hemorrhages, accounting for 73.4%. Spinal injuries followed with 16.4% and internal injuries ranked third with 7.8%. As stated previously, the years from 1961 through 1970 were associated with changes in blocking and tackling techniques that involved the player making initial contact with the head and/or face when executing these fundamental skills. Players were taught to make initial contact with the head/face and the brunt of the blow was to the head and brain. Players also were lowering their heads before contact and thus making contact with the top of the helmeted head causing cervical vertebrae fractures, and in a number of cases, permanent paralysis. The 1960s was also the decade in which spearing played a major role in the number of fatal injuries. Spearing was the act of a player making contact with the helmeted head into an opposing player, with the final outcome being a serious head or neck injury to the player initiating the spearing. Spearing was taught in order to punish the ball carrier, but it actually caused more harm to the player doing the spearing. A rule was initiated in 1965 that stated no player may deliberately and maliciously use his helmet or head to unnecessarily butt or ram an opponent. The penalty was 15 yards, but in the opinion of the injury report authors, it did not do much to eliminate this activity. The 1970 rule book defined spearing as the deliberate and malicious use of the head and helmet in an attempt to punish a runner after his momentum has stopped. During this time there was also some discussion of removing the facemask from the helmet in order to stop the use of the head in blocking and tackling. This discussion did not get very far and the face mask continued to be a part of the helmet. After the 1968 football season and the dramatic rise in fatalities to 36, both coaches and administrators showed great concern, and as will be shown, made progress to help reduce football deaths. It is interesting that after the 1968 season there were no changes to the safety recommendations from the previous year.

Indirect fatalities also increased during this decade, but the area of main concern was the number of heat stroke deaths. The first heat stroke death was not recorded until 1955, and in 1970 there were eight stroke deaths—the highest number ever recorded. There were recommendations to reduce or eliminate the number of heat stroke fatalities, but heat stroke continued to create problems in future decades.

The 1960s saw an introduction to football head and face tackling and blocking, butt tackling and blocking, spearing, and an increase of heat stroke deaths. These types of tackling and blocking fundamental skills were actually being taught as the correct way to perform these skills, and they were thought of as being the most efficient. The end result of these fundamental skills was the most dramatic increase in head and neck fatalities since the beginning of data collection in 1931.

There were also continuous recommendations to form a scientific committee to evaluate the football helmet in order to reduce the number of serious brain injuries and fatalities. In 1967, the Equipment and Rules Committee recommended the establishment of minimum standards for football helmets by an organization capable of undertaking this project. There was no movement in this area during the 1960s.

References

1. American Football Coaches Association: Proceedings of the Thirty-Ninth Annual Meeting of the American Football Coaches Association, January, 11, 1962, Chicago, IL.

2. American Football Coaches Association: Proceedings of the Fortieth Annual Meting of the American Football Coaches Association, January 8, 1963, Los Angeles, CA.
3. American Football Coaches Association: Proceedings of the Forty-First Annual Meeting of the American Football Coaches Association, January 6, 1964, New York, NY.
4. American Football Coaches Association: Proceedings of the Forty-Second Annual Meeting of the American Football Coaches Association, January 10, 1965, Chicago, IL.
5. American Football Coaches Association: Proceedings of the Forty-Third Annual Meeting of the American Football Coaches Association, February 1, 1966, Washington, DC.
6. American Football Coaches Association: Proceedings of the Forty-Fourth Annual Meeting of the American Football Coaches Association, January 12, 1967, Houston, TX.
7. American Football Coaches Association: Proceedings of the Forty-Fifth Annual Meeting of the American football Coaches Association, January 10 1968, New York, NY.
8. American Football Coaches Association: Proceedings of the Forty-Sixth Annual Meeting of the American Football Coaches Association, January 8, 1969, Los Angeles, CA.
9. American Football Coaches Association: Proceedings of the Forty-Seventh Annual Meeting of the American Football Coaches Association, January 14, 1970, Washington, DC.
10. American Football Coaches Association: Proceedings of the Forty-Eighth Annual Meeting of the American Football Coaches Association, January 13, 1971, Houston, TX.
11. National Federation of State High School Associations: Football Rules Books, 1961–70.
12. Nelson DM: *The Anatomy of a Game: Football, the Rules, and the Men Who Made the Game.* University Press, DE. 1994.

Chapter 5

Fatalities and Catastrophic Injuries, 1971–1980

Introduction

Injury data from the decade 1961–70 revealed the highest number of direct football fatalities since the study was initiated in 1931, with a total of 244, which included 37 in sandlot, 5 in professional, 178 in high school, and 24 in college. The number of direct fatalities from 1971 through 1980 were reduced dramatically from 244 to 127, partly due to the great concern among coaches, athletic directors, physicians, equipment manufacturers, and others, plus a major rule change and helmet standard implementation (American Football Coaches Association (AFCA 1976)). The 1960s had five years in which the number of direct fatalities was in the 20s. The 1970s were associated with only two years of 20 fatalities and, in fact, had four years of single-digit injuries and one year with only 4.

As illustrated in Table 5.2, the number of indirect fatalities was reduced from the 1960s to the 1970s. The 1960s had 125 indirect fatalities, and the 1970s had 86—a reduction of 39.

The 1970s saw a major rule change in 1976 that eliminated initial contact with the head or face while tackling and blocking. In addition to this major rule change, a helmet standard went into effect at the college level in 1978 and at the high school level in 1980. These two changes were given credit for the major reduction of direct fatalities in the 1970s.

Fatalities and Catastrophic Injuries, 1971–1980

In 1971 there were 20 direct football fatalities with 2 at the sandlot level, 3 in college, and 15 at the high school level (AFCA 1972). This was a reduction from the 29 fatalities recorded in 1970. Direct fatalities were defined as those deaths which resulted from participation in football. This definition changed

Table 5.1 Direct Football Fatalities 1971–80

Year	Sandlot	Professional	High School	College	Total
1971	2	0	15	3	20
1972	3	1	16	2	22
1973	2	0	7	0	9
1974	0	0	10	1	11
1975	1	0	13	1	15
1976	3	0	15	0	18
1977	1	0	8	1	10
1978	0	0	9	0	9
1979	0	0	3	1	4
1980	0	0	9	0	9
TOTAL	12	1	105	9	127

over the next decade, however. The 1971 incidence per 100,000 participants was very low for direct fatalities. The incidence rate was 1.25 for high school, and 4.00 for the colleges. Thirteen of the direct fatal injuries in 1971 resulted from injuries to the head (brain), four were to the spinal cord, and three were to the abdomen. The activities most involved with direct football fatalities in 1971 were tackling (8), being tackled (2), blocking (2), and collision (2). The activity of six fatalities was unknown. A majority of the fatal injuries were also associated with defensive football, but there were seven unspecified in this category. For an unknown reason there was no data related to the positions played by the injured athletes in 1971 (AFCA 1972).

Table 5.2 Indirect Football Fatalities 1971–80

Year	Sandlot	Professional	High School	College	Total
1971	2	1	7	2	12
1972	0	0	10	1	11
1973	0	0	5	3	8
1974	0	0	5	3	8
1975	2	0	3	3	8
1976	1	0	7	2	10
1977	0	0	6	0	6
1978	0	0	8	1	9
1979	1	0	8	1	10
1980	0	0	4	0	4
TOTAL	6	1	63	16	86

In addition to the direct fatalities in 1971, there were also 12 indirect fatalities. Indirect were those fatalities which were caused by systemic failure as a result of exertion while participating in football activity or by a complication which was secondary to a nonfatal injury. At this time in the history of indirect fatal injuries, most deaths were related to heart failure and infection, but heat stroke deaths were increasing. In 1971 heart-related deaths numbered seven, heat stroke numbered four, and there was one case of a blood clot in the lung (AFCA 1972).

In the Discussion and Recommendation section of the 1971 report, it was pointed out that 85% of the fatalities were associated with the head and neck and that these injuries must be reduced. Spearing, or driving the head into an opponent, should be condemned by all responsible persons associated with the game of football. When using the head as a battering ram there is the danger of hyperflexion, hyperextension, or compression of the cervical vertebra, as well as the possibility of concussion. It was recommended that coaches and officials in both practice and games enforce the rules prohibiting spearing. The three recommendations to help reduce head and neck injuries were enforcing the rules prohibiting spearing, wearing properly fitted helmets, and ensuring excellent physical conditioning for players (AFCA 1972).

Most of the past reports, including the 1971 report, stated that protective equipment was satisfactory and did not play a role in any of the fatal injuries. The 1971 report stated that it was imperative that old and worn equipment be renovated or discarded and that equipment should be properly fitted (AFCA 1972). Manufacturers, coaches, trainers, and physicians were encouraged to work together and individually toward this end.

A major recommendation that had been in a majority of the reports is for all football players to receive a complete medical examination and medical history at the beginning of each season. The exam and medical history should be kept on file with the proper authorities before a player is allowed to participate in any phase of the game. In addition, it was recommended that it be mandatory for a physician to give written approval before a player was allowed to return to practice or a game after an injury, and that the physician be on the field during game and practice sessions. If the physician is not able to be at practice and/or games, arrangements must be made to contact a physician during an emergency. In addition to a physician, athletic trainers should be members of the medical staff and be qualified in treating and preventing injuries.

In 1971, heat stroke was responsible for 4 of the 12 indirect deaths. Heat stroke deaths had been on the rise, and in 1970 there were eight heat stroke deaths. The following were recommendations from the 1971 report to help prevent heat stroke deaths:

1. Schedule practice sessions in hot weather during the early morning or evening.
2. Acclimatize athletes to hot weather through carefully graduated practice sessions.
3. Provide rest periods of 15 to 30 minutes during practice session of 1 hour.
4. Furnish extra water and salt in recommended amounts (salt recommendation changes in future decades).
5. Watch athletes for signs of trouble (fatigue, lethargy, inattention, stupor, awkwardness, etc.).
6. Remember, temperature and humidity, not the sun, are the important factors and heat stroke and heat exhaustion can occur in the shade.
7. In case of a possible heat stroke injury, contact a physician at once and do not wait.
8. Conduct continued research concerning the safety factor in football (rules, facilities, equipment, etc.) (AFCA 1972).

The 1972 report showed a slight increase of direct fatalities from 20 in 1971 to 22 in 1972 (AFCA 1973). Sixteen fatalities were at the high school level, three were in sandlot football, one was at the professional level, and one was in college. As in previous reports, head and spine injuries were the major cause of death with 19, or 86% of the direct fatalities. Of the 19, 16 were head injuries and 3 were related to the spinal cord. The remaining three fatalities were injuries to the abdomen. Tackling was associated with nine of the direct deaths, being tackled with three, blocking with three, being blocked with one, and the activity of six was unknown. Eleven of the injuries were associated with playing defensive football, five with offensive football, three while participating in fundamental skills during practice, and three were unknown activities. Participation numbers in 1972 were 1,200,000 high school players and 75,000 college players, which gave an incidence rate per 100,000 participants at 1.62 direct fatalities for high school and 2.67 for college.

Indirect fatalities in 1972 numbered 11, 1 fewer than the 1971 report. The 1972 report included a special Editor's Note which stated that in that year's survey, 7 of the 11 indirect fatalities resulted from heat illness (AFCA 1973). The 1970 report was associated with the greatest number of heat stroke deaths (eight) since the study was initiated in 1931. The 1972 report was associated with the second greatest number of heat stroke deaths with seven. Heat stroke deaths have continued to increase since the first case was recorded in 1954. During the 1960s and early 1970s, football coaches thought that not providing water for the players made them tough. This mentality began to change as the number of heat stroke deaths continued. A major recommendation in the 1972 report, as in the 1971 report, stated that all coaches, trainers, and physicians should continue their efforts toward eliminating athletic fatalities resulting from physical activity in hot weather (AFCA 1973). All of the other recommendations in 1972 were the same as those in 1971.

In 1973, the number of direct fatal football injuries numbered 9, a dramatic reduction over the 22 in 1972 and 20 in 1971 (Table 5.1). Two of the fatalities were in sandlot football, and seven were at the high school level. There were none in professional or college football. Head and spinal cord injuries accounted for all nine of the injuries. A variety of activities was associated with the 1972 direct fatalities, but tackling led the list with four followed by one each in blocking, being tackled, and in a pile-up. The activity of two was unknown. Three of the injured players were playing defensive football, three were playing offensive football, two were practicing fundamentals, and one was unknown. The direct fatality incidence per 100,000 participants was 0.58 for high school football and 0.00 for college football (AFCA 1974).

Indirect football fatalities in 1973 numbered eight, a reduction of three from 1972 (Table 5.2). Heart-related deaths numbered five, and heat-related deaths were associated with three. Since the first recorded football heat stroke death in 1955, there had been 61 heat stroke deaths in football. From 1970 to 1973 there were 22 cases of heat stroke death. Heat stroke deaths had been a major concern in all levels of football.

The discussion section of the 1973 report stated that it was difficult to suggest reasons for the reduction of fatalities from the previous year, but it was the opinion of the authors that the following may have played a major role:

1. Better equipment and increased research on the helmet.
2. Increased emphasis on physical conditioning by both athletes and coaches.
3. Medical and health care for the athlete had improved during the last several years.
4. Improved coaching techniques as well as emphasis on rule changes increased protection of the athlete.

The report also mentioned that continued surveillance of athletic injuries would hopefully help in the reduction of injuries and fatalities, and that if previous safety suggestions were followed, the decline would continue. Recommendations for the reduction of fatalities were again very similar to the two previous reports, with special emphasis on eliminating heat stroke deaths in football participants. In bold letters it was stated that all coaches, trainers, and physicians should continue their efforts toward eliminating athletic fatalities resulting from physical activity in hot weather (AFCA 1974). Recommendations for eliminating heat stroke fatalities were repeated from previous reports.

The 1974 football season was associated with 11 direct fatalities, which is 2 more than the 9 in 1973. This number is still low when compared to earlier years and the 36 in 1968. The authors of the 1974 report stated that in the 43 years of the fatality study, there were only 3 years with fewer fatalities (1945, 1952, and 1973) (AFCA 1975). Ten of the fatalities in 1974 were in high school players and one was in a college player (Table 5.1). Head and spinal injuries continued to be the leading cause of death in 1974 with nine head injuries and one spinal injury at the high school level. The one death at the college level was an internal injury (ruptured spleen). Tackling continued to be the main cause of football fatalities, and in 1974 accounted for 7 of the 11 deaths, followed by 1 each for blocking and being tackled. The activity of two was unknown. Seven of the injured players were playing defense, one was playing offense, one was in fundamentals, and two were unknown. Participation numbers in 1974 were 1,200,000 high school players and 75,000 college players with an incidence rate per 100,000 participants of 0.83 for the high schools and 1.33 for the colleges.

Indirect fatalities numbered eight in 1974, which is the same as in 1973 (Table 5.2). Four of the indirect fatalities were associated with complications related to the injury, one was related to sickle cell disease, one with embolism, one heat-related, and one with an unknown cause. The one heat stroke death was a major reduction over the past six years.

The 1974 report repeated the possible reasons for the reduction of direct fatalities in 1973 and 1974 (physical conditioning, medical and health care, and improved coaching), but also credited better equipment, particularly the increased research on the helmet by the National Operating Committee on Standards for Athletic Equipment (NOCSAE). Background information and the history of NOCSAE will be covered in a later chapter. There were no new recommendations added to the previous report.

In the 1975 football season there was a slight increase of direct fatalities over the previous year, from 11 to 15 (Table 5.1). The increases were three at the high school level and one in sandlot football. This is still a major reduction when compared to the 22 fatalities in 1972. Head injuries in 1975 accounted for 13 of the direct injuries, and spinal injuries were associated with 2. In 7 of the 15 direct fatalities the participants were tackling, two were caused by a collision, one while blocking, and the activity of five was unknown. For the first time a fatality was related to a tackling dummy. The dummy was spring-loaded and traveled down a chute to the tackler. The dummy had a large metal bar down the middle and was quite hard. This was the only fatal injury related to this piece of equipment; but there were a number of other serious injuries, and the equipment was taken off the market. Being on the defensive side of the ball continued to be associated with most of the injuries, but there were also six unknowns. Participation numbers stayed constant in 1975 with 1,200,000 high school players and 75,000 college players. The incidence rate per 100,000 participants in 1975 was 1.08 for the high schools and 1.33 for the colleges (AFCA 1976).

Indirect fatalities numbered eight in 1975 for the third consecutive year. Heart-related deaths were associated with four fatalities, brain aneurysm with one, sickle cell disease with one, complication of an injury with one, and the cause of one was unknown. For the first time since the 1958 season there were no heat stroke deaths in 1975. From the 1959 season through the 1974 season, there was a total of 61 heat stroke deaths, with 8 being the greatest number in 1970. The 1975 report stated that the reduction of heat related deaths in 1975 was the result of the educational programs of many organizations and groups including the American Football Coaches Association, the National Collegiate Athletic Association, The National Federation of State High School Associations, the National Athletic Trainers Association, and team physicians.

In the discussion phase of the 1975 report it was noted that football equipment continued to improve under the guidance of NOCSAE, who continued their research on improving helmets not only for football, but also ice hockey and baseball. The recommendation section of the 1975 report was identical to the 1974 report.

In 1976, the number of direct fatalities increased by 3 to 18 (Table 5.1). That was an increase of 3 over the 15 in 1975. The high schools showed an increase of two, sandlot also had an increase of two, and the colleges decreased by one. Fourteen of the fatalities were caused by injuries to the head and spine, with the head being involved in 13. Three injuries were listed as internal, and the cause of one was unknown. One of the internal injuries was related to a blow to the chest while being blocked, which caused cardiac arrest. It was not stated in the report, but this injury was most likely a commotio cordis death. Tackling again led the list of activities the participants were involved in at the time of the injury with five, and followed closely with three being tackled. There were a greater number of unknowns in 1976 with seven. Playing defensive football accounted for 8 of the 18 fatalities, offensive football four, and the activity of six was unknown. Fatality rates per 100,000 participants continued to be low at both the high school and college levels. The high school fatality rate was 1.15, and for the colleges was 0.00 (AFCA 1977).

Indirect fatal injuries in 1976 numbered 10, which was an increase of 2 over the past three seasons. Heart-related deaths were associated with two, aneurysm with one, sickle cell disease with one, complications of injury with three, and heat stroke was again associated with one death after having none in 1975. The cause of two indirect deaths was unknown.

The authors of the 1976 report stated that the number of fatalities continued to remain low when compared to the reports of the past 20 years (AFCA 1977). A major rule change designed to reduce direct injuries was mentioned in the discussion section of the 1976 report. The rule change was made to eliminate the head as a primary and initial contact area in blocking and tackling. The rule change will be discussed in the Football Rules section of this chapter. Recommendations for reducing fatalities were again exactly the same as in the previous report. There is a strong possibility that the authors of the Football Fatalities Report felt that, if the recommendations made in the 1976 and earlier reports were followed by coaches, administrators, medical staff, game officials, players, equipment manufacturers, and others, the number of fatalities would be reduced and the game would be safer for the participants. The problem was getting all of these groups to follow the recommendations that were based on reliable data.

In 1977, direct fatalities were reduced by eight over 1976 (Table 5.1). There was a total of 10 direct fatalities in 1977, which was a major reduction. High school fatalities went from 15 in 1976 to 8 in 1977. Eight of the fatal injuries resulted from injuries to the head and spine—four in each. There were also two internal injuries. One of the internal injuries was related to a torn intestine after a player was hit while passing the ball in a practice session. The second internal injury took place in a game when the player was struck in the chest by the opponent's helmet during a kickoff, which injured the heart. It is a possibility that this heart death was related to commotio cordis. Tackling was the main activity resulting in fatal injuries during the 1977 season with five, followed by being tackled with two. The activities of two fatalities were collisions not otherwise specified, and the activity of one was unknown. Five of the participants were playing defensive football when injured. The high school incidence rate per 100,000 participants dropped to 0.61 and the college rate was 1.33. The 10 direct deaths in 1977 was the lowest number since the 9 deaths in 1973 and the 6 deaths in 1952.

Indirect fatalities numbered six in 1977, which was a reduction of four from the preceding year (Table 5.2). Heat stroke again was the cause of one death, followed by one heart-related death and two deaths related to complications of the injury. The cause of one indirect death was unknown. The six indirect deaths was the lowest number since the five deaths in 1967.

Partial credit for the reduction of direct fatalities in 1977 was given to the football rules governing bodies and administrative organizations for the rule change in 1976 which eliminated the head as a primary and initial contact while blocking and tackling (AFCA 1978). The authors of the 1977 report stated that credit for the reduction of direct fatalities should also be given to NOCSAE and their helmet research. As in previous reports there were two sets of recommendations: one for the elimination of heat stroke deaths, and one for the overall reduction of fatalities. These recommendations had not changed in the 1970s, with the exception of the 1974 report which mentioned the importance of the NOCSAE helmet research.

The 1978 football fatality research report showed continued reduction of direct fatalities that began in 1977 with a reduction of eight direct fatalities over the 1976 data (Table 5.1). There were nine direct fatal injuries in 1978, which equaled the number in 1973, and was the only other single-digit number since the six in 1952. It was interesting that all nine fatalities were associated with high school football. Seven of the nine fatalities involved the head and neck, and the remaining two were internal injuries. One of the internal injuries involved a ruptured colon resulting from being tackled, and the second cause of death was an internal chest hemorrhage due to trauma. Five of the direct fatalities involved tackling, one being tackled, one a collision with another player, and the activity of two was unknown. Defensive football was associated with five of the fatalities, offensive football with one, kickoffs with two, and one was unknown. The fatality incidence rate of high school football remained low with a rate of 0.69 per 100,000 participants.

Indirect fatalities in 1978 numbered nine, with eight at the high school level and one at the college level (Table 5.2). After three years of only two heat stroke deaths, the 1978 report listed four. Heart-related deaths were listed as the remaining five indirect deaths. In the discussion section of the 1978 report, the authors stated that there was a dramatic increase in the number of heat stroke deaths and that these deaths could be prevented by careful control of various factors in the conditioning of the athletes (AFCA 1979). They again emphasized a number of preventive recommendations that should be followed by coaches, trainers, and physicians. The recommendations had been listed in a number of previous reports and played a role in reducing heat stroke deaths to zero in 1975, one in 1976, and one in 1977. The overall recommendations to reduce the number of football fatalities in all of football were identical to the previous year.

The 1979 fatality report illustrates a continued reduction of direct fatal injuries with four (Table 5.1). Three were at the high school level and one was at the college level. This was the lowest number of direct fatalities since the beginning of the study in 1931. The three high school fatalities reached the record low of three from 1945. There had been only five years since 1931 when

Image 5.1 Head Down Tackling, c. 1979
Photo courtesy of Don McCauley.

the number of direct fatal injuries in football was in single digits. Two of the high school deaths involved the head and one involved the spine. The college death was a head injury. Tackling accounted for two of the injuries, being tackled for one, and the activity of one was unknown. Three of the injuries were on the defensive side of the ball, and one was a ball carrier being tackled. High school participation numbers were 1,300,000 and the fatality rate was 0.23 per 100,000 participants. The college incidence rate in 1979 was 1.33 per 100,000 participants (75,000 total participants).

There were also 10 indirect fatalities in 1979 with 8 being at the high school level, 1 at the college level, and 1 in sandlot (Table 5.2). Indirect deaths outnumbered direct deaths by six, and this occurrence was the beginning of a trend for a greater number of indirect deaths. There were two heat stroke fatalities in 1979, and the cause of eight was unknown. This was the first year for such a large number of indirect deaths with unknown causes.

The authors again stated that they were convinced the reduction of fatalities in football was directly related to the 1976 rule change eliminating the head in blocking and tackling and the helmet research of NOCSAE (AFCA 1980). It had been suggested that the increased protection of the helmets and face masks encouraged football participants to take undue risks when executing

Table 5.3 Direct Football Fatalities Incidence
per 100,000 Participants 1971–80

Year	High School	College
1971	1.25	4.00
1972	1.33	2.67
1973	0.58	0.00
1974	0.83	1.33
1975	1.08	1.33
1976	1.15	0.00
1977	0.61	1.33
1978	0.69	0.00
1979	0.23	1.33
1980	0.69	0.00

the fundamental skills of the game, but the fatality data did not indicate this to be true. Heat stroke deaths continued to be a problem since there was at least one heat stroke death every year since 1959, with the exception of 1975 when there were none. The 1979 report continued to offer suggestions for football activity carried on in hot and humid weather. Recommendations resulting from the 1979 report were identical to the previous year.

The 1980 report revealed an increase of five direct football deaths when compared to the 1979 data (Table 5.1). All nine of the fatalities were at the high school level, which was an increase of six when compared to the three in 1979. There was an increase in fatal injuries, but the numbers continued to stay in single digits, and there were only six years since 1931 where the fatal injuries were in single digits. All of the nine injuries involved the head and neck (seven head and two neck). Being tackled accounted for four injuries, tackling for three, and the activity of two was unknown. For the first time in a number of years, offensive football accounted for more injuries than defensive football, with four. Fatality rates per 100,000 participants were low for both high school and college football with the high school rate being 0.69 and the college rate being 0.00. In the Discussion section of the report, it was emphasized that past data show that years of fatal injury decreases had been followed by increases (1945, 1952, 1973), and an effort must be made to avoid another rise in direct fatalities.

Indirect fatal injuries in 1980 numbered four, which was a reduction of six when compared to the 1979 data (Table 5.2). The causes of three indirect fatalities were unknown and the fourth was a heat stroke death. Since 1959 there had been only one year with no heat stroke deaths (1975). Recommendations

Table 5.4 Direct Football Injuries Cause of Death 1971–80

Cause	Sandlot	Professional	High School	College	Total
Cerebral Hemorrhage	9	0	78	3	90
Spinal Cord	1	1	15	5	22
Internal Abdominal	1	0	12	1	14
Unknown	1	0	0	0	1
TOTAL	12	1	105	9	127

Table 5.5 Direct Football Fatalities Activity 1971–80

Activity	Frequency	Percentage
Tackling	55	43.3
Tackled	18	14.2
Blocking	9	7.1
Collision	7	5.5
Blocked	2	1.6
Pile-Up	1	0.8
Spring-Loaded Equipment	1	0.8
Unknown	34	26.7
TOTAL	127	100.0

for preventing heat stroke fatalities were again emphasized in the 1980 report, along with general recommendations for the prevention of all injuries and fatalities (AFCA 1981).

In the 1970s, cerebral hemorrhages were the number one cause of direct fatalities with a total of 90, and accounted for 70.9% of all direct fatalities for the decade (Table 5.4). Spinal cord injuries were associated with 22 (17.3%), internal injuries with 14 (11.0%), and there was one unknown. High school football cerebral hemorrhage deaths numbered 78 and accounted for 74.3% of the total (Table 5.4).

Table 5.5 shows that tackling again led the list of activities with 55 (43.3%) of the direct fatalities in the 1970s. Tackling was followed by being tackled with 18 (14.2%), blocking with 9 (7.1%), and smaller numbers for collision, blocked, and pile-up. There was also a death related to a spring-loaded tackling dummy. Fifty-seven percent of the fatalities were caused by tackling and being tackled.

In the 1970s, defensive football accounted for 43.3% of all direct fatalities, with offensive football associated with 19.7%. Fundamentals were associated with 7.9%, kickoff plays had 1.6%, and 27.5% were unknown (Table 5.6).

Table 5.6 Direct Football Fatalities Offensive vs. Defensive 1971–80

Activity	Frequency	Percentage
Offensive	25	19.7
Defensive	55	43.3
Fundamentals	10	7.9
Kickoff	2	1.6
Not Specified	35	27.5
TOTAL	127	100.0

Table 5.7 Indirect Football Fatalities Cause of Death 1971–80

Cause	Frequency	Percentage
Heart Attack	27	31.4
Heat Stroke	23	26.7
Complications of Injury	10	11.6
Aneurysm	3	3.5
Sickle Cell	3	3.5
Blood Clot Lung	2	2.3
Embolus	1	1.2
Other	17	19.8
TOTAL	86	100.0

Heart-related deaths and heat stroke were related to 58% of the indirect deaths during the 1970s. Heart attacks accounted for 27 (31.4%) and heat stroke accounted for 23 (26.7%) (Table 5.7). Complications of an injury were associated with 10 fatalities, followed by a variety of other causes.

Catastrophic (Disability) Football Injuries

The 1970s were associated with a lower number of football fatalities, but a new concern surfaced in the form of disability or paralyzing cervical spine injuries. Schneider (1973) reported 56 injuries to the cervical spine involving fracture-dislocations from 1959 through 1963, and 30 of these injuries involved permanent quadriplegia. Torg et al.'s (1979) data collection system recorded 259 cervical spine and spinal cord injuries with fractures or dislocations from 1971 to 1975, and 99 of these injuries involved permanent quadri-

Table 5.8 Torg Registry Data Cervical Spine Injuries

Years	Cervical Injuries	Quadriplegia
1971–75	259	99
1976	115	34

Source: Torg et al. 1979.

plegia. In 1976, the numbers included 115 cervical cord injury cases and 34 cases of permanent quadriplegia (Table 5.8). His data also indicated that 52% of all cervical spine quadriplegia from 1971 to 1975 were the result of spearing. Seventy-two percent of the high school cases and 78% of the college cases during this period of time involved tackling. Being tackled accounted for the next highest percentage of permanent injuries. The position with the greatest number of permanent cervical cord injuries was the defensive back, followed by linebackers, special team players, offensive backs, defensive lineman, and offensive lineman. The data also illustrate that in most of the disability injuries the subject used his head as a battering ram and made initial contact with the top or crown of the helmet in a high-impact situation. Torg was given credit for stating that the cause of cervical spine injuries was due to axial loading of the spinal column.

In 1977, Frederick O. Mueller and Carl S. Blyth initiated a survey of catastrophic head and neck injuries for the National Federation of State High School Associations (NFHS), the National Collegiate Athletic Association (NCAA), and AFCA. The area of concern was the steady increase of catastrophic head and neck injuries since the late 1950s and the data collected by Torg's Head and Neck Injury Registry (Torg et al. 1979). In 1976, the Rules Committees of the NFHS and the NCAA changed their rules to prohibit "butt blocking" and "spear tackling" (AFCA 1972–81; NFHS 1971–80). Both of these techniques involved making initial contact with the face and helmet. The new rule prohibited the use of the helmeted head as the initial point of contact when blocking and tackling. To determine the effectiveness of the 1976 rule, data on all catastrophic head and neck injuries were collected during the 1977 football season. Fatalities had been collected since 1931, so this additional data included players with a permanent disability. The first year of data collection included 12 players with varying degrees of cervical cord paralysis, with 10 being high school players and 2 college players. Eight of the injured players were playing defense when the injury occurred, and nine were tackling or attempting to tackle the ball carrier. Data for the catastrophic injuries continued to be updated and the collection process improved over the years. Tables 5.9–5.11

Table 5.9 Permanent Cervical Cord Injuries 1977–80

Year	High School	Professional	College	Total
1977	10	0	2	12
1978	13	1	0	14
1979	8	0	3	11
1980	11	0	2	13
TOTAL	42	1	7	50

Source: Mueller and Blyth 1979–80.

Table 5.10 Permanent Cervical Cord Injuries Incidence
per 100,000 Participants 1977–80

Year	High School	College
1977	0.77	2.67
1978	1.00	0.00
1979	0.62	4.00
1980	0.85	2.67

Based on 1,300,000 high school players and 75,000 college players.
Source: Mueller and Blyth 1979–80.

Table 5.11 Permanent Cervical Cord Injuries Offensive vs.
Defensive Football 1977–80

Position	1977	1978	1979	1980	TOTAL
Defense	7	9	7	11	34
Offense	1	0	1	1	3
Unknown	4	5	3	1	13
TOTAL	12	14	11	13	50

Source: Mueller and Blyth 1979–80.

illustrate the permanent cervical cord injuries collected from 1977–80 (including updates). The data indicated no dramatic rise in the number of permanent disability cervical cord injuries from 1977–80 and continued to demonstrate a reduction from data published in the late 1950s, 1960s, and early 1970s. Injury rates were low, as shown in Table 5.10, and Table 5.11 indicates, when looking at cervical cord injuries, that it was much safer playing offensive football versus defensive football. A majority of the injured players were tackling at the time of the injury, and most were defensive backs.

Football Rules 1971–1980: Safety and Equipment

Football rules and player protective equipment continued to play a major role in the reduction of fatal injuries during the 1970s. Information was taken from the NCAA and NFHS rule books and from the book *The Anatomy of a Game: Football, the Rules, and the Men Who Made the Game*, by David M. Nelson (1994).

There were some major equipment rule changes in the 1970s related to the helmet, and these changes were directly related to the reduction of head injuries and deaths. Starting in 1971, a rule made it illegal for a player five yards or more outside the legal clipping area, or in motion toward the ball, to block below the waist in the legal clipping area. This rule addition was made to help reduce the number of knee injuries. Spearing was also prohibited, and flagrant offenders were disqualified. This was an important change to help prevent the increased number of catastrophic neck injuries. In 1972, the fair catch was again redefined to require lateral movement of only one arm at full length above the head. It was also ruled illegal to strike an opponent's head, face, or neck with an extended forearm and elbow. The 1972 rules also made it clear that in 1973 mouth protectors would be mandatory. The 1973 rules made head protectors mandatory with a secured chin strap. Also, a single intraoral mouth protector comprised of at least two portions—teeth portion and lip portion— was made mandatory. Any projection of metal or other hard substance from a player's artificial legs, arms, or hands was prohibited. The fair catch was again redefined in 1973 by adding "and waving the arm and hand from side to side." The term "limited substitutions" was deleted from the rules and any number of legal substitutions for either team was allowed to enter the game between periods, after a score or try, and during the interval between downs.

In 1974, it was legal to use the palm of the hand to strike the opponent's head, neck, or face. Blocking below the waist was now prohibited during a free kick except against the runner. There were so many problems with the blocking-below-the-waist rule, that in 1974 this action was prohibited anywhere on the field. A valid fair catch was redefined again, stating that the player must wave his arm side to side more than once, and only the player making the fair catch had the protection of no tackling or blocking by the kicking team. Because certain position players had not been wearing shoulder pads, the 1974 rules made the wearing of shoulder pads a requirement. The shoulder pad requirement took place at the high school level in 1976. Shoulder pads with the leading edge of the epaulet rounded, with a radius greater than half the thickness of the material used, were prohibited. A medically prescribed hearing aid was permitted. The 1974 rules also made coaches aware that beginning in 1975, it was recommended that all institutions purchase head protectors that meet the NOCSAE test standard, and that in 1978 all players must wear head protectors that meet the NOCSAE test standard. The helmet standard went into effect at the college level in 1978 and the high school level in 1980. The NOCSAE helmet standard is often cited as one of the equipment changes that helped make the game of football safer for participants.

In 1975, the rules stated that in 1976 the four-point chin strap would be mandatory, and the high school rules made spearing an automatic disqualification. The open hand used on the face mask of the opposing player was legal if it was part of an attempt to get at the ball or runner. Another addition to the fair catch rule stated that a player who has made the fair catch signal and does not touch the ball cannot block an opponent during that down. The rules also made it clear that the referee may temporarily suspend the game when conditions warrant such action. Such conditions could be a violent thunderstorm with severe lightning.

The 1976 rule book redefined spearing as the deliberate use of the helmet in an attempt to punish an opponent. Intentionally striking with the top of the helmet was a 15-yard penalty. According to the rules, the player does not have to be malicious when he spears the opponent with his helmet, but it has to be deliberate. This continued to be a very difficult decision for the officials to decide if a spear was deliberate or not. The high school rule book defined "butt blocking" as a technique involving a blow with the face mask, frontal area, or top of the helmet driven directly into an opponent as the primary point of contact, either in close line play or in the open field. Face tackling was defined as driving the face mask, frontal or top of the helmet, directly into the runner. Both butt blocking and face tackling were listed as personal fouls. Also, the 1976 high school rules required players to wear hip and shoulder pads. The college rules required hip and thigh pads in 1976 and prohibited the use of artificial hands and arms.

The open hand rule was changed in 1977, and players were allowed to use the open hand on the face mask of the opponent without being part of a legal attempt to get at the ball carrier or runner. High school players were required to wear thigh guards in 1977. The 1978 rules left it up to the umpire to decide if an artificial limb would endanger other players. High school rules left it up to individual states to decide if a player may participate with a below-the-knee artificial limb. Players wearing illegal equipment were not permitted to play and had to change the equipment between downs, leave the game, or be charged a free time-out. The 1978 high school book, as a point of special emphasis, mentioned the crack-back blocks and blocking below the waist.

The 1979 rules stated that striking an opponent with a knee, striking an opponent's face, head, or neck illegally and spearing would result in a 15-yard penalty and a first down. Adding the first down language was a change. In regard to an interception of a forward pass, backward pass, or a fumble, all players were prohibited from blocking below the waist except against the runner. Defensive players were also prohibited from charging into the passer when it was obvious that the ball had been thrown. Also in 1979, it was against the rules to block the kicker of a free kick before he had advanced five yards beyond his restraining line or the ball had touched the ground, a player, or an official. The high school rule book in 1979 defined legal shoes and made it illegal especially for kickers to wear ski or logger boots, ballerina slippers, etc. The high school rule book, as a point of special emphasis, mentioned that the NOCSAE helmet requirement was to begin in 1980.

The major rule addition for the high schools in 1980 was the requirement to wear NOCSAE-approved helmets. The colleges began using these helmets in 1978. It was also illegal in 1980 to grasp an opponent's face protector or any edge of the helmet opening. A "chop block" was defined as an illegal delayed block at the knee or below against an opponent who is in contact with a teammate of the blocker. It was also required in 1980 to wear soft pads over the knees and covered by the football pants. The high schools approved the use of hinged braces that contain metal, provided the hinges are covered with a minimum of half an inch of soft material.

Discussion

The decade 1971–80 started with some fairly high numbers of direct fatalities, but there was a dramatic decline in 1973 to nine, followed by three years of increases, and again dramatic declines in the final four years of the decade (Graph 5.1). The four fatalities in 1979 were the lowest number since the beginning of the research in 1931. The four years of single-digit fatalities in the 1970s were the first years since 1952 when there were six. From 1931 through 1980, there had been only six years with single-digit injuries, and four of those years were in the 1970s. When the data from the 1970s was compared to the data of the 1960s, there was a dramatic reduction of 117 fatalities. Credit for this reduction was given to the data collection initiated in 1931, the 1976 rule change eliminating initial contact with the head and face while tackling and blocking, helmet research conducted by NOCSAE, the helmet standard mandated for the colleges in 1978 and the high schools in 1980, coaches' awareness of the proper teaching of blocking and tackling skills, and improved

Graph 5.1 Direct Fatalities 1971–80

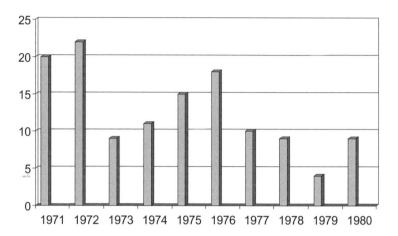

medical care at both practice and games. There was a 59% reduction of football fatalities from 1965–70 (pre-NOCSAE standard), when there were 161 fatalities, to 1971–76 (post-NOCSAE), when there were 95 fatal injuries.

The 1970s also saw a reduction of indirect injuries from 125 in the 1960s to 86. Heart- and heat-related deaths continued to be the major causes of indirect fatalities.

For the 50-year period from 1931 through 1980, there was a total of 871 direct football fatalities. High school football accounted for 556, sandlot for 165, college for 75, and professional for 75. The head was the body part most injured, accounting for 60.5% of the fatalities; spinal injuries accounted for 16.4%, followed by internal injuries with 15.4%, and other injuries with 7.7%. The number of internal injuries continued to decline from the 1930s. During this 50-year period, tackling was associated with 34.2% of the fatalities, being tackled with 15.5%, blocking with 9.4%, being blocked with 2.2%, and a variety of other activities and unknowns accounted for 38.7%.

As shown on Graph 5.2, the collection of direct football fatalities was initiated in 1931 with 214 fatalities. The following two decades saw a reduction of direct fatal injuries, with 144 in the 1940s and 142 in the 1950s. The 1960s was associated with initial head contact, while tackling and blocking and a dramatic increase of fatalities to 244. The 1970s started with great concern for the safety problems in the 1960s and will be remembered for the football rule changes of 1976, the NOCSAE helmet standard going into effect, and the dramatic reduction of direct fatalities to 127 (a reduction of 117 from the 1960s). While there was a reduction of fatalities in the 1970s, there was a new concern

Graph 5.2 Direct Fatalities by Decade

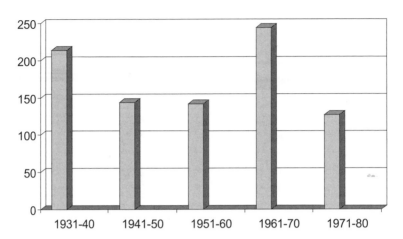

Graph 5.3 Indirect Fatalities by Decade

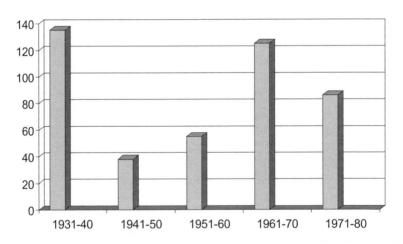

related to catastrophic (permanent neck and brain disability) injuries. The catastrophic injuries led to a number of court cases against the helmet manufacturers, schools, coaches, and administrators.

For the 50-year period from 1931 to 1980 there was a total of 439 indirect fatalities. The 1930s had 135 and were followed by a reduction to 38 in the 1940s, and 55 in the 1950s. Mirroring data for direct fatalities, the 1960s saw a dramatic increase of indirect fatalities to 125. Indirect fatalities in the 1970s accounted for 86. Cause of indirect injury data during the decade of the 1930s was not adequate, and consequently, only the 40-year cause of injury data from 1941–80 was used. Heart-related indirect deaths accounted for 118 (38.8%), heat stroke for 68 (22.4%), and a variety of other causes and unknowns accounted for 118 (38.8%). There were no heat stroke deaths during the 1940s, but there were eight in the 1950s. Heat stroke became a major problem in the 1960s and continued in the 1970s.

The 1970s were considered the decade when fatalities were reduced and safety measures in the form of rule changes, helmet standards, and other equipment requirements were mandated. The question in 1980 was whether these safety measures would continue reductions in both direct and indirect fatalities.

References

1. American Football Coaches Association: Proceedings of the Forty-Ninth Annual Meeting of the American Football Coaches Association, January 1972, Hollywood, FL.
2. American Football Coaches Association: Proceedings of the Fiftieth Annual Meeting of the American Football Coaches Association, January 1973, Chicago, IL.
3. American Football Coaches Association: Proceedings of the Fifty-First Annual Meeting of the American Football Coaches Association, January 1974, San Francisco, CA.
4. American Football Coaches Association: Proceedings of the Fifty-Second Annual Meeting of the American Football Coaches Association, January 1975, Washington, DC.
5. American Football Coaches Association: Proceedings of the Fifty-Third Annual Meeting of the American Football Coaches Association, January 1976, St. Louis, MO.
6. American Football Coaches Association: Proceedings of the Fifty-Fourth Annual Meeting of the American Football Coaches Association, January, 1977, Hollywood, FL.
7. American Football Coaches Association: Proceedings of the Fifty-Fifth Annual Meeting of the American Football Coaches Association, January 1978, Atlanta, GA.
8. American Football Coaches Association: Proceedings of the Fifty-Sixth Annual Meeting of the American Football Coaches Association, January 1979, San Francisco, CA.
9. American Football Coaches Association: Proceedings of the Fifty-Seventh Annual Meeting of the American Football Coaches Association, January 1980, New Orleans, LA.

10. American Football Coaches Association: Proceedings of the Fifty-Eighth Annual Meeting of the American Football Coaches Association, January 1981, Miami Beach, FL.
11. Mueller FO, Blyth CS: Fourth Annual Survey of Catastrophic Football Injuries 1977–80, University of North Carolina, Chapel Hill, NC.
12. National Federation of State High School Associations: Football Rules Books, 1971–80.
13. Nelson DM: *The Anatomy of a Game: Football, the Rules, and the Men Who Made the Game.* University Press, DE. 1994.
14. Schneider, RC: *Head and Neck Injuries in Football.* Baltimore, William and Wilkins. 1973.
15. Torg JS, Truex R, Quedenfeld TC, Burstein A, Spealman A, Nichols C: The National Football Head and Neck Injury Registry. *JAMA*, Vol. 241, No. 14, April 6, 1979.

Chapter 6

Fatalities and Catastrophic Injuries, 1981–1990

Introduction

Football fatalities remained steady during the decades that followed a high of 214 in the first decade of data collection. The following two decades—the 1940s and 1950s—were associated with 144 and 142 fatalities. The years from 1961 through 1970 saw a dramatic increase to 244. As mentioned earlier this was a major concern to all involved in the game of football, and many changes did take place in the 1970s when the number of fatalities was reduced to 127. This concern for the safety of the participants continued from 1981 through 1990, and as illustrated in Table 6.1, there was another major reduction in the number of fatal football injuries to 61. There was only one year in the 1980s—1986—with double digit fatalities. High school football saw the greatest reduction from 105 in the 1970s to 49 in the 1980s.

As illustrated in Table 6.2, the number of indirect fatalities was also reduced during the 1980s to 73.

The first year of the 1990s was historic in that there were no direct fatalities in all levels of football. Going back to 1931 and forward to 2008 this was the only year that there were no direct fatal injuries. However, another injury problem—paralyzing cervical cord injuries—outnumbered direct fatalities in the 1990s. These injuries were a major concern and led to a number of lawsuits. There were 100 cervical cord injuries with paralysis compared to 61 direct fatalities.

Fatalities and Catastrophic Injuries, 1981–1990

In 1981 there were nine direct fatalities with five at the high school level, two in college football, and two in sandlot play. This is the lowest number since the four fatal injuries in 1979. The definition of direct fatalities contin-

Table 6.1 Direct Football Fatalities 1981–90

Year	Sandlot	Professional	High School	College	Total
1981	2	0	5	2	9
1982	2	0	7	0	9
1983	0	0	4	0	4
1984	1	0	4	1	6
1985	2	0	4	1	7
1986	0	0	10	1	11
1987	0	0	4	0	4
1988	0	0	7	0	7
1989	0	0	4	0	4
1990	0	0	0	0	0
TOTAL	7	0	49	5	61

ued to be defined as those fatalities which resulted directly from participation in football. In 1981, the incidence rate for high school football was 0.38 per 100,000 participants, and for college football it was 2.67. Eight of the direct fatalities in 1981 resulted from injuries to the head (brain), and one was the result of an injury to the spinal cord. The activities most involved with direct football fatal injuries were tackling (seven), being tackled (one), and unknown (one). As in previous reports, a majority of the fatal injuries were taking place in games. In 1981, six of the nine injuries occurred in games and three in practice.

In addition to the nine direct fatalities in 1981, there were also six indirect fatalities and all were at the high school level. During this time period in the history of football, most indirect deaths were associated with heart failure. Three of the six were related to the heart, two to heat stroke, and one resulted from acute chronic asthma. Heat stroke deaths continued to be a problem in the 1980s. From 1960 through 1981 there had been 68 heat stroke cases which resulted in death.

In the discussion and recommendations section of the 1981 report, the authors stated that the number of direct fatalities remained stable with no dramatic increase or decrease in any area (AFCA 1982). The trend for fewer fatalities, when compared to the data collected for the past 25 years, continued in 1981. Full effort was recommended to continue this trend and to avoid another rise in direct fatalities. Since head and neck injuries accounted for all of the direct deaths in 1981, it was also recommended that the rule changes for the 1976 season, which eliminated the head as a primary and initial contact area for blocking and tackling, should again be emphasized. Several suggestions for reducing head and neck injuries were as follows:

Table 6.2 Indirect Football Fatalities 1981–90

Year	Sandlot	Professional	High School	College	Total
1981	0	0	6	0	6
1982	1	0	7	3	11
1983	0	0	6	3	9
1984	0	0	3	0	3
1985	0	0	1	1	2
1986	0	0	7	1	8
1987	0	0	3	3	6
1988	1	0	10	0	11
1989	0	0	9	2	11
1990	0	0	3	3	6
TOTAL	2	0	55	16	73

Table 6.3 Direct Football Fatalities Incidence
per 100,000 Participants 1981–90

Year	High School	College
1981	0.38	2.67
1982	0.54	0.00
1983	0.30	0.00
1984	0.30	1.33
1985	0.30	1.33
1986	0.77	1.33
1987	0.30	0.00
1988	0.54	0.00
1989	0.27	0.00
1990	0.00	0.00

1. Athletes must be given proper conditioning exercises to strengthen their necks so they will be able to hold their heads firmly erect when making contact.
2. Coaches should drill the athletes in the proper education of the fundamentals of football skills, particularly blocking and tackling.
3. Coaches and officials should discourage the players from using their heads as battering rams when blocking and tackling. The rules prohibiting spearing should be enforced in practice and in games. The players should be taught to respect the helmet as a protective device and that the helmet should not be used as a weapon.

4. All coaches, physicians, and trainers should take special care to see that the players' equipment is properly fitted, particularly the helmet.

Another important effort continued to be the improvement of football protective equipment under the guidance of the National Operating Committee on Standards for Athletic Equipment (NOCSAE). The NOCSAE organization continued their research on improving helmets for football. It was imperative that old and worn equipment be properly renovated or discarded. Continued emphasis should be placed on developing the best equipment possible (AFCA 1982).

In addition to these recommendations, it was deemed important, whenever possible, for a physician to be on the field during game and practice sessions. When this was not possible, arrangements were to be made in advance to obtain a physician's immediate service when emergencies arise. Each institution was also instructed to have a team trainer who was a regular member of the institution's staff and who was qualified in treating and preventing injuries.

Heat stroke fatalities continued to be a problem in 1981, when there were two cases. Suggestions for heat stroke prevention were listed as follows:

1. Provide physical examinations with a medical history for each athlete and an annual health history update.
2. Acclimatize athletes to heat gradually for the first 7 to 10 days.
3. Know both the temperature and humidity. Use of a sling psychrometer was recommended to measure the relative humidity, and anytime the wet-bulb temperature was over 78°F, practice should be altered.
4. Rest periods of 15–30 minutes should be provided during workouts of 1 hour. Players should rest in cool shaded area and remove helmets and loosen jerseys.
5. Provide water replacement during practice. Water should be available and in unlimited quantities. Give water regularly.
6. Salt should be replaced daily, and liberal salting of the athletes' food will accomplish this purpose. Coaches should not provide salt tablets during practice.
7. Athletes should weigh themselves each day before and after practice and weight charts should be checked in order to treat the athletes who lose excessive weight each day. Generally, a 3% weight loss through sweating is safe, and a 5% loss is in the danger zone.
8. Clothing is important and players should never wear long sleeves or excess clothing. Never use rubberized clothing or sweatshirts.
9. Some athletes are more susceptible to heat injury and should be watched closely.

10. Observe athletes for signs of heat illness. Some signs are nausea, incoherence, fatigue, weakness, vomiting, cramps, weak rapid pulse, visual disturbance, and unsteadiness (AFCA 1982).

Specific recommendations resulting from the 1981 survey data are as follows:

1. Provide mandatory medical examinations and medical history before an athlete participates in football.
2. Emphasize gradual and complete physical conditioning.
3. Have a physician present at all games and practices. If not possible emergency measures provided.
4. All personnel should be cognizant of problems and safety measures related to physical activity in hot weather.
5. Have a team trainer who is a regular member of the staff.
6. Have a cooperative liaison between all members of sports medicine staff.
7. Exhibit strict enforcement of game rules. Coaches and school officials must support game officials.
8. Employ well trained athletic personnel; provide excellent facilities; and secure the safest and best equipment available.
9. Continue research concerning the safety factor in football.
10. Coaches should continue to teach and emphasize the proper fundamentals of blocking and tackling. Keep the head out of football (AFCA 1982).

Nine fatalities were directly related to football during the 1982 season. Seven of the fatalities occurred in high school football, and two in sandlot football. There were no college or professional football direct deaths in 1982. For the approximately 1,575,000 football participants in 1982, the injury rate per 100,000 participants was 0.57. As shown in Table 6.3, the high school fatality rate for the 1,300,000 participants was 0.54. Most football fatal injuries usually occur in games, and in 1982 eight happened in games and one in practice. Tackling caused three deaths, being tackled caused four, blocking a punt caused one, and one cause was unknown. As in past reports, a majority of the fatal direct injuries resulted from injuries to the head. In 1982, seven of the nine deaths resulted from head injuries, one from internal injuries, and the cause of one was unknown. Running backs were associated with four of the nine direct fatalities. Linebackers, defensive linemen, defensive backs, and offensive linemen were all associated with one fatal injury each.

In addition to the direct fatalities in 1982, there were also 11 indirect fatalities. Indirect fatalities are those caused by a systemic failure as a result of exertion while participating in football activity or by a complication which was secondary to a nonfatal injury (AFCA 1983). Two of the indirect fatalities in 1982 were the result of heat stroke, five were related to heart failure, one resulted from an asthma attack, one from a sickle cell crisis, one from a congenital brain defect, and one from natural causes. The 11 indirect deaths were an increase of 5 over the 1981 data.

The recommendations based on the 1982 final report were very much the same as in the 1981 report. There was one additional general recommendation in the 1982 report that was related to head trauma, stating that when a player has experienced or shown signs of head trauma (loss of consciousness, visual disturbances, headache, inability to walk correctly, obvious disorientation, memory loss), he should receive immediate medical attention and should not be allowed to return to practice or game without permission from the proper medical authorities (AFCA 1983).

The 1983 fatality report shows four deaths directly related to football, and all four were in high school football. This is the lowest number since 1979 and one of the lowest numbers since the initiation of research in 1931. The incidence rate for the 1,575,000 participants in 1983 was 0.25 per 100,000 participants. The incidence rate for high school football was 0.30 per 100,000, and there were no fatalities in college football. Three of the four direct fatal injuries occurred in games and one occurred in practice. Two of the injuries happened in October, one in August, and one in September. As in previous reports, defensive play was involved in most injuries. Two of the injuries in 1983 involved defensive play, but the exact activity was unknown. One of the other injuries involved head-to-head contact while being tackled, and one player was participating in a one-on-one blocking drill. All four of the fatal injuries involved injuries to the head. Of the four injured players, one was a running back, one was a defensive end, one was a defensive lineman, and one was a defensive back.

Indirect fatalities in 1983 numbered nine—six at the high school level and three at the college level. All six of the high school deaths were heart-related; college included one heart-related injury, one congenital brain defect, and one heat stroke.

In addition to the direct and indirect fatalities in 1983, there were three deaths listed as not related to football. Two were in high school (lightning and natural causes) and one was in college (lightning).

The 1983 survey showed a reduction in direct fatalities from nine in 1982 to four in 1983. The report stated that progress has been made and full effort must be made to continue this trend and to avoid another rise in fatal injuries (AFCA 1983).

Recommendations that helped reduce the number of direct fatalities to single digits in 1978 were repeated in the 1983 report. Heat stroke fatalities continued to be a problem, and there had been at least one heat stroke fatality since 1976. The report again emphasized the importance of following the heat stroke prevention and emergency procedures.

There were six direct fatalities in 1984, which was a slight rise of two from the 1983 report. Four of the fatalities occurred in high school football, one in college, and one in sandlot play. For the 1,575,000 football participants in all levels of play in 1984, the direct incidence rate per 100,000 participants was 0.38. The high school incidence rate was 0.30 per 100,000 participants, and the college rate was 1.33. Most direct injuries occurred in games, and in 1984 two of the injuries occurred in games and four in practice. Two injuries took place in August, three in September, and one in October. Tackling accounted for two of the fatal injuries and there were four unknown causes. As in past reports, all six of the fatalities were the result of injuries to the head.

All three of the indirect fatalities in 1984 were caused by heat stroke. Indirect deaths were reduced by six from the nine in 1983, but heat stroke deaths continued to be a major concern. The report stated that there must be a continuous effort to reduce heat stroke deaths and to follow the suggestions and precautions previously recommended when football is played in hot weather (AFCA 1984).

Recommendations from the 1984 report were the same that had been suggested for the past number of years due to the fact that the number of deaths had been reduced dramatically since the late 1960s and early 1970s.

In the 1985 report, the definition of direct fatalities was changed from "those fatalities which resulted from participation in football" to "those fatalities which resulted from participation in the fundamental skills of football" (AFCA 1986). There were seven direct fatalities in 1985, one more than in 1984. Four of the direct fatalities occurred in high school football, one in college, and two in sandlot football. The direct fatality incidence rate for the 1,575,000 football participants in 1985 was 0.44 per 100,000. For the 1,300,000 high school participants, the direct fatality incidence rate was 0.30 per 100,000, and for college football it was 1.33 per 100,000. Direct fatalities in 1985 show five deaths in games and two in practice sessions. Usually, direct fatalities take place in games. One of the fatal injuries took place in the off-season in April, one occurred in August, four occurred in September, and one occurred in November. Three of the fatalities took place while the player was tackling, two while being tackled, and the activity of two was unknown. Injuries to the head continued to result in the majority of deaths with six in 1985, and one was related to a spleen injury. Two of the fatalities took place on kickoff plays: one in a ball carrier and one in a tackler. Other positions with fatalities were a linebacker, a tight end, a lineman, and two unknown.

In 1985, there were only two indirect fatalities. One was related to heart failure and one was related to sickle cell crisis. There were no heat stroke fatalities in 1985, which was the first time since the 1975 report was published.

The 1985 report included a chart illustrating the percent reduction of head-related fatalities from 37.4% in 1965–74, to a low of 15.99% in 1975–84. During the same time periods, cervical spine fatalities were reduced from a high of 37.9% to a low of 12.6%. The 1976 rule change that prohibited the head as the primary and initial contact area for blocking and tackling was given the majority of credit for this dramatic reduction

During the 1986 football season there were 11 fatalities. This was the first time since 1977 when the number of fatal injuries was in double digits. Ten of the injuries occurred in high school and one was at the college level. The incidence rate for the 1,575,000 participants in all levels of football was 0.69 per 100,000. The high school rate was 0.77 and the college rate was 1.33 per 100,000. Ten of the fatalities occurred in games and one occurred in practice. One of the fatal injuries took place in August, two in September, seven in October, and one in November. Two of the players were injured while tackling, two were tackled, one was blocking on a punt return, and the six were unknown activities. In the six cases listed as unknown it was not possible to identify the activity due to the athlete collapsing on the field or sideline. Nine of the direct fatalities resulted from injuries to the head, one from a neck injury, and one from an injury to the spleen. The positions of the players when injured included two ball carriers, two tacklers, one defensive back, one linebacker, two interior linemen, one quarterback, and the position of two was unknown.

There were also eight indirect fatalities in 1986—seven in high school and one in college. Six of the high school indirect fatalities were associated with heart failure and one with an enlarged spleen due to mononucleosis. The one college player autopsy report stated he died from sickle cell disease and an enlarged heart.

The 1986 report also listed four deaths not related to football. Two died at home from natural causes, one from malignant hyperthermia (the coroner stated it was not related to football), and one died from cardiac arrest while lifting weights.

In the recommendation section of the report, the authors stated that after an eight-year trend of fewer football fatalities, the 1986 research showed an increase (AFCA 1987). They also stated that the numbers were still low when compared to the late 1960s, but any increase in football fatalities is a concern. The recommendations for reducing head and neck fatalities, heat stroke fatalities, and general recommendations were repeated from past reports.

Four fatalities were directly related to football during the 1987 season, and all four were at the high school level. The direct fatality incidence rate for all levels of football in 1987 was 0.25 per 100,000 participants. The incidence rate for high school direct fatalities based on 1,300,000 participants was 0.30 per 100,000 players. Three of the four injuries occurred in games and one occurred in practice. Two fatalities occurred in September, one in October, and one in November. Tackling had been the activity associated with the majority of fatalities over the years, and in 1987 three of the four injuries were again associated with tackling, and one was unknown. Two of the fatal injuries were caused by injuries to the head and two by neck injuries. Defensive backs were associated with two of the injuries, a defensive tackle with one, and the position of one was unknown. The four fatalities in 1987 were considered a significant reduction from the 11 fatal injuries in 1986.

High school indirect fatalities accounted for three deaths in 1987, and college football also had three indirect deaths. Two of the high school indirect injuries were heart-related and one was listed as a heat stroke death. Two of the college indirect deaths were also heart-related and one was listed as acidosis (a decrease of alkalinity in bodily fluids in proportion to the content of acid). The high school heat stroke death was the first since 1984.

Four deaths of football players in 1987 were listed as not related to football. One was a college athlete who was working out on his own, and collapsed and died of cardiac arrest. A second was a college player who died in his dormitory room from an asthma attack. A third was a high school player who suffered cardiac arrest during knee surgery and died three months later. A fourth was a high school player who collapsed on the practice field, but the medical findings were inconclusive and the death was listed as being not related to football.

The recommendations for the 1987 report were the same as listed in previous reports in the 1980s, with one exception. A new recommendation for heat stroke prevention was added, mentioning a new treatment for heat stroke. The treatment involved applying either alcohol or cool water to the victim's skin followed by vigorous fanning. The fanning causes evaporation and cooling. This method was published in *The First Aider* in September 1987 (AFCA 1988). (7) An addition to the 1987 report was a graph illustrating the major decline of head and neck fatalities from 1945 through 1987. It was an excellent illustration of the dramatic decrease of head and neck fatalities from the high in 1968 to the low numbers in the 1980s.

Direct fatalities increased slightly from four in 1987 to seven in 1988. All seven were at the high school level. For the past 11 years there was only 1 year with double-digit direct fatalities and that was in 1986 with 11. The incidence rate for direct fatalities in all levels of football in 1988 was 0.44 per 100,000 players exposure basis. High school football, with 1,300,000 participants, had a direct fatality incidence rate of 0.54 per 100,000. Four of the direct fatal injuries occurred in games, two occurred in practice, and one occurrence was unknown. One of the fatalities occurred in August, two in September, one in October, two in November, and one was unknown. One of the November injuries actually happened in September, but the player died in November. The fatal injury listed as unknown happened during the 1988 season, but the athlete was in a coma and died in 1990. In 1988, two players were injured while tackling, one was tackled, one was blocked, one was in a pile-up, and the activity of two was unknown. In 1988, head and neck injuries continued to be the major cause of fatal injuries in football. Five of the seven fatalities resulted from injuries to the head, one from a fractured cervical vertebra, and one from a blow to the chest from the helmet of an opponent causing an irregular heartbeat and cardiac arrest (in later years this type of injury was listed as commotio cordis). Three of the injured athletes were playing defensive back at the time of the injury, one was an offensive back, one a linebacker, and the position of two was unknown.

Also in 1988, there were 11 indirect football deaths. Ten were associated with high school football and one with sandlot football. Six of the high school indirect deaths were related to heart failure, two to heat stroke, one to an asthma attack, and one to a ruptured spleen associated with mononucleosis. The sandlot indirect fatality was related to an asthma attack. The 1988 indirect fatal injuries showed an increase of five from the 1987 report.

There were also four deaths in 1988 that were not attributed to football— two in high school players and two in college players.

Recommendations for prevention were not changed from former reports, but there was one area that received special emphasis and was listed separately from the other recommendations. It was listed under the heading "Keep the Head Out of Football" and stated the following: "A 1976 rule change that eliminated the head as the initial contact point in blocking and tackling has significantly reduced head and neck injuries in the sport of football. Coaches can do their part to continue that trend by teaching correct techniques and emphasizing proper fundamentals at all times. That way, players can avoid catastrophic injury and coaches can avoid lawsuits. Keep the head out of football" (AFCA 1989). Another addition to the 1988 report was a statement from the AFCA titled, "Adopt 'Safety First' Coaching Techniques" (AFCA 1989). It stated that, according to legal experts, "failure to warn" (coaches failing to warn players about potential dangerous play) is one of the primary accusations made against coaches in litigation involving catastrophic injury to a player. To help prevent what could result in the destruction of a coaching career, as well as massive financial loss, adopt these "safety first" coaching techniques:

1. Have a clear and complete understanding of the intent of correct application of safety rules.
2. Make graphically clear to players the risk of violating these rules and use the available printed material as a constant authoritative reminder to them of the importance of correct techniques.
3. Point out in exact terms the risk of an accidental catastrophic injury in athletics before the first practice (AFCA 1989).

The foregoing recommendation was a direct response to the great number of lawsuits in the 1970s and 1980s against coaches, administrators, schools, and helmet manufacturers.

The 1989 football season was associated with four direct fatalities, and all four were in high school football. The direct fatality incidence rate for all levels of football, based on the increased number of 1,800,000 participants, was 0.22 per 100,000 players. The previous number of participants at all levels of football was 1,575,000. The number of high school and junior high school participants also increased from 1,300,000 to 1,500,000 for the 1989 report. The direct fatality incidence rate for high school participants in 1989 was 0.27 per 100,000 players. All four of the direct fatal injuries occurred in games, with three occurring in September and one in October. Two of the injuries happened while being tackled, one while blocking, and the activity of one was unknown. Two of the injured players were offensive backs, one was a lineman, and one was a wide receiver. All four of the injuries were head injuries.

Indirect fatalities in 1989 numbered 11, which was equal to the 1988 number. Nine of the indirect fatalities were in high school football and two were in college. Six of the high school indirect injuries were heart-related, two were heat strokes, and one was caused by lightning. The two college injuries were heart-related. Heat stroke fatalities continued to be a problem; over the past three years there were five heat stroke deaths. If football personnel followed the recommendations that were included in all of the previous reports, including the 1989 report, the number of heat stroke deaths could have been reduced or eliminated.

In addition to the direct and indirect fatal injuries in 1989, there were two high school deaths that were not related to football. One was caused by a congenital brain-spinal cord defect, and one was related to cardiac arrest that occurred at the player's home.

Preventive recommendations were not changed from the 1988 report and again included emphasis on keeping the head out of football, the AFCA section on adopting safety first coaching techniques, and the chart illustrating head and neck fatalities from 1945 through 1989.

The 1990 football season was historic in that there were no direct fatalities. This was the first time since the research began in 1931 that there had not been a direct fatality at any level of football. The 1990 report illustrated the importance of data collection and analysis in making changes in the game of football which helped reduce the incidence of serious injuries. The report stated that the elimination of direct fatalities in 1990 could be directly related to information presented in the *Annual Survey of Football Injury Research 1931–90*.

There were six indirect fatalities in 1990; three were associated with high school football and three with college football. Two of the high school indirect fatalities were related to heart failure and one to an asthma attack. One of the college injuries was related to the heart, one to heat stroke, and one to exertion-induced rhabdomyolysis with sickle cell disease being a possible contributor. There were six heat stroke deaths during the previous four years. Repeated calls were made for heat stroke to be eliminated in football, and the report repeated the recommendations that had been in past reports.

The report also stated that past efforts that were successful in reducing direct fatal injuries, and the elimination of them in 1990, must again be emphasized (AFCA 1991). Rule changes for the 1976 season, which eliminated the head as a primary and initial contact area for blocking and tackling, was cited as of the utmost importance in reducing head and neck deaths. Recommendations for reducing head and neck injuries, and general recommendations, were repeated from past reports. One safety addition to the 1990 report was a new section titled "Make Safety a Commitment and Your Number 1 Priority." Following is a list of recommendations for a coach's safety checklist written by Dick Schindler for the *National Federation of State High School News*:

- Keep the head up.
- Discuss the risk of injury.
- Keep the head out of contact.
- Explain how serious injuries occur.
- Involve parents in early season meeting.
- Have a set plan for coaching safety.
- Clearly explain and demonstrate safe techniques.
- Provide the best medical care possible.
- Monitor blocking and tackling techniques every day.
- Repeat drills which stress proper and safe techniques.
- Admonish and/or discipline users of unsafe techniques.
- Receive clearance by a doctor for an athlete to play following head trauma.
- Stress safety every day.

- Don't glorify "head hunters"—player always looking to hit with his helmeted head.
- Support officials who penalize illegal helmet contact.
- Don't praise or condone illegal helmet contact.
- Provide conditioning to strengthen neck muscles.
- Ensure that entire staff is tuned in to safety program.
- Check helmet condition regularly.
- Be aware that improper technique causes spinal cord injuries.
- Ensure that helmets fit properly.
- Be prepared for a catastrophic injury.
- Know that the game doesn't need abusive contact.
- Know that player safety is your responsibility.
- Remember, it's a game—not a job—for the players (AFCA 1991).

As illustrated in Table 6.4, head injuries were responsible for 49 (80.3%) of the 61 head-related fatal injuries from 1981 to 1990. Spinal cord injuries were related to five (8.2%), and internal injuries accounted for four (6.6%). There were also three unknowns (4.9%).

Table 6.5 shows that tackling is associated with the greatest number of fatal football injuries (21, or 34.4%), followed by being tackled (12, or 19.7%).

Table 6.4 Direct Football Fatalities Cause of Death 1981–90

Cause	Sandlot	Professional	High School	College	Total
Head	6	0	38	5	49
Spinal	0	0	5	0	5
Internal	0	0	4	0	4
Other	1	0	2	0	3
TOTAL	7	0	49	5	61

Table 6.5 Direct Football Fatalities Activity 1981–90

Activity	Frequency	Percentage
Tackling	21	34.4
Tackled	12	19.7
Blocking	4	6.6
Blocking Punt	1	1.6
Blocking Drill	1	1.6
Collision	4	6.6
Unknown	18	29.5
TOTAL	61	100.0

Table 6.6 Direct Football Fatalities Offensive vs. Defensive 1981–90

Activity	Frequency	Percentage
Offensive	15	24.6
Defensive	24	39.3
Not Specified	22	36.1
TOTAL	61	100.0

Table 6.7 Indirect Football Fatalities Cause of Death 1981–90

Cause	Frequency	Percentage
Heart	43	58.9
Heat	14	19.2
Asthma	5	6.8
Sickle Cell	3	4.1
Congenital Brain	2	2.7
Natural Causes	1	1.4
Mononucleosis	1	1.4
Lightning	1	1.4
Rhabdomyolysis	1	1.4
Unknown	2	2.7
TOTAL	73	100.0

There was a dramatic decrease in the other activities listed and a large number of unknowns.

Defensive football, as would be expected with tackling being the major risk factor, was associated with 39.3% of the 61 direct fatalities in the 1980s. A problem with this data was the fact that there were 22 unspecified activities, shown in Table 6.6.

Heart-related indirect deaths were responsible for 43 (58.9%) of the 73 reported incidents in 1981–90, followed by heat stroke with 14 (19.2%). Heart-related and heat stroke deaths were followed by a number of other causes, as shown in Table 6.7.

Catastrophic (Disability) Football Injuries

As mentioned in the previous chapter, a new concern for football emerged in paralyzing cervical spine injuries and permanent disability injuries to the brain. The National Center for Catastrophic Sports Injury Research data collection for cervical cord injuries was initiated in 1977, and data collection for brain injuries was initiated in 1984. In 1987, researchers also started to collect catastrophic injury data with complete recovery. It was deemed important to collect nondisability injury data since many of these injuries involved the same type of activities that caused disability injuries. There is now a database of fatalities, dating back to 1931, of catastrophic injuries (disability) dating back to 1977, and of catastrophic nondisability injuries dating back to 1987. This chapter includes all catastrophic injuries for the decade 1981–90.

As illustrated in Table 6.8, permanent cervical cord injuries during the 1980s numbered 100 with 82 at the high school level, 13 at the college level, 2 at the professional level, and 3 at the sandlot level. The year with the greatest number was 1989 when there was a total of 15 permanent cervical cord injuries. The lowest number was in 1986 with four, but there was a steady increase during the final four years of the decade. High school football accounted for the most cervical cord injuries, but there were also many more participants at that level. Table 6.9 shows the incidence rate at the high school level to be less than 1.00 injuries per 100,000 participants for all 10 years, but just one injury at the college level had an incidence rate of 1.33 per 100,000 participants. In 1984 the incidence rate at the college level was 4.00 per 100,000 participants.

Table 6.8 Permanent Cervical Cord Injuries 1981–90

Year	Sandlot	Professional	High School	College	Total
1981	1	0	6	2	9
1982	1	1	7	2	11
1983	0	0	11	1	12
1984	1	0	6	0	7
1985	0	0	6	3	9
1986	0	0	4	0	4
1987	0	0	9	0	9
1988	0	0	10	1	11
1989	0	1	12	2	15
1990	0	0	11	2	13
TOTAL	3	2	82	13	100

Table 6.9 Permanent Cervical Cord Injuries Incidence
per 100,000 Participants 1981–90

Year	High School	College
1981	0.46	2.67
1982	0.54	2.67
1983	0.85	1.33
1984	0.46	0.00
1985	0.46	4.00
1986	0.31	0.00
1987	0.69	0.00
1988	0.77	1.33
1989	0.80	2.67
1990	0.73	2.67

From 1981–88. Based on 1,300,000 senior high school and junior high school players, and 75,000 college players. In 1989, senior high school and junior high school figures increased to 1,500,000.

As was true with the fatal football injuries in the 1980s, a majority of the injured players were participating in defensive activity when injured. Seventy-nine were on defense, and only 15 were playing offense. Tackling was the cause of almost half of the cervical cord injuries, followed by being tackled. Players were also injured more in games than in practice. Also approximately one-third of the injuries were to defensive backs.

Table 6.10 Permanent Cervical Cord Injuries Offensive vs.
Defensive Football 1981–90

Year	Offense	Defense	Unknown	Total
1981	3	5	1	9
1982	3	8	0	11
1983	2	10	0	12
1984	1	5	1	7
1985	1	8	0	9
1986	0	3	1	4
1987	1	6	2	9
1988	2	9	0	11
1989	0	14	1	15
1990	2	11	0	13
TOTAL	15	79	6	100

Table 6.11 Permanent Brain Injuries 1984–90

Year	Sandlot	Professional	High School	College	Total
1984	0	0	5	2	7
1985	0	0	4	1	5
1986	0	0	2	0	2
1987	0	0	2	0	2
1988	0	0	4	0	4
1989	0	0	6	0	6
1990	0	0	2	0	2
TOTAL	0	0	25	3	28

Table 6.12 Catastrophic Injuries Recovery 1987–90

Injury	High School	College	Total
Fracture CV	23	8	31
Subdural	15	4	19
Transient Cord	9	5	14
Lumbar Fracture	2	0	2
Other	1	1	2
TOTAL	50	18	68

In addition to the 100 cervical cord injuries with permanent paralysis in 1981–90, there were also 28 brain injuries with permanent disability. Twenty-five were at the high school level and three were in college football (Table 6.11).

In 1987, the collection of catastrophic injuries with full recovery was initiated. In just a four-year period there were 68 catastrophic football injuries with full recovery. Many of these injuries could have resulted in permanent disability, but either the player had excellent medical care on site and in the hospital or he was very fortunate that his spinal cord missed being severely damaged by a fraction of an inch.

Recommendations to help prevent catastrophic football injuries were listed in the 1990 report as follows:

1. Rule changes that were initiated for the 1976 football season, which eliminated the head as a primary and initial contact area for blocking and tackling, were of the utmost importance. Coaches should drill the players in the proper execution of the fundamentals of football, particularly in blocking and tackling. *Shoulder block and tackle with the head up—keep the head out of football.*

2. Athletes must be given proper conditioning exercises to strengthen their necks so they can hold their heads firmly erect while making contact during a tackle or block. Strengthening of the neck muscles may also protect the neck from injury.

3. Coaches and officials should discourage players from using their heads as battering rams when blocking and tackling. The rule prohibiting spearing should be enforced in practice and games. The players should be taught to respect the helmet as a protective device and that the helmet should not be used as a weapon.

4. Football officials can play a major role in reducing catastrophic football injuries. The use of the helmet in making initial contact while blocking and tackling is illegal and should be called for a penalty. Officials should concentrate on helmet contact and call the penalty. If more of these penalties are called, there is no doubt that both players and coaches will get the message and discontinue this type of play. A reduction in helmet contact will result in a reduction of catastrophic football injuries.

5. All coaches, physicians, and trainers should take special care to see that the players' equipment is properly fitted, particularly the helmet.

6. It is important, whenever possible, for a physician to be on the field during game and practice. When this is not possible, arrangements must be made in advance to obtain a physician's immediate services when emergencies arise. Each institution should have a team trainer who is a regular member of the institution's staff and who is qualified in the emergency care of both treating and preventing injuries.

7. Coaches must be prepared for a possible catastrophic head or neck injury. Everyone involved must know what to do. Being prepared and knowing what to do may be the difference that prevents permanent disability.

8. When a player has experienced or shown signs of head trauma (loss of consciousness, visual disturbances, headache, inability to walk correctly, obvious disorientation, memory loss) he should receive immediate medical attention and should not be allowed to return to practice or game without permission from the proper medical authorities.

9. Both past and present data show that the football helmet does not cause cervical cord injuries, but that poorly executed tackling and blocking technique is the major problem (Mueller and Blyth 1990).

The report goes on to say that catastrophic injuries may never be totally eliminated, but continued research has resulted in rule changes, equipment standards, improved medical care both on and off the playing field, and changes in teaching the fundamental techniques of the game. These changes were the result of a united effort by coaches, administrators, researchers, equipment manufacturers, physicians, trainers, and players. Research based on reliable data is essential if progress is to be made. Research provides data that indicate the problems and reveal the adequacy of preventive measures (Mueller and Blyth 1990).

Football Rules 1981–1990: Safety and Equipment

In the 1980s, football rules and player protective equipment continued to play a major role in the reduction of fatal and catastrophic injuries. Information was taken from the National Collegiate Athletic Association (NCAA) and the National Federation of State High School Associations (NFHS) rule books and from David Nelson's book, *The Anatomy of a Game: Football, the Rules, and the Men Who Made the Game.*

In 1981, new rules permitted the use of molded-sole shoes with nonremovable cleats no more than half an inch in length made of nonabrasive material with no cutting edge. The trend of wearing nondetachable cleats (soccer shoes) required a new section in the equipment rule because of the materials and shapes of the shoes' cleats. Safety rules in 1981 included making blocking below the waist only legal in the free blocking zone, and defined a "chop block" as a delayed block at the knee or below against an opponent who is in contact with a teammate of the blocker in the free blocking zone. Another important safety rule was the revised spearing definition that included the intentional use of the helmet in an attempt to punish an opponent. The word "intentional" caused concern for referees deciding between what was intentional and what was not intentional. Officials were also given the authority to delay a game when weather conditions were hazardous. In the kicking game it was ruled illegal for a player to be on the back or shoulders of a defensive teammate to try and block an extra point or field goal. It was also illegal to step, jump, or stand on a teammate or an opponent; place hands on a teammate to get leverage for additional height; or to be picked up by an opponent.

Equipment changes in the 1982 rules included requiring pants as player's equipment, requiring players to wear knee pads, making tear-away jerseys illegal, and requiring jerseys to fully cover shoulder pads and any extensions to them. A penalty for wearing illegal equipment was reduced from 15 to 5 yards, and the coach was responsible for verifying before the game that players are legally equipped.

In 1983, the mandatory disqualification for spearing was changed so that disqualification was mandatory only when the act was considered flagrant, and

Image 6.1 Curt Warner, Penn State University
Photo courtesy of NCAA.

the penalty was to be similar to other illegal helmet contact fouls. Also, in 1983, the head coach was responsible for having his team on the field for the mandatory three-minute warm-up at the end of the halftime intermission. The Rules Committee included a "Points of Emphasis" section in the 1983 rules in an attempt to communicate to officials, coaches, and players the committee's concern about a number of rules being violated and not properly enforced. The only equipment change for the 1983 season was the requirement that all players wear an intraoral mouthpiece that covers all upper jaw teeth (changed from two-piece mouthpiece).

Equipment changes in 1984 stated that hip pads must include tailbone pads. The reason for this change was not stated and it was not known if there was an injury problem related to the tailbone. Hand protectors (casts or splints) were permitted only to protect a fracture or dislocation. Preventive knee braces were illegal in 1984 unless covered from direct external exposure. The committee's major concern in 1984 was unsportsmanlike conduct and the failure of coaches and players to adhere to the Football Code, which was established in 1916. The code began with the following statement:

> Both in play and by tradition football is a distinctively academic game—
> the game of the schools and the colleges. The friends of the game must
> accordingly rely on the schools and colleges for the preservation of its
> past traditions and the maintenance of the high standards of sports-

Image 6.2 Herschel Walker, University of Georgia
Photo courtesy of NCAA.

manship in its play, which are to be expected in a distinctively academic game. (AFCA 1985)

Another safety rule established in 1984 prevented those in the back position to clip in the free blocking zone. The rule widened the clipping zone from four yards to five, and prohibited players on the line and in the legal clipping zone from leaving the zone and circling back to clip. It was also illegal for players to block below the waist toward the ball if they were seven or more yards from the middle lineman. This action prevented what is known as the crackback block.

Equipment changes in 1985 included adopting specifications for the face protector and clarifying the padding requirement on knee braces. A major job of the Rules Committee in 1985 was the recodification of the rule book for the first time in the past 35 years. According to one of the committee members, it was now the most readable and understandable rule book in the history of the game. It took approximately three years for the changes to occur.

A major move in the offensive use of hands made blocking with the hands open and fully extended permissible at any time in all areas of the field, which made blocking safer and easier to teach. Another safety change was to make it illegal for a back in motion to block below the waist in the free blocking zone.

David Nelson, Secretary and Editor of the Rules Committee, made personal observations on the status of the game in 1985, stating:

> Our present dilemma is fivefold—the game's foundation of educational football is eroding: (1) the football code is being ignored, (2) rules violations are being taught, (3) (some) officials are officiating as the coaches are teaching (not by the rules), (4) the players are not always playing by the rules, (5) the television interests (supported by home management) blatantly ignore the rules. (NFHS 1981–90)

In 1986, the rule book stated that preventive knee braces must be worn under the pants. The only other equipment change in 1986 stated that the helmet of each player must have an exterior warning label regarding the risk of injury. There were no new significant safety rules.

The rule changes for 1987 were few and 1987 was actually considered a slow year for the Rules Committee. In regard to equipment, new rules stated that knee braces, if worn, must be worn under and not over the pants. It was also ruled legal for a participant to play with an artificial limb or arm, and a new rule stated that tooth protectors must cover all upper teeth.

During the past several years, there had been a controversy over the injury potential of synthetic turf, which motivated the Rules Committee to request research on the subject from the NCAA Committee on Competitive Safeguards and the Medical Aspects of Sports (CCSMAS). The NCAA Committee appointed a special committee to study the effects of synthetic and natural turf and the severity of injuries in games and practices. A report was scheduled for the 1998 Rules Committee meeting.

A second controversial topic concerned the claims made for the reduction of knee injuries if knee braces were worn. The Rules Committee had been petitioned for a number of years to make the knee brace mandatory equipment. The Rules Committee again requested the CCSMAS to appoint a special committee to research the topic. At the time of this request there was a similar study initiated at Wake Forest University Medical Center. Both studies concluded that preventive knee braces do not consistently prevent knee injuries and may actually increase the possibility of knee problems. Manufacturers of knee braces continued to support research that reached more positive conclusions for their products.

Equipment additions to the rules in 1988 included the mandatory covering of any part of the knee brace which extended below the pants, the prohibition of the use of ceramic material in cleats, and the prohibition of any player from intentionally using his helmet to butt or ram an opponent. This rule made it difficult for the officials to decide what was intentional and what was not. Also, gloves that were the same color as the ball were declared illegal. An additional equipment safety change was the decision to use colored mouth protectors so there would be no question of whether a player was wearing one. The color yellow was selected and brought immediate protests. To satisfy all critics and still meet the general purpose, the 1989 rule stated that any visible color could be used. Another rule related to equipment safety, but not to player's equipment, was the padding of the goal posts.

General safety rules in 1988 included making the open hand and extended arm blocking legal, and the authorization of state associations to allow teams totally composed of deaf or partially deaf players to use a drum to establish a rhythmic cadence.

According to one Rules Committee member, the committee's major problem in 1988 was getting the attention of officials and coaches on the Points of Emphasis to solve the game's shortcomings.

The 1989 safety changes in the rules lifted the final restriction in offensive use of the hands and arms. The requirement that a blocker's hand and arms be within the frame of the body was eliminated. It was still illegal for a defensive lineman to slap and strike the offensive blocker, but a technique that put the hand under the chin and facemask, pushing the head back and in some cases knocking the helmet off, was made illegal in the 1989 rules. Clipping was also defined as using the hands to push an opponent in the back.

There were also a few equipment changes in the 1989 rules, one being that in 1992, face protectors would have to meet the NOCSAE standard. Jerseys could not be taped, tied, or altered to produce a knot or knot-like protrusion. It was also recommended for 1989, and mandatory by 1990, that the goalposts be padded with resilient shock absorbing material to a height of at least six feet above the ground.

In 1990, there were three safety rules enacted. First, the onside kick was eliminated and the kicking team was not permitted to touch a free kick until it traveled 10 yards or it was touched by a receiving team member. Second, the committee rejected a proposal to exempt a player from a "roughing" or "running into" penalty when blocked into the kicker by an opponent. Included in this rule was giving the placekick holder on a free kick the same protection as the kicker. A final safety rule was the enforcing a personal foul for an offensive player for continuous contact to the head of a defensive player. This same rule against a defensive player was passed in 1989 and was expanded to include the offensive player in 1990.

The only equipment rule changes involved adding hard hand, wrist, forearm, and elbow guards and brace materials to the illegal equipment list. Support wrap was legalized if it was nonhardening, nonabrasive, and used to protect an injury. A single-color plain towel was the only uniform adornment that was legal in 1990.

Discussion

As shown in Graph 6.1, direct fatalities during the 1980s were up and down with a high of 11 in 1986, and the historic low of 0 in 1990. The only year with double digits was in 1968 with 11 fatalities. This dramatic reduction in direct fatalities was again related to the data collection that began in 1931 and continued every year since, with the exception of 1942 during World War II. The rule change in 1976 that prohibited initial contact with the head and face while tackling and blocking received major credit for the reduction, along with the NOCSAE helmet standard that was mandated by colleges in 1978 and high schools in 1980. The research was also important to the coaching community in that it made them aware of the dangers associated with improper tackling and blocking techniques. In addition, it was important to the medical community to understand the importance of proper medical care for athletes injured in football practices and games and the importance of having athletic trainers available for both prevention and treatment of injuries.

The decade 1981–90, as illustrated in Graph 6.2, was associated with the lowest number of direct fatalities (61) since the beginning of research in 1931. This continued the major reduction of direct football fatalities from the 1960s with 244 direct fatalities, to the 1970s with 127 direct fatalities, to the 1980s with 61 direct fatalities. The greatest reduction was in high school football from 105 fatalities in the 1970s to 49 in the 1980s.

For the 60-year period from 1931 to 1990, there were 932 direct football fatalities. High school football was associated with the greatest number (605), followed by sandlot (172), college (80), and professional (75). Head injuries accounted for 61.8% of the direct fatalities, followed by spinal injuries with 15.9%, internal injuries with 14.8%, and a variety of other causes accounting for 7.5%. During this same period, tackling was responsible for 34.2% of the direct fatalities, being tackled for 15.8%, blocking for 9.2%, being blocked for 2.0%, and unknown causes were responsible for 38.7%.

Indirect fatalities were also associated with a reduction of fatalities in 1981–90 when compared to the 1970s, and for the first time there were more indirect fatalities than direct fatalities. As shown in Graph 6.3, indirect fatalities in the 1980s went from a high of 11 to a low of 2 in 1985.

Graph 6.4 compares indirect fatalities by decade and illustrates a slight reduction from 86 in the 1970s to 73 in the 1980s. The 1930s and 1960s were

Graph 6.1 Direct Fatalities 1981–90

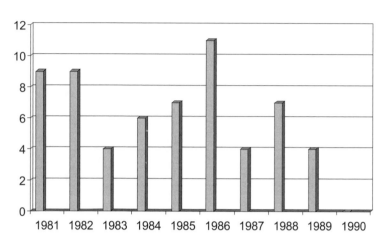

Graph 6.2 Direct Fatalities by Decade

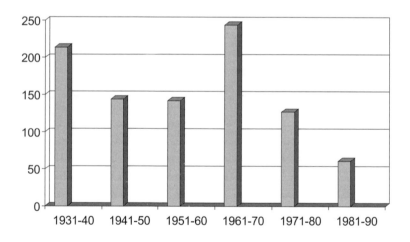

associated with the greatest number of indirect fatalities. Heart-related indirect deaths accounted for 43% and heat stroke accounted for 14%. Heat stroke deaths continued to be a problem.

From 1931 to 1990, there were 512 indirect football fatalities in all levels of football, as illustrated in Graph 6.4. High school football had 315, sandlot had 98, college had 82, and professional had 17. Heart-related deaths accounted for

Graph 6.3 Indirect Fatalities 1981–90

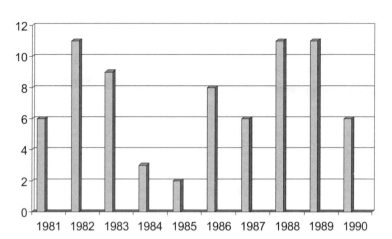

Graph 6.4 Indirect Fatalities by Decade

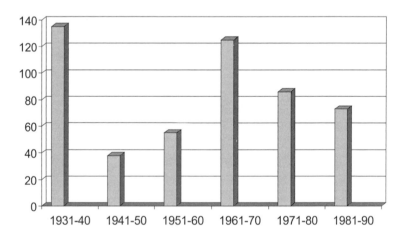

the greatest number of indirect fatalities with 161, followed by heat stroke with 85. There were no heat stroke deaths until 1955, and since that time they have been a problem. As an example, there were eight heat stroke deaths in 1970, an all-time high.

As reported in the previous chapter, the reduction of direct football fatalities brought on a new concern: catastrophic football injuries (permanent neck and brain disabilities). The decade 1981–90 was associated with 100 catastrophic cervical vertebrae injuries and 28 brain injuries with permanent disability. In addition to the disability injuries, there were an additional 68 head and neck injuries with complete recovery at the high school and college levels. For the 14-year period from 1977 through 1990, there were a total of 150 permanent disability cervical cord injuries, 28 permanent disability brain injuries, and 68 catastrophic injuries with complete recovery. Catastrophic injuries, both disability and recovery, were a major concern during this period of time. There were many lawsuits filed against both the helmet manufacturers and coaches, stating the causes of these injuries were related to poor helmet design and the improper teaching of tackling and blocking skills by the coaches.

Safety rules continued to emphasize not using the head in blocking and tackling, and changes in the spearing definition in 1981 stated that it was the intentional use of the helmet in an attempt to punish the ball carrier. As will be seen in later chapters, the word "intentional" created problems for the officials. The football rules continued to mandate specific pieces of protective equipment to prevent injuries to the participants.

The 1980s was associated with a dramatic reduction in direct fatalities, and a continued concern for catastrophic head and neck injuries. Indirect fatalities were associated with a decline, but heart and heat stroke deaths continued to be a concern. From 1980 through 1989, there were 283 changes in the football rules, but only a small portion of these were directly related to player safety.

References

1. American Football Coaches Association: Proceedings of the Fifty-Ninth Annual Meeting of the American Football Coaches Association, January 1982, Houston, TX.
2. American Football Coaches Association: Proceedings of the Sixtieth Annual Meeting of the American Football Coaches Association, January 1983, Los Angeles, CA.
3. American Football Coaches Association: Proceedings of the Sixty-First Annual Meeting of the American Football Coaches Association, January 1984, Dallas, TX.
4. American Football Coaches Association: Proceedings of the Sixty-Second Annual Meeting of the American Football Coaches Association, January 1985, Nashville, TN.

5. American Football Coaches Association: Proceedings of the Sixty-Third Annual Meeting of the American Football Coaches Association, January 1986, New Orleans, LA.

6. American Football Coaches Association: Proceedings of the Sixty-Fourth Annual Meeting of the American Football Coaches Association, January 1987, San Diego, CA.

7. American Football Coaches Association: Proceedings of the Sixty-Fifth Annual Meeting of the American Football Coaches Association, January 1988, Atlanta, GA.

8. American Football Coaches Association: Proceedings of the Sixty-Sixth Annual Meeting of the American Football Coaches Association, January 1989, Nashville, TN.

9. American Football Coaches Association: Proceedings of the Sixty-Seventh Annual Meeting of the American Football Coaches Association, January 1990, San Francisco, CA.

10. American Football Coaches Association: Proceedings of the Sixty-Eighth Annual Meeting of the American Football Coaches Association, January 1991, New Orleans, LA.

11. Mueller FO, Blyth CS: *Fourth Annual Survey of Catastrophic Football Injuries—1981–1990*, University of North Carolina, Chapel Hill, NC.

12. National Federation of State High School Associations: Football Rules Books, 1981–90.

13. Nelson DM: *The Anatomy of a Game: Football, the Rules, and the Men Who Made the Game*. University Press, DE. 1994.

Chapter 7

Fatalities and Catastrophic Injuries, 1991–2000

Introduction

As stated in the previous chapters, there was a steady decline of football fatalities at all levels following the high of 214 in the first decade of data collection 1931–40. The following two decades, the 1940s and 1950s, were associated with 144 and 142 direct fatalities, respectively. The years from 1961 through 1970 were associated with a dramatic increase to 244. Concern for the safety of participants received a major emphasis during the 1970s, and the result was a major reduction of direct fatal injuries to 127. This reduction continued in the 1980s with 61 direct fatalities. As illustrated in Table 7.1, this reduction continued in the 1990s when there were 42 direct football fatalities at all levels. Sandlot direct fatalities were reduced from 7 in the 1980s, to 1 in the 1990s, professional football had 0 in both decades, high school football was reduced from 49 to 36, and college football had 5 for both decades. There was a total reduction of 19 direct fatalities in the 1990s.

Indirect fatalities in the 1990s were more than double the number of direct fatalities (Table 7.2). There were 90 indirect fatalities from 1991 to 2000. There had been a trend during the later decades for the number of indirect deaths to be greater than direct deaths. Indirect fatalities in the 1990s increased by 17 over the 1980s.

Fatalities and Catastrophic Injuries, 1991–2000

In 1991, there were three football fatalities, and all three were at the high school level (Table 7.1). For the 1,800,000 participants the incidence of direct football fatalities was 0.17 per 100,000 participants. The incidence at the senior high school and junior high school level was 0.20 per 100,000 participants (Table 7.3). All three of the fatalities occurred in games, with two taking place in September

Table 7.1 Direct Football Fatalities 1991–2000

Year	Sandlot	Professional	High School	College	Total
1991	0	0	3	0	3
1992	0	0	2	0	2
1993	0	0	3	1	4
1994	0	0	0	1	1
1995	0	0	4	0	4
1996	0	0	5	0	5
1997	0	0	6	1	7
1998	0	0	6	1	7
1999	1	0	4	1	6
2000	0	0	3	0	3
TOTAL	1	0	36	5	42

and one in October. Head injuries continued to be involved with most fatal injuries, and in 1991 all three of the deaths were related to the head/brain. One of the players was injured while tackling, one while blocking on a kickoff, and one while being tackled.

Indirect fatalities were associated with four deaths in 1991—three at the high school level and one at the college level. All four of the indirect fatalities were heart-related. There were also two college fatal injuries that were not related to football. One was related to a bacterial virus, and the second was due to medical complications of an injury. Lightning continued to be a problem in

Table 7.2 Indirect Football Fatalities 1991–2000

Year	Sandlot	Professional	High School	College	Total
1991	0	0	3	1	4
1992	1	0	9	1	11
1993	0	0	8	1	9
1994	1	0	2	2	5
1995	1	0	7	1	9
1996	0	1	10	1	12
1997	1	0	7	0	8
1998	1	0	6	1	8
1999	1	0	11	0	12
2000	0	0	10	2	12
TOTAL	6	1	73	10	90

Table 7.3 Direct Football Fatalities Incidence
per 100,000 Participants 1991–2000

Year	High School	College
1991	0.20	0.00
1992	0.13	0.00
1993	0.20	1.33
1994	0.00	1.33
1995	0.26	0.00
1996	0.33	0.00
1997	0.40	1.33
1998	0.40	1.33
1999	0.26	1.33
2000	0.20	0.00

1991 when an assistant coach was struck and killed on the practice field. Two other coaches suffered minor injuries and a player was sent to the hospital in serious condition.

Discussion and recommendations from the 1991 report mentioned the 1990 report when there were no direct fatalities in all of football, and only three injuries in 1991 (AFCA 1992). These data illustrate the importance of collection and analysis of the data in making changes that help reduce the incidence of serious injuries and fatalities. Emphasis was placed on a full effort to keep the number of fatalities low and to strive for the elimination of fatal football injuries. Recommendations that proved effective in the past concerning head and neck injuries, heat stroke deaths, and general recommendations were again emphasized and repeated in the 1991 report.

The football season of 1992 continued the low number of direct football fatalities with two at the high school level. The rate of direct fatal injuries was very low for the 1,800,000 participants in all levels of football. The incidence rate for all levels of football was 0.11 per 100,000 participants, and the high school rate was 0.13. One of the high school injuries took place in a practice scrimmage, and the place of the other injury was unknown. Tackling was associated with one of the fatal injuries, and the activity of one was unknown. One of the deaths was caused by an injury to the head and the cause of the second death was unknown.

Table 7.2 illustrates an interesting change in which there were more indirect fatalities than direct fatalities. In 1992, there were 11 indirect fatalities—9 at the high school level, 1 in sandlot football, and 1 at the college level. Five of the nine high school indirect injuries were associated with heart failure, one with heat stroke, one with a rare bacterial disease, one with an aneurysm, and the cause of one was unknown. The sandlot death was related to a seizure, and the college death was heart-related. In addition to the above fatalities, a high school player died of heart failure while attending a football camp. In later years this type of injury would be included in the overall data. There was also one high school death due to complications after knee surgery that was listed as not related to football.

In the Discussion section of the 1992 report, it was emphasized that the 1990, 1991, and 1992 data illustrate the importance of data collection and analysis. A strong recommendation was made that contact should always be made with the head up and never with the top of the head/helmet. Initial contact should never be made with the head/helmet. Additional recommendations were repeated from previous reports (AFCA 1993).

After three years of reduced direct fatalities, the 1993 season saw a slight increase to four. Three were associated with high school and one with college. For the approximately 1,800,000 football participants at all levels of play, the rate of direct fatalities was 0.22 per 100,000 players. The rate for senior high and junior high school football was 0.20, and for college football the rate per 100,000 exposures was 1.33. Two of the fatal injuries took place in games, and two were in practice. One of the direct fatalities took place in August, two in September, and one in October. As in past reports, tackling was associated with the majority of fatal injuries. In 1993 tackling accounted for two of the injuries, one with being tackled, and the activity of one was unknown. The head and neck continued to be the body parts most injured with three head deaths and one neck fatality.

Indirect fatalities were associated with nine fatalities in 1993 with eight being at the high school level and one in college football. Seven of the high school indirect injuries were heart-related, and one was associated with an asthma attack. The college indirect death was also heart-related. Indirect fatalities were again associated with a higher number of cases than direct fatalities.

A recommendation in the 1993 report emphasized the importance of an all-out effort to keep the number of fatal injuries low, and to strive for the elimination of football fatalities as was done in 1990 (AFCA 1994). Additional recommendations were repeated from past reports without changes.

The 1994 football season was historic in that there were no direct football deaths in sandlot, professional, or high school football, and only one in college. The rate of direct fatal injuries for the 1,800,000 participants in 1994 was 0.05 per 100,000 participants. The rate for the college level was 1.33 per 100,000 participants. The one direct fatality occurred in a practice session during March (spring practice). The cause of the injury was unknown, but it was listed as an injury to the head and the position was linebacker.

In 1994, there were also five indirect fatalities with one being in sandlot football, two in high school, and two at the college level. Both of the high school fatalities and the sandlot death were heart-related. One of the college fatal injuries was heart-related, and the second was listed in the autopsy report as neurogenic pulmonary edema. There were no heat stroke deaths in 1994. As in the four previous reports, indirect fatalities outnumbered direct fatalities.

Recommendations made from the results of the 1994 report and past reports were successful in reducing direct fatalities and were repeated (AFCA 1995).

There were four direct fatalities in 1995, and all four were associated with high school football. For the approximately 1,800,000 football players in 1995, the rate of direct fatalities was 0.22 per 100,000 participants. The rate of direct fatalities for the 1,500,000 players at the senior high and junior high levels was 0.26 per 100,000 participants. All four of the deaths occurred in games, with three taking place in October and one in September. Blocking and tackling in football account for the greatest number of fatalities, and in 1995, one was associated with being tackled on a kickoff return, and the activity of three was unknown. All four of the fatalities resulted from injuries to the head.

Indirect fatalities numbered nine in 1995. Seven were associated with high school football, one with the college level, and one in sandlot football. Four of the high school injuries were heat-related, one was heart-related, one was due to an asthma attack, and one was due to lightning. The cause of the college death was unknown, but the report stated it could have been related to the heat. The one sandlot fatality was heart-related.

In the Discussion and Recommendation section of the report, it was emphasized that heat-related deaths were a major concern and that the heat stroke deaths in 1995 accounted for the most since the 1978 season (AFCA 1996). It also emphasized that from 1990 through 1995, the number of direct fatalities was low, illustrating the importance of data collection and analysis. An all-out effort was recommended to keep these numbers low and to strive to eliminate football fatalities (AFCA 1996).

In the Recommendation section for head and neck injuries, it was mentioned that coaches who are teaching helmet or face tackling and blocking techniques are not only breaking the rules but are placing their players at risk for permanent paralysis or death (AFCA 1996). In addition, if a catastrophic injury case went to a court of law, there was no defense for teaching this type of tackling and blocking technique. Since 1960, most of the direct fatalities had been caused by head and neck injuries. Recommendations for the prevention of head and neck fatalities were repeated from past reports.

Recommendations for the prevention of heat stroke deaths were also repeated from past reports, with an emphasis on the four cases in 1995 being the greatest number since 1978. The discussion continued by stating that there was no excuse for increased heat stroke deaths since they are preventable with the proper precautions (AFCA 1996).

Five direct fatalities were reported in the 1996 Annual Survey of Football Injury Research, and all five were in high school football. For the approximately 1,800,000 players in 1996, the rate of direct fatalities was 0.28 per 100,000 participants. The senior high and junior high school rate, based on 1,500,000 players, was 0.33 per 100,000 participants. A majority of direct fatalities happen in games and in 1996 all five of the deaths took place in games. Four of the fatal injuries took place in September and one was in October. The 1996 report showed one fatality happened while being tackled, one while blocking on a kickoff, one while tackling; the activity of two was unknown. Four of the five direct fatalities were the result of injuries to the head, and one was the result of a blow to the chest (commotio cordis) while tackling.

In 1996 there were also 12 indirect fatalities with 10 being associated with high school football, one college, and one semi-professional football. Five of the high school deaths were related to the heart, one was related to the heat, one to an asthma attack, one to a blood infection (septicemia) after surgery, and one to a pulmonary embolism. The cause of the college indirect fatality was heart-related, and the semi-professional cause was heat stroke.

The 1996 data continued the trend of single-digit direct fatalities that started in the 1978 football season. The one exception was in 1986 when there were 12 direct fatalities. As in previous reports, indirect fatalities continued to outnumber direct fatal injuries. Recommendations for preventing head and neck injuries and heat stroke deaths were repeated from previous reports. One of the general recommendations from the present and past reports was related to head injuries, and emphasized the importance of immediate medical attention for the injured athlete and that he should not be allowed to return to practice or games without permission from the proper medical authorities (physician) (AFCA 1997).

Seven direct fatalities were recorded in the 1997 football injury report. Six were associated with high school football and one with the college level. The rate of direct fatal injuries was very low for the 1,800,000 football participants in 1997, with a rate of 0.38 per 100,000 participants. The senior high and junior high school rate was 0.40 and the college rate was 1.33 per 100,000 participants. Five of the seven fatal injuries occurred in games, and one took place in a practice scrimmage. Three of the injuries occurred in September, three were in October, and one was unknown. One of the fatalities happened while tackling, one while being blocked, and the activity of the other five was unknown. The large number of unknowns was due to the fact that with many head injuries it was difficult to know when the fatal hit actually took place. Five of the direct fatal injuries were the result of injuries to the head/brain, one was from a blow to the chest while being blocked (most likely commotio cordis), and the cause of one was unknown.

Indirect fatalities numbered eight in 1997, with seven at the high school level and one in sandlot football. Six of the high school deaths were heat-related and one was heat-related. The cause of the sandlot death was heat-related. Heart-related deaths continued to be the number-one cause of indirect deaths, and heat stroke deaths continued to be a problem despite the recommendations for prevention.

Recommendations from the 1997 Annual Survey of Football Injury Research were identical to previous years (AFCA 1998). The authors felt that the recommendations for the prevention of both direct and indirect fatalities had proven effective in most cases and should be emphasized in present and future reports.

The fatality report for 1998 was identical to the 1997 report in that there were seven direct fatalities. Six of the fatalities were associated with senior high and junior high school football, and one was at the college level. The direct fatality rate per 100,000 participants for the 1,800,000 players at all levels in 1998 was 0.38. The rate for high schools was 0.40 per 100,000 participants, and for college the rate was 1.33. Four of the seven fatal injuries took place in games, and three were in practices. Two of the injuries took place in September, three were in October, one was in November, and one was in a May spring practice. Three of the injured players were tackling when injured, one was in a tackling drill, one in a defensive drill, and the activity of two was unknown. The head/brain continued to be the body part most injured, and in 1998 all seven of the fatalities were related to brain injuries.

There were also eight indirect fatalities in 1998, with six being associated with high school football, one with college football, and one with sandlot football. Four of the high school deaths were heat-related, and two were heart-related. Both of the other deaths, college and sandlot, were heart-related.

In the recommendation section of the 1998 report, it was pointed out in bold letters that there were four heat stroke deaths and that there was no excuse for any number of heat stroke deaths since they were all preventable with the proper precautions. It also stated that four heat stroke deaths in one year should never happen, and that every effort should be made to continuously educate coaches concerning the proper procedures and precautions when practicing or playing in the heat (AFCA 1999). The preventive measures concerning heat stroke and head and neck injuries were repeated from past reports.

Six direct fatalities were associated with football in 1999, with four being at the high school level, one in college, and one in sandlot play. It was estimated that there were 1,800,000 players in all levels of play, and the rate of direct fatal injuries was 0.33 per 100,000 participants. The rate of direct fatalities at the senior high and junior high school levels was 0.26 per 100,000 participants, and the rate at the college level was 1.33. Five of the six fatalities took place in games, and one occurred in practice. Three fatal injuries happened in September, two in October, and one in August. Two of the fatalities occurred while tackling, one while being tackled, one while being blocked on a kickoff, one while blocking, and the activity of one was unknown. All six of the injuries resulted from injuries to the brain.

There were also 12 indirect fatalities in 1999. Eleven of the indirect deaths took place in high school football, and one took place at the sandlot level. Seven of the high school deaths were heart-related, two were heat-related, one was associated with sickle cell disease, and one was listed as a natural death. The sandlot death was heart-related.

In the Discussion section of the report related to head and neck injuries, it was pointed out that a number of players who suffered brain trauma complained of headaches or had a previous concussion prior to their deaths (AFCA 2000). It was emphasized that players should be made aware of these signs by the team physician, athletic trainer, or the coach, and that players should also be encouraged to inform the team physician, athletic trainer, or coach if they are experiencing any of these signs of brain trauma. It was also mentioned that coaches should never make the decision whether a player returns to a game or active participation in a practice if the player experiences brain trauma (AFCA 2000).

Another area of concern was the number of heat stroke deaths—13 in the past five years. The report stated, as it had in past reports, that there was no excuse for any number of heat stroke deaths since they were all preventable with the proper precautions (AFCA 2000). Every effort should be made to educate coaches continuously concerning the proper procedures when practicing or playing in the heat. Other recommendations were repeated from past reports.

The 2000 fatality report reported the lowest number of direct fatal injuries (three) since the 1994 report, when there was one. All three of the injuries were at the high school level. For the approximately 1,800,000 players in 2000, the rate of direct fatalities per 100,000 participants was 0.17. The rate for high school football was 0.20 per 100,000 participants. All three of the direct fatalities took place in games, and all three happened in September. Two of the injuries took place while tackling, and the activity of the third was unknown.

Table 7.4 Direct Football Fatalities Cause of Death 1991–2000

Cause	Sandlot	Professional	High School	College	Total
Head	1	0	30	4	35
Spinal	0	0	1	0	1
Chest (Heart)	0	0	4	0	4
Other	0	0	1	1	2
TOTAL	1	0	36	5	42

One of the fatal injuries was related to an injury to the brain, and two were the result of cardiac concussion or commotio cordis. There had been commotio cordis injuries in past reports, but this was the first report that actually stated that the deaths were commotio cordis injuries.

Indirect deaths numbered 12 in 2000. Ten were associated with high school football and two with college football. The main cause of indirect deaths had been heart-related, and in 2000 eight of the high school indirect deaths were heart-related. The remaining two indirect deaths were heat-related. Both of the college indirect fatalities were also heat-related.

The head and neck recommendations were repeated from previous reports since the results had been positive. From 1991 through 2000, there were 18 heat stroke deaths in football. This had been a major concern, and most health professionals believed that there was no excuse for any heat stroke deaths in football since they were all preventable with the proper precautions. The 12 heat stroke prevention measures had been part of previous reports and were included in the 2000 report (AFCA 2001). It had become obvious that coaches and others responsible for the health of their players had not been following the preventive recommendations provided by current and past reports.

As illustrated in Table 7.4, of the 42 direct deaths from 1991 through 2000, head/brain injuries led the list with 35 followed by chest injuries with 4, spine injuries with 1, and injuries listed as other with 2. Even with the dramatic reduction of direct fatalities, brain injuries continued to be a problem accounting for 83.3% of the direct fatal injuries. One of the reasons for the great number of brain injuries could well have been related to the data in Table 7.5, which shows that 42.8% of the injuries were related to either tackling or being tackled. A large percentage of football deaths were caused by "football activity," which meant that the exact activity of the injured player was unknown but that he was participating in some type of football activity.

When looking at the position played, Table 7.6 shows that linebackers and defensive backs accounted for 35.8% of the fatal injuries in the 1990s. Since linebackers and defensive backs account for most of the tackles, it would seem log-

Table 7.5 Direct Football Fatalities Activity 1991–2000

Activity	Frequency	Percentage
Football Activity	18	42.9
Tackling	14	33.3
Tackled	4	9.5
Blocking KO	3	7.1
Blocked KO	1	2.4
Tackle Drill	1	2.4
Blocking	1	2.4
TOTAL	42	100.0

ical that they would also account for a large percentage of the fatal injuries. Fifty percent of the fatalities were also related to defensive football, and an interesting fact is that 9.5% were related to the kickoff (KO) or KO return team. It should also be noted that 14.3% were listed as unknowns.

When discussing the cause of indirect fatalities, a majority of the injuries were heart-related (63.5%), as illustrated in Table 7.7. As already mentioned, heat-related deaths continued to be a major concern during the 1990s, and as shown in Table 7.7, they accounted for 20% of the indirect fatalities. Heart and heat stroke deaths were followed by a small number of other causes, but the main concern in all of the reports continued to be the heart and the heat. It should

Table 7.6 Direct Football Fatalities Position 1991–2000

Position	Frequency	Percentage
Linebacker	8	19.1
Defensive Back	7	16.7
Running Back	3	7.1
Football Drill	3	7.1
Defensive End	3	7.1
Defensive Line	3	7.1
KO Return Team	3	7.1
Quarterback	2	4.8
Fullback	2	4.8
Offensive Line	1	2.4
KO Team	1	2.4
Unknown	6	14.3
TOTAL	42	100.0

Table 7.7 Indirect Football Fatalities Cause of Death 1991–2000

Cause	Frequency	Percentage
Heart	57	63.5
Heat	18	20.0
Asthma	3	3.3
Aneurysm	1	1.1
Bacterial Disease	1	1.1
Seizure	1	1.1
Pulmonary Edema	1	1.1
Lightning	1	1.1
Blood Clot	1	1.1
Pulmonary Embolism	1	1.1
Blood Infection	1	1.1
Sickle Cell	1	1.1
Natural	1	1.1
Unknown	2	2.2
TOTAL	90	100.0

also be mentioned at this point that even though heart-related deaths accounted for a majority of the indirect deaths, there was a total lack of preventive measures in the Recommendation section of all past reports. The reason for this is unknown.

Catastrophic (Disability) Football Injuries

There was a major decline in the number of permanent disability cervical cord injuries in the years from 1991 through 2000. In the previous decade there were 100 cervical cord injuries with disability, and in the 1990s there were 69. Fifty-five of the injuries were at the high school level, nine at the college football level, four in the professional game, and one in sandlot football (Table 7.8). There was only one year (1999) when the number was not in single digits. The incidence rate per 100,000 participants for high school football was below 1.00 for all 10 years, and the college rate was 4.00 in 1996 and 2.66 in 2000 (Table 7.9). Most catastrophic injuries take place in games and in the 1990s, 43 injuries took place in games, 17 in practice, and 9 were unknown.

As was true with direct football deaths, a majority of the cervical cord injured players were playing defensive football when injured (63.8%). Only 15

Table 7.8 Permanent Cervical Cord Injuries 1991–2000

Year	Sandlot	Professional	High School	College	Total
1991	0	1	1	0	2
1992	0	1	6	0	7
1993	0	1	8	0	9
1994	0	0	1	1	2
1995	0	0	8	1	9
1996	0	0	6	3	9
1997	0	1	7	1	9
1998	0	0	4	0	4
1999	1	0	8	1	10
2000	0	0	6	2	8
TOTAL	1	4	55	9	69

players (21.8%) were playing on the offensive side of the ball, and the activity was often unknown (Table 7.10). As was true with the fatality data, a majority of the catastrophically injured players were tackling at the time of the injury. Forty-two of the players were tackling, seven were tackled, three were blocking, two were being blocked, two were in a tackling drill, three were on kickoff teams, one was in a drill, and the activity of nine was unknown. Defensive backs were involved in 21 of the 69 catastrophic injuries, followed by a variety of other positions. As stated, most of the injured players were playing defense.

Table 7.9 Permanent Cervical Cord Injuries Incidence
per 100,000 Participants 1991–2000

Year	High School	College
1991	0.07	0.00
1992	0.40	0.00
1993	0.53	0.00
1994	0.07	1.33
1995	0.53	1.33
1996	0.40	4.00
1997	0.47	1.33
1998	0.27	0.00
1999	0.53	1.33
2000	0.40	2.66

Table 7.10 Permanent Cervical Cord Injuries Offensive vs.
Defensive Football 1991–2000

Year	Offense	Defense	Unknown	Total
1991	1	1	0	2
1992	2	3	2	7
1993	0	7	2	9
1994	0	2	0	2
1995	0	6	3	9
1996	1	6	2	9
1997	4	5	0	9
1998	1	3	0	4
1999	3	7	0	10
2000	3	4	1	8
TOTAL	15	44	10	69

As illustrated in Table 7.11, there were also 50 permanent disability brain injuries in the 1990s. Forty-six of the injuries were in high school football and four were at the college level. This was the first decade with a full 10 years of permanent disability brain injury data. The previous decade had data collection start in 1984 with a total of seven years of data. In those seven years there were 28 permanent disability brain injuries—an average of 4 per year. The activity of a majority of the cerebral injuries was unknown due to the fact that it was very difficult to know which hit caused the injury. The first female cat-

Table 7.11 Permanent Brain Injuries 1991–2000

Year	Sandlot	Professional	High School	College	Total
1991	0	0	3	1	4
1992	0	0	4	0	4
1993	0	0	5	0	5
1994	0	0	4	1	5
1995	0	0	4	0	4
1996	0	0	5	0	5
1997	0	0	7	1	8
1998	0	0	4	0	4
1999	0	0	4	0	4
2000	0	0	6	1	7
TOTAL	0	0	46	4	50

astrophic injury was recorded on October 18, 1999, when a 13-year-old suffered a fractured cervical vertebra while playing junior high school football.

Football Rules 1991–2000: Safety and Equipment

The 1990s continued the emphasis on player safety with the addition of new safety rules and changes and additions to protective equipment. Information was taken from the National Collegiate Athletic Association (NCAA) and National Federation of State High School Associations (NFHS) rule books, and from the book, *The Anatomy of a Game: Football, the Rules, and the Men Who Made the Game*, by David M. Nelson (1994).

The Football Rules Committee felt that in 1991 there was no drastic need to change the football rules, but it did refer to cost containment and NCAA infractions as major issues. There were no drastic changes, but one of the most important rules made in 1991 stated that an unconscious or apparently unconscious player, as determined by the officials, may not return to the game without written authorization from a physician (NCAA 1990–2000; NFHS 1991–2000). The definition of "unconscious" as applied to a person who was unable to receive information and/or unable to respond to questions or whose responses were inappropriate. The injured player may or may not be motionless and his eyes may be closed or open. If there was doubt as to whether the player was unconscious, the officials should rule that he appeared to be unconscious. The officials should record the player's number so there would be no problem regarding his return (NCAA 1990–2000; NFHS 1991–2000).

Intentionally kicking or attempting to strike an opponent with a fist, locked hands, or elbows were listed as disqualifying fouls in 1991. Also important in 1991 was the rule that stated that, when in doubt, the referee shall stop the clock for an injured player. There was only one rule addition that involved protective equipment—rib and back pads covering by the jersey was made mandatory. Points of emphasis in 1991 included player safety, sportsmanship (ethics and integrity), and player's positions at the snap of the ball. An important point in player safety stated that it is unconscionable to teach or condone spearing techniques and unworthy for an official to ignore such action (NCAA 1990–2000; NFHS 1991–2000).

The 1991 Rules Committee, like many before, considered a number of rule changes that did not pass the preliminary vote but which could eventually be approved in future years. In 1991, there were the following future safety rule possibilities:

1. A block in the back is an illegal block and not clipping.
2. All blocking below the waist is prohibited during a down.
3. Blocking below the waist toward the ball is prohibited from the position of the tight end.
4. All face mask penalties are 15 yards.
5. A roughing-the-passer penalty was added to the end of the last run.
6. Hands are required to be within the frame of the blocker's body when making contact with an opponent.
7. The total time of the game was reduced.

In 1992, a block in the back was made illegal. Safety rules pertaining to protective equipment required that the National Operating Committee on Standards in Athletic Equipment (NOCSAE) seal be required on the face mask, and removable shoe cleats were no longer approved. Points of Emphasis in the 1992 rules book covered pass interference, illegal contact, and identifying eligible receivers. The important point of emphasis for player safety was illegal contact—late tackle, piling on, spearing, butt blocking, face tackling, and contact out of bounds. The rule book stated that football is a game of contact and enough legal contact is permitted by rule, and that officials and coaches must do everything in their power to see illegal contact is not permitted. The 1992 rules also clarified the section on mandatory equipment. Mandatory equipment was listed as a face mask which met the NOCSAE test standard, a helmet which met the NOCSAE test standard and secured by a properly fastened chinstrap, hip pads with a tailbone protector, a jersey, knee pads worn over the knee and under the pants, pants which cover the knees and knee pads, shoes, shoulder pads fully covered by the jersey, thigh guards, and a tooth and mouth protector (NCAA 1990–2000; NFHS 1991–2000).

An important rule change in 1993 specified that a player who was bleeding, had an open wound, or had excessive blood on his uniform must leave for at least one down. There was also a special section on communicable disease procedures concerning blood-borne infectious diseases and procedures for reducing their potential transmission. The chop block was defined as at the thigh or below. Related to equipment, jerseys could not be altered to produce a knot-like protrusion or tear-away type jersey, penalty-flag colored gloves and pads were illegal, and player's towels were restricted to only white in color with absolutely no markings. Points of Emphasis in 1993 covered protection for the snapper, roughness during onside kicks, and legal protection of hand/wrist injuries. The Rules Committee was concerned that opponents were charging into the snapper with illegal contact when the snapper was positioned in an unprotected position (head down for the long snap). When the snapper

Image 7.1 #44 with Head Down Tackle
Photo courtesy of NFHS.

was in this position his head and neck were in a vulnerable position and could result in a serious injury.

The 1994 rules involved a number of unsportsmanlike changes. Taunting was added to the rule prohibiting baiting, a substitute entering the playing field during a fight would be disqualified, and it was specified as unsportsmanlike conduct for a player to attempt to focus attention upon himself with any delayed, excessive, or prolonged act. One of the equipment rules stated that gloves designed for athletic competition should have an interior label securely attached or an interior stamp (NFHS/NCAA specifications) indicating voluntary compliance with test specifications on file with the Sporting Goods Manufacturers Association as of January 1, 1994. Hard materials were allowed on hand, wrist, forearm, or elbow, when padded as specified, if directed in writing by a licensed medical physician to protect an injury. In 1994, jerseys were also required to be tucked into the pants. An important rule to combat heat stroke injuries gave the officials the right to call an official's time out for heat and humidity conditions. This was an important rule even though most severe heat stroke injuries took place in early season practice. Points of Emphasis in 1994 involved helmet contact and defining the free blocking zone. In regard to helmet contact, it was stated that coaches should continue to insist on proper tackling technique—and for players to use their shoulder pads and keep their head up. It was also stated that officials should strongly enforce the rules related to illegal helmet contact.

In 1995, fighting was defined, and disqualification was the penalty. Also, a second unsportsmanlike foul resulted in disqualification. Equipment changes included the rule that players on the same team must wear helmets of the same color, and players were prohibited from removing their helmets. The only other equipment rule stated that jewelry was illegal equipment. This rule was made since more players were beginning to wear all kinds of jewelry that could be unsafe for their opponents or teammates. Points of Emphasis in 1995 covered roughing the kicker/passer/holder, taunting and baiting (which was getting out of hand), and shifts/false starts. In regard to roughing the passer, kicker, and holder, the committee was concerned that even though the rule and purpose was very clear, they felt that nonpenalized roughing occurred too frequently to be ignored and was increasing.

In 1996, it was illegal for the defense to charge directly into the snapper when the offense was in a scrimmage kick formation until the snapper was in a position to defend himself or when he moved to participate in the play. This rule was important since the snapper had his head in a down position prior to the snap of the ball. An important equipment rule stated the ball becomes dead when the runner's helmet comes off during the play. Also in 1996, a player wearing illegal cleats would be disqualified, and all hard surface shoulder pad auxiliary equipment attachments had to be covered by the jersey. Points of Emphasis in 1996 covered illegal helmet contact, safety and ethics, and sideline management and control. Illegal helmet contact had been a point of emphasis for a number of years. Illegal helmet contact was listed as spearing, butt blocking, and face tackling. The number of catastrophic injuries had declined dramatically since these rules were put in place, but the committee felt the problem might be on the increase. Safety and ethics were Points of Emphasis since the committee felt there was a general apathy toward the rules and the enforcement of the rules. The committee listed several potential problem areas for coaches:

1. Teaching illegal techniques that jeopardize the safety of players.
2. Teaching illegal techniques that violate the principles of sportsmanship and fair play.
3. Reacting critically to an official's call for enforcing the rules for safety precautions (NCAA 1990–2000; NFHS 1991–2000).

The committee also listed several problem areas for officials:

Image 7.2 Illegal Helmet Contact
Photo courtesy of Don McCauley.

1. Selectively enforcing rules based on personal opinions about the rule.
2. Selectively enforcing rules based on the perceived severity of the penalties involved.
3. Personally interpreting rules (NCAA 1990–2000; NFHS 1991–2000).

The 1997 rules provided an automatic first down for roughing the snapper in a kick formation. An editorial change stated that all players involved in blocking below the waist must be in the free blocking zone at the snap. Related to equipment, the ball became dead when the helmet came completely off of a player in possession of the ball. Also, the rules prohibited the use of eye shields which prevented visual examination of an injured player's eyes. State associations could also authorize, through a licensed physician, use of a device to enhance efficiency of a required hearing aid. The use of tobacco or smokeless tobacco resulted in an unsportsmanlike foul and disqualification. Open-hand blocking and sportsmanship were included in the Points of Emphasis in 1997.

The two main rule changes in 1998 that involved safety stated that no defensive player could use the hand(s) to slap a blocker's head, and the other prohibited the use of eye shields with less than 100% allowable light transmission. Points of Emphasis in 1998 were all related to player safety and included the following:

1. Actions against the runner
2. Unnecessary contact with players away from the play
3. Legal and illegal equipment
4. Illegal contact below the waist (NCAA 1990–2000; NFHS 1991–2000)

The 1999 rules clarified the prohibition on the use of an eye shield with less than 100% allowable light transmission. Gloves or hand pads were required to be gray in color, effective August 1, 2000, and jerseys had to be full length and tucked into the pants, effective August 1, 1999. An interesting rule stated that visible bandanas worn on the field of play or end zones were illegal. Points of Emphasis were as follows:

1. Free blocking zone and blocking restrictions
2. False starts and neutral zone infractions
3. Sportsmanship and conduct
4. Safety and equipment

In 2000, gloves or hand pads were required to be gray in color. A new rule stated that one of two penalties was now applicable for a player who grasps an opponent's face mask or helmet opening—5 or 15-yard penalty. The face mask penalty depended on whether the act was intentional or just a glancing blow. It was also illegal in 2000 for a player to be in position to receive a hand-to-hand snap from between the snapper's legs during a scrimmage kick formation. There was only one point of emphasis in 2000, and it stated that a new emphasis on reducing risk must rest in the hands of those who have the most direct control of the game—the administrators, coaches, officials, parents, and student-athletes.

Discussion

The years from 1991 through 2000, as shown in Graph 7.1, illustrated a low of one fatal injury in 1994 followed by a steady increase to seven in both 1997 and 1998. The decade closed in 2000 with three fatalities. Graph 7.2 shows the 1990s were associated with the lowest number of direct fatalities since the beginning of the study in 1931. The number of direct fatalities in the 1930s was high with 214, but data collection during that period was questionable as indicated by the reduction of direct fatalities to 144 in the 1940s and 142 fatalities in the 1950s. The 1960s were associated with the greatest number of direct

Graph 7.1 Direct Fatalities 1991–2000

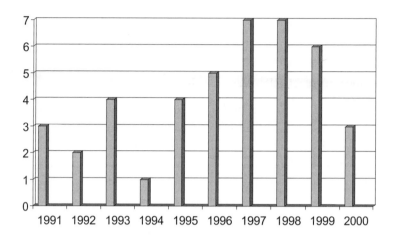

fatalities with 244. The cause of this dramatic rise in fatal injuries was mentioned in earlier chapters and will not be repeated here. There was a steady decline in direct fatalities, with 127 in the 1970s, 61 in the 1980s, and a low of 42 in the 1990s.

It is interesting that in the first 50 years of research, the percentage of direct fatalities related to head injuries was 60.5%, increased slightly after 60 years to 61.8%, and increased again after 70 years to 62.7%. Spinal cord fatalities saw a percentage decline from 16.4% in the first 50 years, 15.9% after 60 years, and 15.3% after 70 years. A possible explanation of these percentages is that football players continued to use their heads in making initial contact, but were more apt to keep their head in an up position during contact. The percent changes were so small that it was difficult to place any relationship between the increases or reductions. Table 7.12 clearly points out the importance of the rule changes that were made in the 1970s. It shows the dramatic increase in the number and percentage of head and spinal cord injuries during the 10 years from 1965 to 1974 when tackling and blocking involved initial contact with the head and face. It then shows the dramatic decrease in the number and percentage of head and spinal cord fatalities from 1975 to 1984 when the major rule changes concerning blocking and tackling techniques took place. The number of head and spinal cord fatalities continued to decrease over the next 10 years from 1985 to 1994.

Graph 7.3 illustrates the number of indirect fatalities for each year in the 1990s. It was interesting to note that during the early decades, direct fatalities outnumbered indirect fatalities, but the 1980s showed just the opposite. There

Graph 7.2 Direct Fatalities by Decade

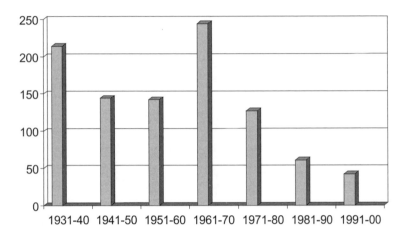

were 61 direct fatalities in this decade, but the number of indirect fatalities numbered 73. This was also true in the 1990s, but the difference was much larger with only 42 direct fatalities and 90 indirect fatalities. These differences could be accounted for in the increases in the number of heart-related and heat-related deaths. The percentage of heart-related deaths increased from 38.8% of indirect deaths for 1941–80 (40 years), to 42.7% for 1941–90 (50 years), to 46.7% for 1941–2000 (60 years). The emphasis had always been on reducing the number of direct fatal injuries, which was successful, but there had not been as great an effort on reducing the indirect fatalities, with the exception of heat stroke deaths.

Graph 7.4 illustrates the highest number of indirect fatalities in the first decade of data collection (1931–40), but the data were not reliable in that the report included deaths that were not related to football. There was a dramatic

Table 7.12 Head and Cervical Spine Fatalities

Years	Head		Cervical Spine	
	Frequency	%	Frequency	%
1945–54	87	18.7	32	27.6
1955–64	115	24.7	23	19.8
1965–74	162	34.9	42	36.2
1975–84	69	14.8	14	12.1
1985–94	32	6.9	5	4.3
TOTALS	465	100.0	116	100.0

Graph 7.3 Indirect Fatalities 1991–2000

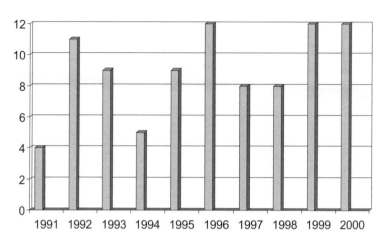

decline in the next two decades followed by a dramatic rise in 1960s. The next three decades were fairly stable with a slight increase in the 1990s.

As in past years, major rule changes in the 1990s were put in place to make the game of football safer for participants. One of these was aimed at reducing the number of serious medical complications after a player suffers a concussion. The rule stated that when a player is unconscious, or apparently unconscious, he cannot return to the game without the written authorization

Graph 7.4 Indirect Fatalities by Decade

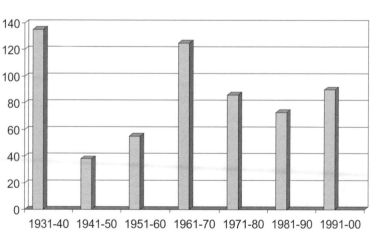

of a medical physician. This rule was important since there had been a major emphasis on concussion injuries and the possibility of death related to second impact syndrome. This rule did not apply to the college game. Players who were bleeding were also not allowed to continue playing due to concerns related to communicable diseases. An official was also allowed to call an official timeout for heat and humidity conditions that may have made continued play unsafe for the participants. Equipment changes were minor during this decade, but the section on mandatory equipment was clarified. The major Point of Emphasis was related to illegal helmet contact, which had played a major role in reducing deaths and catastrophic injuries in football. The Rules Committee members that had served during the past 70 years should be applauded for their time and effort in making the game of football safer for the participants.

References

1. American Football Coaches Association: Proceedings of the Sixty-Ninth Annual Meeting of the American Football Coaches Association, January 1992, Dallas, TX.
2. American Football Coaches Association: Proceedings of the Seventieth Annual Meeting of the American Football Coaches Association, January 1993, Atlanta, GA.
3. American Football Coaches Association: Proceedings of the Seventy-First Annual Meeting of the American Football Coaches Association, January 1994, Anaheim, CA.
4. American Football Coaches Association: Proceedings of the Seventy-Second Annual Meeting of the American Football Coaches Association, January 1995, Dallas, TX.
5. American Football Coaches Association: Proceedings of the Seventy-Third Annual Meeting of the American Football Coaches Association, January 1996, New Orleans, LA.
6. American Football Coaches Association: Proceedings of the Seventy-Fourth Annual Meeting of the American Football Coaches Association, January 1997, Orlando, FL.
7. American Football Coaches Association: Proceedings of the Seventy-Fifth Annual Meeting of the American Football Coaches Association, January 1998, Dallas, TX.
8. American Football Coaches Association: Proceedings of the Seventy-Sixth Annual Meeting of the American Football Coaches Association, January 1999, Nashville, TN.

9. American Football Coaches Association: Proceedings of the Seventy-Seventh Annual Meeting of the American Football Coaches Association, January 2000, Anaheim, CA.
10. American Football Coaches Association: Proceedings of the Seventy-Eighth Annual Meeting of the American Football Coaches Association, January 2001, Atlanta, GA.
11. National Collegiate Athletic Association, Football Rule Books 1991–2000. Indianapolis, IN.
12. National Federation of State High School Associations: Football Rule Books, 1991–2000. Indianapolis, IN.
13. Nelson DM: *The Anatomy of a Game: Football, the Rules, and the Men Who Made the Game,* University Press, DE. 1994.

Chapter 8

Fatalities and Catastrophic Injuries, 2001–2008

Introduction

A short summary of previous chapters will show the steady decline of direct football fatalities at all levels of play following the high of 214 in the first decade of data collection 1931–40 (with the exception of the decade 1961–70). The following two decades, the 1940s and 1950s, were associated with 144 and 142 direct fatalities, respectively. The years from 1961 through 1970 were associated with a dramatic increase to 244. Concerns for the safety of participants received major emphasis during the 1970s, and the result was a major reduction of direct fatal injuries to 127. This reduction continued in the 1980s and 1990s with 61 and 42 direct fatalities, respectively. The data collection for the next decade includes only eight years (2001–08) and the number of direct fatalities numbered 38. One could only estimate that there was a strong possibility that in the years from 2001 through 2010 there would be a slight increase of direct fatal injuries compared to the 1990s.

As illustrated in Table 8.1, during the eight years of data collection from 2001 through 2008, there was a total of 38 direct fatal injuries in all levels of football. Sandlot football accounted for 4, professional football for 3, high school football for 30, and college football for 1. When compared to the previous decade, sandlot and professional football showed an increase of three each, high school football had a decrease of six, and college football a decrease of four. If the years 2009 and 2010 have similar results as 2008, there will be a definite increase of direct fatalities in the decade 2001–10, but only time will reveal those numbers. As illustrated in Table 8.2, indirect fatalities were more than double the number of direct fatalities from 2001 to 2008. This had been the trend starting with the 1980s. The remainder of this chapter will focuses on the eight years of data collection from 2001 to 2008.

Table 8.1 Direct Football Fatalities 2001–08

Year	Sandlot	Professional	High School	College	Total
2001	1	0	8	0	9
2002	1	1	3	1	6
2003	1	0	2	0	3
2004	1	0	4	0	5
2005	0	1	2	0	3
2006	0	0	1	0	1
2007	0	1	3	0	4
2008	0	0	7	0	7
TOTAL	4	3	30	1	38

Fatalities and Catastrophic Injuries, 2001–2008

In 2001 (Table 8.1), there was a total of nine direct fatal injuries—eight at the high school level and one in sandlot football. That is the greatest number since the 12 direct fatalities during the 1986 season. For the 1,800,000 participants in all levels of football, the incidence rate per 100,000 participants was 0.50. As shown in Table 8.3 the incidence rate per 100,000 participants in high school football was 0.53, and for college football was 0.00. The 2001 data continue the trend of single-digit direct fatalities that started in the 1978 football season (with the exception of the 12 in 1986), but there was an increase from 3 in 2000 to 9 in 2001.

A majority of direct fatal injuries occurred in games; in 2001 eight fatalities occurred in games and one was unknown. One injury took place in August, two in September, four in October, one in November, and the date of one was unknown. Tackling was involved with one fatal injury, two with being tackled, one

Table 8.2 Indirect Football Fatalities 2001–08

Year	Sandlot	Professional	High School	College	Total
2001	0	2	10	3	15
2002	1	0	7	3	11
2003	1	1	4	1	7
2004	0	0	7	3	10
2005	1	1	8	2	12
2006	2	0	12	2	16
2007	1	1	6	1	9
2008	3	0	7	3	13
TOTAL	9	5	61	18	93

Table 8.3 Direct Football Fatalities Incidence
per 100,000 Participants 2001–08

Year	High School	College
2001	0.53	0.00
2002	0.20	1.33
2003	0.13	0.00
2004	0.27	0.00
2005	0.13	0.00
2006	0.07	0.00
2007	0.20	0.00
2008	0.47	0.00

with being blocked on a kickoff, two with being tackled on a kickoff, one falling on the ball, and two in other collisions. Six of the fatalities involved injuries to the brain, one from a fractured cervical vertebra, one from a ruptured spleen, and one from a ruptured aorta.

Football cannot be directly responsible for all football fatalities, and in 2001 there were 15 indirect fatal injuries: 10 in high school, 3 in college, and 2 in professional. Six of the high school deaths were heart-related, one was heat-related, and the cause of three was unknown. One of the college indirect fatalities was heart-related, one heat-related, and one was due to an asthma attack. The professional football fatalities included one heat stroke, and the cause of one was unknown. The 2001 report mentioned that the heat stroke deaths continued to be a concern since they were preventable with the proper precautions (American Football Coaches Association 2002).

The 2001 report emphasized the importance of eliminating initial contact with the head and face in blocking and tackling and stated that coaches who were teaching helmet and face contact in tackling and blocking were not only breaking the rules but also placing their players at risk for permanent paralysis or death (AFCA 2002). That type of tackling and blocking was the direct cause of 36 football fatalities and 30 permanent paralysis injuries in 1968. It was also pointed out that if a catastrophic football injury went to a court of law, there was no defense for using this type of tackling or blocking technique. Recommendations for reducing head and neck injuries, as well as heat stroke deaths, were repeated from past reports (AFCA 2002).

The 2002 football season was associated with six direct fatal injuries. Three of the deaths were at the high school level, one at the professional level, one in sandlot (one of three females in the database), and one at the college level. The injury rate per 100,000 participants was 0.33 for the 1,800,000 participants at all levels of football. The high school injury rate was 0.20 and the college rate was 1.33. Three of the deaths occurred in games, two in practice, and one was unknown. Five of the injuries took place during September and one happened in July. Brain injuries were involved in all six direct fatalities. Tackling and being tackled were associated with two of the injuries, and the activity of the other four was unknown. In many of the cases where the activity was listed as unknown, the athletes were involved in a number of collisions; but the one collision that caused the death could not be identified.

Indirect fatalities numbered 11 in 2002, with 7 in high school, 3 in college, and 1 at the sandlot level. Five of the high school indirect fatalities were heart-related, one was due to an asthma attack, and the cause of one was unknown. One of the heart-related deaths was related to an over-the-counter herbal stimulant that contained ephedra. The college indirect deaths were caused by heart failure, heat stroke, and an unknown cause. The sandlot death was heart-related (AFCA 2003).

In 2003, football accounted for three direct deaths—two at the high school level and one in sandlot football. This was the lowest number since the three direct deaths in 2000, one in 1994, and zero in 1990. The incidence rate per 100,000 was 0.17 for the 1,800,000 participants in 2003. The high school rate was 0.13, and the college rate was 0.00. All three of the fatalities occurred in games, with one taking place in September, one in October, and one in November. One of the injuries occurred while tackling, and the activity of the other two was unknown. Two of the fatalities were brain injuries, and one involved an injury to an artery in the player's neck.

In 2003, the seven indirect fatalities continued the trend for indirect injuries outnumbering direct fatalities. For the first three years from 2001 through 2003, there were 33 indirect deaths and 18 direct. Six of the seven high school indirect fatalities were heart-related, and the cause of the college death was unknown.

Recommendations for the reduction of direct fatalities were the same as in 2002. The recommendations for indirect heat stroke deaths emphasized that in the past nine years there were 21 young football players who died from heat stroke, and from 1960 through 2003 there were 101 heat stroke deaths. There were no heat stroke fatalities in 2003. The report pointed out that every effort should be made to continuously educate coaches concerning the proper procedures and precautions when practicing or playing football in the heat. Eleven recommendations for heat stroke prevention were listed, which were the same recommendations as in previous reports (AFCA 2004).

Five fatalities were directly related to football during the 2004 season: one in sandlot football and four at the high school level. The rate for direct fatalities in the 1,800,000 participants at all levels was 0.28 per 100,000 players. The high school exposure rate was 0.27. Four of the direct fatalities took place in games and one was in practice. One of the injuries happened in August, two in September, and two in November. As usual, three fatalities occurred while being tackled, one while tackling, and one in a tackling drill. Four of the injuries involved helmet-to-helmet contact, and four resulted in brain injuries (AFCA 2005).

Also in 2004, there were 10 indirect fatalities: 7 associated with high school football and 3 with college football. Heat stroke was related to three of the high school indirect deaths, one was caused by lightning, and the cause of three was unknown. Two of the college indirect deaths were heart-related, and one was related to sickle cell disease (AFCA 2005).

There were also two deaths that were not listed as football deaths. One was a high school player who had a seizure at home and later died. The second was a sandlot player who was trying to make a mandatory weight class and died of heat stroke after being in a sauna and walking on a treadmill at home (AFCA 2005).

The only change in the 2004 recommendations was related to the 24 football players who died from heat stroke from 1995 through 2004. The new recommendation for treatment was immersing the athlete in ice water to help bring down the temperature. It was also mentioned that some schools were placing baby pools or tubs of ice water at their practice facilities in order to treat heat stroke cases. This treatment had been successful in a number of cases (AFCA 2005).

There were three direct fatalities during the 2005 football season: two at the high school level and one in professional football. The incidence rate for the 1,800,000 players at all levels was 0.17 per 100,000 participants. The rate for high school players was 0.13 per 100,000 participants. All three of the fatal injuries occurred in games with one taking place in September, one in October, and one in April. Tackling is usually associated with a majority of the injuries, but in 2005 one of the injuries happened while being blocked, one while blocking on a kickoff, and one while tackling on a kickoff. The high school player being blocked was in helmet-to-helmet contact. The high school player blocking lowered his head when making contact with the opponent's chest. The professional player was tackling on a kickoff with his head in a down position and contact was made with the leg of the opponent to the top of his head. The high school deaths resulted from brain injuries, and the professional player died from a fractured cervical vertebra (AFCA 2006).

Indirect fatalities in 2005 numbered 12: 8 in high school football, 2 at the college level, 1 in professional football, and 1 at the sandlot level. The causes of the high school indirect fatalities included three heart-related incidents, one from heat stroke, one was a lightning strike, and the cause of three was unknown.

The college deaths were related to one heat stroke case and one viral meningitis case. Both the sandlot and professional players' deaths were heart-related (AFCA 2006).

Most recommendations for prevention in 2005 were repeated from past reports, but it was emphasized that since 1995 there were 26 young football players who died from heat stroke (20 high school, 4 college, and 2 professional). It was also emphasized that there is no excuse for heat stroke deaths since it is preventable with proper precautions. The 11 recommendations for heat stroke prevention were again listed and again mentioned immersing the athlete in ice water in order to help reduce the body temperature (AFCA 2006).

Under general recommendations, keeping the head out of football again received major emphasis, along with the recommendation that a player with a concussion should receive immediate medical attention and should not be allowed to return to practice or a game without permission from the proper medical authorities. The 2004 and 2005 reports included a statement concerning the increase over the years in the number of indirect deaths and recommended that schools have automated external defibrillators (AEDs) available for emergency situations (AFCA 2006).

There was only one direct fatality in all levels of football during the 2006 season, and that one fatality was in high school football. The last time there was only one direct fatality was in 1994 and it was a college death. For the approximately 1,800,000 participants in 2006, the rate of direct fatalities was 0.06 per 100,000 participants. The high school rate was 0.07 and the college rate was 0.00. The one fatal injury took place in a September practice, and the athlete was tackled while running the ball. The cause of death was a cervical vertebra injury.

The trend continued in 2006 for indirect fatalities outnumbering direct fatal injuries. There were 16 indirect fatalities in 2006: 12 in high school, 2 in college, and 2 in sandlot. The high school fatalities were caused by eight heart-related cases, three heat stroke cases, and one was unknown. The college deaths were caused by one heat stroke and one sickle cell disease. The sandlot or youth league fatalities had one heat stroke and one related to sickle cell disease. Indirect fatalities had been in double figures since 1999 with the exception of 2003. The 16 deaths in 2006 were the highest number since the 24 indirect deaths in 1965 (AFCA 2007).

The report pointed out that since 1995 there had been 31 football players who died from heat stroke (23 in high school, 5 in college, 2 in professional, and 1 in sandlot). A strong statement was given that every effort should be made to educate coaches continuously concerning the proper procedures and precautions when practicing or playing in the heat. The 11 recommendations for the prevention of heat stroke fatalities were repeated from the 2005 report (AFCA 2007).

There were four direct fatalities during the 2007 football season. Three fatalities were at the high school level and one was at the professional level. As was true during the past 10 years, the rate of direct fatal injuries was very low on a 100,000 player exposure basis. For the approximately 1,800,000 participants in 2007, the rate of direct fatalities was 0.22. per 100,000 participants. The rate for senior high and junior high school was 0.20 per 100,000 participants. All four of the fatalities in 2007 took place in games, with three in October and one in February. Two of the injuries happened while tackling and two while being tackled. Brain injuries accounted for two of the deaths, one was due to a spinal cord injury, and one to an internal injury.

Indirect fatalities numbered nine in 2007 with six at the high school level, one in college football, one in sandlot, and one in semi-professional. The causes of the high school indirect fatalities were two heart-related cases, two heat strokes, one pulmonary embolism, and one unknown. The college and sandlot deaths were both heart-related, and the professional death was related to the individual being diabetic. The professional player did not have a medical exam but signed a waiver in order to play.

There was a slight increase from one to four direct fatalities in 2007, and a reduction of seven indirect fatalities. Indirect fatalities had been in double figures since 1999, with the exceptions of 2003 and 2007.

Since 1960, most of the direct fatalities had been caused by brain and neck injuries, and, in fact, since 1990, all but five of the direct deaths had been brain injuries. A recommendation for reducing head and neck injuries stated that a number of players with brain trauma complained of headaches or had a previous concussion prior to their deaths (AFCA 2008). The team physician, athletic trainer, or coach should make players aware of the signs for concussion, and players were encouraged to inform the team physician, athletic trainer, or coach if they are experiencing any signs of concussion. It was also stated that coaches should never make the decision whether a player returns to a game or practice if that player experiences brain trauma (AFCA 2008).

The 2007 data show two cases of heat stroke death at the high school level with another one possible, but there was no autopsy performed. Since 1995, there were 33 football players who died from heat stroke (25 high school, 5 college, 2 professional, and 1 sandlot). The 11 recommendations to help prevent heat stroke deaths were repeated from previous years (AFCA 2008).

In 2007, there were also three deaths that were not related to football. One was a 14-year-old high school player who died in his sleep from a torn aorta that could have happened from trauma or natural causes. The second was a 17-year-old high school player who also died in his sleep. He complained his head hurt the night before he died. The third player was also a high school player participating in a touch football game after a summer weight lifting workout. The cause of death was an aortic aneurysm.

The 2008 football season was associated with seven direct football fatalities, and all seven were at the high school level. For the 1,800,000 participants at all levels, the 2008 rate of direct fatalities was 0.39 per 100,000 participants. The high school rate was 0.47 and the college rate was 0.00. Five of the seven deaths happened in games, one in practice, and one in a scrimmage game. Three of the injuries took place in August, three in September, and one in October. Tackling had always been involved in a majority of the fatal injuries and in 2008 three of the injuries involved tackling, one involved being tackled, one involved being blocked, and two were involved in a collision. Brain injuries accounted for five of the injuries, one was due to an abdominal injury, and one was an injury to the chest. Since 1960, most of the direct fatalities had been caused by brain and neck injuries, and in fact, since 1990, all but six of the head and neck injuries involved injuries to the brain.

Several suggestions for reducing head and neck injuries were listed in the 2008 report, as follows:

1. Athletes must be given proper conditioning exercises that will strengthen their neck so they will be able to hold their heads firmly erect when making contact.
2. Coaches should drill the athletes in the proper execution of the fundamental football skills, particularly blocking and tackling. *Contact should always be made with the head up and never with the top of the head/helmet. Initial contact should never be made with the head/helmet or face mask.*
3. Coaches and officials should discourage the players from using their heads as battering rams when blocking and tackling. The rules prohibiting spearing should be enforced in practice and in games. The players should be taught to respect the helmet as a protective device and that the helmet should not be used as a weapon.
4. All coaches, physicians, and trainers should take special care to see that the player's equipment is properly fitted, particularly the helmet.
5. When a player has experienced or shown signs of head trauma (loss of consciousness, visual disturbances, headache, inability to walk correctly, obvious disorientation, memory loss), he should receive immediate medical attention and should not be allowed to return to practice or game without permission from a physician.
6. A number of the players associated with brain trauma complained of headaches or had a previous concussion prior to their deaths. The team physician, athletic trainer, or coach should make players aware

of these signs. Players should also be encouraged to inform the team physician, athletic trainer, or coach if they are experiencing any of the aforementioned signs of brain trauma.

7. Coaches should never make the decision to return a player to a game or active participation in a practice if that player experiences brain trauma (AFCA 2009).

Of the five brain injuries in 2008, two were diagnosed as second impact syndrome. Players with second impact syndrome received an initial concussion and returned to play before being fully healed.

The trend continued in 2008 for indirect fatalities to outnumber direct injuries. Indirect deaths had been in double figures since 1999 with the exceptions of 2003 and 2007. Indirect fatalities in 2008 numbered 13, with 7 being at the high school level, 3 in college football, and 3 in sandlot football. Four of the high school indirect injuries were associated with heat stroke, and three were heart-related. Two of the college injuries were heat strokes and one was a sickle cell death. All three of the sandlot indirect deaths were heart-related. The 2008 data show six cases of heat stroke (four high school and two college), which is the third highest number since the eight in 1970 and the seven in 1972. Since 1995, there had been 39 football players die from heat stroke (29 high school, 7 college, 2 professional, and 1 sandlot). There were 12 recommendations for heat stroke prevention listed in the 2008 report, as follows.

Heat stroke and heat exhaustion are prevented by careful control of various factors in the conditioning program of the athlete. When football activity is carried on in hot weather, the following suggestions and precautions should be taken:

1. Each athlete should have a complete physical examination with a medical history and an annual health history update. History of previous heat illness and type of training activities before organized practice begins should be included.
2. Acclimatize athletes to heat gradually by providing graduated practice sessions for the first 7 to 10 days and other abnormally hot or humid days. Obey the rules pertaining to when full football uniforms may be used.
3. Know both the temperature and the humidity, since it is more difficult for the body to cool itself in high humidity. Use of a sling psychrometer is recommended to measure the relative humidity, and anytime the wet-bulb temperature is over 78°F, practices should be altered.
4. Adjust activity level and provide frequent rest periods. Rest in cool, shaded area with some air movement and remove helmets and loosen

or remove jerseys. Rest periods of 15–30 minutes should be provided during workouts of 1 hour.

5. Provide adequate *cold* water replacement during practice. *Water should always be available and in unlimited quantities to the athletes. Give Water Regularly.* Athletes should drink water before, during, and after practice.

6. Salt should be replaced daily and liberal salting of the athletes' food will accomplish this purpose. Coaches should not provide salt tablets to athletes. Attention must be directed to water replacement.

7. Athletes should weigh each day before and after practice and weight charts should be checked in order to treat the athlete who loses excessive weight each day. Generally, a 3% body weight loss through sweating is safe, and a 5% loss is in the danger zone.

8. Clothing is important and a player should avoid using long sleeves, long stockings, and any excess clothing. Never use rubberized clothing or sweat suits.

9. Some athletes are more susceptible to heat injury. These individuals are not accustomed to working in the heat, may be overweight, and may be the eager athlete who constantly competes at his capacity. Athletes with previous heat problems should be watched closely.

10. It is important to observe for signs of heat illness. Some trouble signs are nausea, incoherence, fatigue, weakness, vomiting, cramps, weak rapid pulse, flushed appearance, visual disturbances, and unsteadiness. Heat stroke victims, contrary to popular belief, may sweat profusely. If heat illness is suspected, seek a physician's immediate service. Recommended emergency procedures are vital. A plan should be in writing and all personnel should have copies.

11. An increasing number of medical personnel are using a treatment for heat illnesses that involves immersing the athlete in ice water. This technique will help bring down the body temperature and has proven to be effective. Some schools have plastic outdoor swim pools filled with ice water available at practice facilities.

12. The National Athletic Trainers Association also has a heat illness position statement on their web site with recommendations for prevention (AFCA 2009).

Specific recommendations resulting from the 2008 survey data were as follows:

1. Mandatory medical examinations and medical history should be taken before allowing an athlete to participate in football. The National Collegiate Athletic Association (NCAA) recommends a thorough medical examination when the athlete first enters the college athletic

program and an annual health history update with use of referral exams when warranted. If the physician or coach has any questions about the athlete's readiness to participate, the athlete should not be allowed to play. High school coaches should follow the recommendations set by their State High School Athletic Associations.

2. All personnel concerned with training football athletes should emphasize proper, gradual, and complete physical conditioning. Particular emphasis should be placed on neck strengthening exercises and acclimatization to hot weather.

3. A physician should be present at all games and practice sessions. If it is impossible for a physician to be present at all practice sessions, emergency measures must be provided. Written emergency procedures are recommended for both coaches and medical staff.

4. All personnel associated with football participation should be cognizant of the problems and safety measures related to physical activity in hot weather.

5. Each institution should strive to have a certified athletic trainer who is a regular member of the faculty and who is adequately prepared and qualified.

6. Cooperative liaison should be maintained by all groups interested in the field of Athletic Medicine (coaches, trainers, physicians, manufacturers, administrators, and so forth).

7. There should be strict enforcement of game rules, and administrative regulation should be enforced to protect the health of the athlete. Coaches and school officials must support the game officials in their conduct of the athletic contests.

8. There should be a renewed emphasis on employing well-trained athletic personnel, providing excellent facilities, and securing the safest and best equipment possible.

9. There should be continued research concerning the safety factor in football (rules, facilities, equipment, and so forth).

10. Coaches should continue to teach and emphasize the proper fundamentals of blocking and tackling to help reduce head and neck fatalities. *Keep the head out of football.*

11. Strict enforcement of the rules of the game by both coaches and officials will help reduce serious injuries. Be aware of the 2005 rule change to the 1976 definition of spearing and to the 2007 high school rules concerning illegal helmet contact.

12. When a player has experienced or shown signs of head trauma (loss of consciousness, visual disturbances, headache, inability to walk cor-

Table 8.4 Direct Football Fatalities Cause of Death 2001–08

Cause	Sandlot	Professional	High School	College	Total
Head	3	1	22	0	26
Spinal	1	2	3	0	6
Internal	0	0	5	0	5
Other	0	0	0	1	1
TOTAL	4	3	30	1	38

rectly, obvious disorientation, memory loss), he should receive immediate medical attention and should not be allowed to return to practice or a game without permission from the proper medical authorities.

13. The number of indirect heart-related deaths has increased over the years, and it is recommended that schools have an AED available for emergency situations (AFCA 2009).

Table 8.4 illustrates that of the 38 direct deaths from 2001 through 2008, head/brain injuries led the list with 26, followed by spinal injuries and internal injuries. Head/brain injuries continued to be a problem in the decade 2001–08, accounting for 68.4% of the direct fatal injuries. Almost 50% of the direct fatalities were associated with the player either making a tackle or being tackled (Table 8.5). Injury reports collected during this time period also show that when tackling or being tackled, there were many more cases of helmet-to-helmet contact. Almost 16% of the fatalities were related to kickoff plays.

When looking at position played, Table 8.6 shows that running backs were associated with 26.3% of the direct fatalities from 2001 through 2008. Kickoff coverage was involved in 13.2% of the fatal injuries followed by linebacker play.

Table 8.5 Direct Football Fatalities Activity 2001–08

Activity	Frequency	Percentage
Tackled	10	26.3
Tackling	8	21.1
Football Activity	7	18.4
Kickoff Activity	6	15.8
Blocked	2	5.3
Tackling Drill	2	5.3
Other	3	7.8
TOTAL	38	100.0

Table 8.6 Direct Football Fatalities Position Played 2001–08

Position	Frequency	Percentage
Running Back	10	26.3
Kickoff Coverage	5	13.2
Linebacker	4	10.5
Defensive Back	3	7.9
Defensive End	2	5.3
Quarterback	2	5.3
Offensive End	2	5.3
Other	5	13.1
Unknown	5	13.1
TOTAL	38	100.0

It was interesting that in the previous decade, 1991–2000, linebackers accounted for the most fatalities followed by defensive backs and running backs. Kickoff coverage changed over the years with teams having their fastest players covering kickoffs and breaking the wedge formed by the receiving team. The players try to break the wedge by lowering their heads and going full speed into the wedge. This kind of contact is bound to cause catastrophic injuries.

As shown in Table 8.7, a majority of the indirect fatalities were heart-related (49.5%) and related to heat stroke (22.5%). Heart and heat deaths accounted for 72% of all indirect fatal injuries from 2001 through 2008. As stated in previously, the trend was for indirect deaths to outnumber direct deaths. From 2001 through 2008, indirect deaths outnumbered direct deaths by 2.4 times (93 to 38).

Sickle cell disease was involved in seven indirect deaths during this time period, and more teams were testing players for sickle cell. The National Athletic Trainer's Association (NATA) came out with *Consensus Statement on Sickle Cell Trait and the Athlete* in 2008 due to the number of deaths associated with this condition. The University of Oklahoma sickle cell database showed seven college football players and one high school player dying from sickle cell disease from 2000 to 2008. One of the problems with identifying sickle cell disease is that it could be mistaken for cardiac arrest or heat stroke. Another problem is that in many cases athletes with sickle cell disease had not been screened. If it is known that an athlete has this trait, there are precautions that may prevent deaths. The NATA consensus statement listed a number of precautions for athletes with sickle cell disease, as follows:

1. There is no contraindication to participation in sport for the athlete with sickle cell disease.

Table 8.7 Indirect Football Fatalities Cause of Death 2001–08

Cause	Frequency	Percentage
Heart	46	49.5
Heat	21	22.5
Sickle Cell	8	8.6
Asthma	2	2.2
Lightning	2	2.2
Unknown	14	15.1
TOTAL	93	100.0

2. Screening and simple precautions may prevent deaths and help athletes with sickle cell disease thrive in their sport.
3. Red blood cells can sickle during intensive exertion, blocking blood vessels and posing a grave risk for athletes with sickle cell disease.
4. Efforts to document newborn screening results should be made during the preparticipation exam.
5. In the absence of newborn screening results, institutions should carefully weigh the decision to screen based on the potential to provide key clinical information and targeted education that may save lives.
6. Irrespective of screening, institutions should educate staff, coaches, and athletes of the potential lethal nature of sickle cell disease.
7. Education and precautions work best when targeted at those athletes who need it most; therefore, institutions should carefully weigh this factor in deciding whether to screen. All told, the case for screening is strong.
8. When athletes with sickle cell disease are identified, there must be precautions applied to their workouts (as listed in the NATA statement) (NATA 2008).

Table 8.8 Head and Cervical Spine Fatalities

Year	Head		Cervical Spine	
	Frequency	Percent	Frequency	Percent
1945–54	87	17.1	32	27.3
1955–64	115	22.5	23	19.7
1965–74	162	31.8	42	35.9
1975–84	69	13.5	14	12.0
1985–94	33	6.5	5	4.3
1995–2004	44	8.6	1	0.8
TOTALS	510	100.0	117	100.0

The 2008 report stated that a number of factors played a major role in reducing serious head and neck fatalities in football, including current rules which eliminated the head in blocking and tackling, coaches teaching the proper fundamentals of blocking and tackling, the helmet research conducted by the National Operating Committee on Standards for Athletic Equipment (NOCSAE), and a good data collection system. This change was best illustrated in Table 8.8 which shows the increase in both brain and cervical spine fatalities during the decade 1965–74. This time period was associated with blocking and tackling techniques that involved the head as the initial point of contact. The reduction of brain and cervical spine fatalities is shown in the decade 1975–84. This time was associated with the 1976 rule change that eliminated the head as the initial contact point in blocking and tackling. Data from the 1985–94 decade continues to illustrate the reduction in brain and neck fatalities. A concern was the fact that the 1995–2004 data showed an increase in brain fatalities over the 1985–94 data. There was an increase of 11 brain deaths (2.1%) during 1995–2004. The report stated that this increase was a concern and that the data from 2005 to 2014 will have to be watched closely (AFCA 2009).

Catastrophic (Disability) Football Injuries

Cervical vertebra injuries with permanent disability continued to be a problem in the time period 2001–08 (Table 8.9). In the previous decade (1991–2000), there was a dramatic reduction of cervical cord disability injuries from the prior decade (1981–90), but with only eight years of data, the latest figures (2001–08) show an increase. There were 76 permanent disability cervical vertebrae injuries from 2001 through 2008, with 64 at the high school level, 4 in college football, 6 at the professional level, and 2 in sandlot football. Four of the eight years of data had the total number of injuries in double digits. The incidence rate per 100,000 participants for high school football was below 1.00 for all eight years, and the college rate was 1.33 for 2002, 1.33 for 2003, and 2.66 for 2006. College football had no cervical cord disability injuries in five of the eight years.

A majority of spinal cord injuries take place in games; and for the eight years from 2001 to 2008, 49 of the 76 injuries took place in games, 13 in practice, 8 in scrimmages, and 6 were unknown. Tackling was responsible for a majority of the cervical vertebra injuries, and for the eight years mentioned above, 43 of the 76 injuries were caused by tackling, 10 by being tackled, 4 on kickoffs and punts, 8 to other causes, and 11 were unknown.

As was true when looking at the fatality data, a majority (65.8%) of the cervical cord injured athletes were playing on the defensive side of the football

Table 8.9 Permanent Cervical Cord Injuries 2001–08

Year	Sandlot	Professional	High School	College	Total
2001	0	0	8	0	8
2002	0	0	6	1	7
2003	0	1	9	1	11
2004	1	1	11	0	13
2005	0	0	5	0	5
2006	0	0	8	2	10
2007	1	1	7	0	9
2008	0	3	10	0	13
TOTAL	2	6	64	4	76

when injured. Only 14 (18.4%) of the 76 players were on the offensive side of the ball. Twelve of the injuries were listed as unknown. Defensive backs led the list of injured players, followed by kickoff participants and linebackers.

As shown in Table 8.12 there were 43 permanent brain injuries from 2001 through 2008. During the previous decade (1991–2000), there was a total of 50 permanent brain injuries. High school participants were associated with 86% of the brain injuries from 2001 to 2008. As stated in previous chapters, it is difficult to establish exactly how the brain injuries were taking place due to the fact that in most cases it was not known when the exact hit that caused the injury took place. There is no doubt that tackling and being tackled led the list, along with other collisions that take place in a football game or practice.

In addition to the cervical cord and brain injuries with permanent disability during the eight years from 2001 to 2008, there were 121 catastrophic injuries with complete recovery. These injuries were listed as fractured cervical

Table 8.10 Permanent Cervical Cord Injuries Incidence
per 100,000 Participants 2001–08

Year	High School	College
2001	0.53	0.00
2002	0.40	1.33
2003	0.60	1.33
2004	0.73	0.00
2005	0.33	0.00
2006	0.53	2.66
2007	0.47	0.00
2008	0.67	0.00

Table 8.11 Permanent Cervical Cord Injuries Offensive vs.
Defensive Football 2001–08

Year	Offensive	Defensive	Unknown	Total
2001	0	4	4	8
2002	0	5	2	7
2003	1	9	1	11
2004	1	11	1	13
2005	3	2	0	5
2006	3	5	2	10
2007	3	5	1	9
2008	3	9	1	13
TOTAL	14	50	12	76

vertebrae, brain injuries, transient paralysis, or severe concussions, but the injured athlete had a complete recovery. The authors of the research were not as
confident in the recovery numbers as they were with the disability injuries, but
noted that of these 121 injuries, many could have been disability injuries without the proper medical care received by the participant.

Football Rules 2001–2008: Safety and Equipment

Football rules and improved protective equipment played a major role in
the reduction of football fatalities and catastrophic injuries during the past 50
years. This trend continued in 2001–08. Some of the safety rules changes for
2001 included a referee's timeout declared when the runner's helmet comes

Table 8.12 Permanent Brain Injuries 2001–08

Year	Sandlot	Professional	High School	College	Total
2001	0	0	2	0	2
2002	0	0	1	1	2
2003	0	0	8	1	9
2004	0	0	2	1	3
2005	1	0	4	1	6
2006	0	0	8	0	8
2007	0	0	4	0	4
2008	1	0	8	0	9
TOTAL	2	0	37	4	43

Image 8.1 Blocking Field Goal
Photo courtesy of NCAA.

off, and the exemption of the ball carrier from the rule that prohibits hurdling. There was also a removable cleat standard that was updated to comply with generally accepted manufacturer's standards. Due to an increase in knee injuries from blocks below the waist in the free blocking zone, a rule change stated that players legally blocking below the waist must be on the line of scrimmage and in the free blocking zone at the snap. Points of Emphasis in 2001 included heat and hydration due to an increase in heat stroke deaths, football helmet removal techniques for head/neck injured players, referee's procedure when a player's equipment needs repair, and a section on profanity and sportsmanship.

The 2001 rule book also covered the major rule differences between the National Federation of High Schools (NFHS) and the NCAA. Following are some of the rule differences related to safety and equipment:

1. Block in the back: In high school, it was defined as a block in the back above the waist as clipping, and the college definition was contact against an opponent, other than the runner, occurring when force of initial contact is from behind/above waist.
2. Chop block: In high schools it was defined at knees or below, and in college at the thigh or below.

3. Butt blocking and Face tackling: In high schools it was illegal and defined, and in colleges there was no definition, but butting and ramming were prohibited.

4. Clipping: In high school, defined as both above and below the waist when from behind, and in colleges, defined as a block against an opponent when force of the initial contact was from behind and at or below the waist (exception runner).

5. Injured player: In high school, a player had to leave game for one down, and in colleges, a time-out was charged only if the player remains in game.

6. Roughing the kicker/holder: In high school, there was no foul if a player was blocked into kicker/holder, and in college, a roughing penalty was called even if legally blocked into kicker/holder.

7. Apparently unconscious player: In high school, a physician must authorize return in writing, and in college, no rule.

8. Chin strap: In high school, either a two- or a four-point strap was allowed, and in colleges, a four-point strap was required.

9. Helmets: In high school, similar team color was not required and there was no rule on taking it off. In college, team color and design must be same and it could not be taken off unless in the team box, with the exception for time-outs, etc.

10. Mouth protectors: In high school, there was no color requirement, and in colleges, prohibited from being clear or white.

11. Pants: In high school, must cover knee and have knee pads, and in college, must have same color and design.

12. Shoes: Required in high schools. In colleges not required, but player was disqualified if cleats were longer than half an inch.

13. Both the high school and college rule books listed the player's equipment that was mandatory and the equipment that was illegal. High school mandatory equipment was as follows:
   - face mask meeting NOCSAE standard
   - helmet meeting NOCSAE standard
   - hip pads with tailbone protector
   - jersey
   - knee pads worn over the knee and under pants
   - pants which cover knees and knee pads
   - shoes
   - shoulder pads
   - thigh guards
   - tooth and mouth protector (AFCA 2002)

In 2002, the rules changes included a redefined clipping rule that stated clipping was a block against an opponent when the initial contact was from behind, at or below the waist, and was not against a player who was a runner or pretending to be a runner. It also included language to include a block in the back under the Illegal Blocking rule. The Points of Emphasis in 2002 for safety included late hits and illegal contact (spearing, face tackling, butt blocking) that had been associated with catastrophic head and neck injuries. A second Point of Emphasis was fluid replacement and hydration, which addressed an increasing number of heat stroke deaths. The third Point of Emphasis related to safety was altered mouth guards and other illegal equipment. The rules committee believed that there was a need to reeducate players and coaches on the inherent risks in altering mouth protectors and removing tailbone protectors from hip pads.

The 2003 and 2004 football rules had no changes that were related to safety. The 2003 rules did have a Point of Emphasis on chop blocks, and the 2004 rules had a Point of Emphasis on helmet contact. The 2004 book also had a section on shared responsibility and the helmet warning statement by NOCSAE. The NOCSAE warning statement was attached on all helmets and stated the following:

> Do not strike an opponent with any part of this helmet or face mask. This is a violation of football rules and may cause you to suffer severe brain or neck injury, including paralysis or death. Severe brain or neck injury may also occur accidentally while playing football. NO HELMET CAN PREVENT ALL SUCH INJURIES. YOU USE THIS HELMET AT YOUR OWN RISK. (AFCA 2005)

The 2005 rules book stated that in 2006 it would be mandatory that all helmets be secured with a four-point chin strap. The reasoning was that the four-point chin strap would increase the probability of the helmet staying in place during game action. Also in 2006 it would be mandatory for tooth and mouth protectors to be a color (not clear or white). This warning for 2006 gave teams the opportunity to exhaust their inventories of two-point chin straps and clear/white mouth/teeth protectors. Points of emphasis in 2005 again mentioned heat and hydration and their effect on weight, spearing, butt blocking, face tackling, and chop blocks. The above mentioned Points of Emphasis are important due to the fact that these areas could all be directly related to death or disability injuries.

As mentioned, the 2006 rules stated that at least a four-point chin strap was required to secure the helmet and mouth guards should be of any readily visible color other than white or clear. A major change in 2006 eliminated the word "intentional" from the spearing rule. The rule now stated: "Spearing is the use of the helmet in an attempt to punish an opponent" (AFCA 2008). Prior to this change, the referee had to decide if the hit was intentional or not, and rule makers felt that this was an impossible task. Points of Emphasis in 2006 included the proper procedure for handling apparent concussions and illegal helmet contact. The section on concussions included an action plan if a player was suspected of having a concussion, as well as a segment on signs observed by the coach and symptoms reported by the player. Illegal helmet contact discussed spearing, face tackling, and butt blocking. It also mentioned the reasoning for eliminating the word "intentional" from the spearing rule.

The 2007 rule book placed all of the illegal helmet contact under one section which stated that illegal helmet contact was an act of initiating contact with the helmet against an opponent (AFCA 2008). The rule also stated that there were several types of illegal helmet contact and defined butt blocking, face tackling, and spearing. Points of Emphasis in 2007 again mentioned heat and hydration due to the five heat-related deaths the previous year. Suggestions for prevention were a part of this topic in order to help coaches and others prepare for practice and play in hot and humid weather. A second important Point of Emphasis mentioned mandatory equipment and illegal equipment. Mandatory equipment and definitions were listed as helmets and face masks, hip pads with tailbone protector, pants, jersey, knee pads, and shoes. Illegal equipment included hard-substance casts that were not padded, jewelry, and eye shields that were not totally clear, not molded, and not rigid. Eye shields had to permit 100% light transmission and could not be tinted.

The 2008 rules clarified mandatory equipment that could not be altered: hip pads, tailbone protector, knee pads, and thigh pads. The rule stated that the equipment must not be altered from the manufacturer's original design/production (AFCA 2009). The concerns were that players and coaches were altering mandatory equipment and, therefore, sacrificing safety by changing the original design. The Points of Emphasis in 2008 were Methicillin-resistant *Staphylococcus aureus* (MRSA), which was a new problem for the Rules Committee, but an increasingly more common problem in the sports world. Also included in this Point of Emphasis were communicable skin diseases and their prevention and treatment. Also discussed in the 2008 Points of Emphasis was the purpose of the helmet (not used as a weapon) and the altering of legal football equipment.

Discussion

As shown in Graph 8.1, the eight years from 2001 through 2008 were associated with 38 direct fatalities. The eight-year period started with nine fatalities in 2001 and ended with seven in 2008 with no years having double digits. In 2006 there was only one fatality in all levels of football. The prior decade

(1991–2000) was associated with 42 fatal injuries and accounted for the lowest number of fatalities in a decade since the start of the research in 1931. It will be interesting to see if the final two years of the decade (2009 and 2010) show an increase for the full decade. Tackling and being tackled were associated with 60.6% of the 38 injuries during these eight years, as opposed to 45.2% the prior decade. Kickoff activity—tackling, being tackled, blocking, being blocked—was associated with 15.9% of the 38 fatalities from 2001 to 2008. The kickoff and kickoff return became a dangerous activity due to players running at full speed into the blocking wedge and attempting tackles (in many cases with the head in a down position or making helmet-to-helmet contact). As was true in past decades, head and neck injuries were involved in a majority of the injuries. For the eight-year period mentioned, head injuries accounted for 68% of the fatalities, neck injuries accounted for 15.8%, and internal injuries accounted for 13%.

The trend of indirect fatalities increasing in numbers over direct fatalities that started in the 1980s, continued in the final eight years of the research (Graph 8.2). There were 2.5 times more indirect fatalities than direct fatalities (93 vs. 38) from 2001 through 2008. Forty-three, or almost 50%, of the indirect deaths were heart-related and 21 (22%) were heat-related. Seventy-two percent of the indirect fatalities were related to heart and heat deaths. In approximately 16% of the indirect fatalities, the cause was unknown. Sickle cell disease also played a role in indirect deaths during this time period. There were seven college indirect deaths related to sickle cell disease. NATA came out with a consensus statement on sickle cell disease in June 2007, and exertional sickling was the leading cause of death in college football from 2001 through 2008. The consensus statement includes the following information:

1. There is no contraindication to participation in sport for the athlete with sickle cell disease.
2. Screening and simple precautions may prevent deaths and help athletes with sickle cell disease thrive in their sport.
3. Red blood cells can sickle during intense exertion, blocking blood vessels and posing a grave risk for athletes with sickle cell disease.
4. Efforts to document newborn screening results should be made during the preparticipation exam.
5. In the absence of newborn screening results, institutions should carefully weigh the decision to screen based on the potential to provide key clinical information and targeted education that may save lives.
6. Irrespective of screening, institutions should educate staff, coaches, and athletes of the potentially lethal nature of sickle cell disease.

Graph 8.1 Direct Fatalities 2001–08

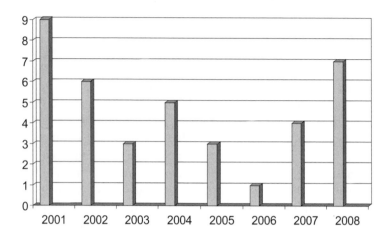

7. Education and precautions work best when targeted at those athletes who need it most; therefore, institutions should carefully weigh this factor in deciding whether to screen. All told, the case for screening is strong.
8. When athletes with sickle cell disease are identified, there must be precautions applied to their workouts (as listed in the NATA statement) (NATA 2007).

Graph 8.2 Indirect Fatalities 2001–08

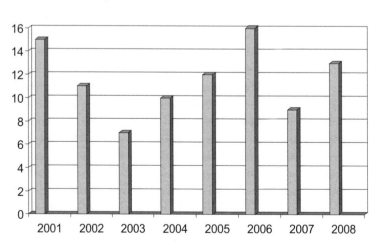

Graph 8.3 illustrates the number of direct fatalities by decade starting from 1931–40 through 2001–08 (eight-year total). There were 1,012 direct deaths over this 78-year period with 671 in high school football, 86 at the college level, 177 in sandlot or recreational play, and 78 at the professional and semi-professional level. There was a decrease in the number of deaths during the 1940s and 1950s when compared to the 1930s, but there was a major increase in the 1960s. The 1960s included the use of the head making initial contact while blocking and tackling, suspect medical care, football helmet manufacturers not having to meet any standards, and fewer rules associated with safety. The 1970s saw a dramatic decrease in the number of direct fatalities from 244 to 127. This decrease was due to the 1976 rule change prohibiting initial contact with the head and face while blocking and tackling, to a helmet standard that went into effect at the college level in 1978 and the high school level in 1980, to improved coaching techniques when teaching the fundamental skills of the game, and to much improved medical care. The 1980s and 1990s continued the decrease of direct fatal injuries to 61 and 42, respectively. The final eight years covered by this book, 2001–08, were associated with 38 direct fatalities.

During the first 50 years of this research, head/brain injuries accounted for 60.5% of the direct deaths, spinal injuries for 16.4%, and internal injuries for 15.4%. After the first 60 years, head/brain injuries increased to 61.8%, spinal injuries were reduced to 15.9%, and internal injuries were reduced to 14.8%. The 70-year totals show an increase of head/brain deaths to 62.7%, a continued reduction of spinal injuries to 15.3%, and a continued reduction of internal injuries to 14.6%. The 78-year totals show an increase of head/brain deaths to 63% and spinal and internal injuries staying about the same. The major football activities involved in direct fatalities were very similar over the decades, and the 78-year totals show tackling involved in approximately one-third of the injuries, followed by being tackled at 16%. These numbers show that approximately 50% of the direct deaths were related to tackling and being tackled. These were followed by blocking (8.6%), being blocked (2.1%), collisions (3.6%), and kickoff activity (1.0%). It is important to mention that approximately one-third of the activities involved in direct deaths were unknown.

Indirect fatalities by decade are illustrated in Graph 8.4. There was a total of 695 indirect deaths from 1931 through 2008. High school football accounted for 449, sandlot/recreational for 113, professional for 23, and college football for 110. Indirect data for the 1930s was suspect due to the fact that many of the deaths classified as indirect football deaths were not actually football-related. The data were not considered reliable, therefore, final calculations did not include the 1930s. For the 40-year totals from 1941 through 1980, heart-related deaths accounted for 38.8% of the indirect deaths, heat stroke deaths for 21.8%,

Graph 8.3 Direct Fatalities by Decade

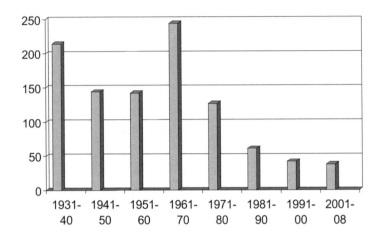

and other/unknowns accounted for 38.8%. The 50-year totals show a slight increase in heart deaths to 42.7% and a slight increase in heat-related deaths to 22.4%. Sixty-year totals show an additional increase in heart-related deaths to 46.7%, and heat-related deaths were approximately the same. Other and unknown accounted for 31.9%. Sixty-eight-year totals show the largest percentage of heart-related deaths at 47.1% and heat-related deaths down to 21.6%. Other and unknown accounted for 31.3%. The 1980s started the trend for in-direct fatalities to outnumber direct deaths (73 indirect to 61 direct). The difference increased in the 1990s from 90 to 42, and in the final eight years from 2001 to 2008, the difference was 93 to 38. There was an explanation for the decrease in direct fatalities over the past couple of decades as shown in previous chapters, but there was no explanation for the increase of indirect fatalities. Heart-related deaths had a steady increase and heat-related deaths stayed about the same. Others and unknowns were about equally divided. As indicated by the 68-year data, heart and heat-related deaths were the major concern accounting for approximately two-thirds of the indirect deaths. Future research will hopefully have answers and preventive measures for heart-related football deaths.

Cervical cord injuries with permanent disability are shown in Graph 8.5. Injuries from 1971 to 1976 were from research conducted by Joseph Torg, M.D. In a five-year retrospective study, he found 99 cases of quadriplegia, which included 77 high school players, 18 college players, and 4 listed as others. In a 1976 prospective study, he listed 34 cases of quadriplegia that included 25 high

Graph 8.4 Indirect Fatalities by Decade

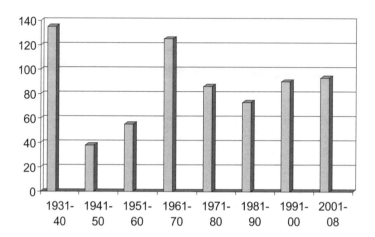

school players, 8 college players, and 1 listed as other. The graph illustrates Torg's data in 1971–76 with a total of 133 cases of quadriplegia, including 102 high school players, 26 college players, and 5 listed as other (Torg et al. 1979). The graph continues with 1977–80 data from Mueller and Cantu and the initial years of the National Center for Catastrophic Sports Injury Research (NCCSIR). Data in 1977–80 show 50 cervical cord injuries with disability. If the 1971–80 data were combined, there would have been a total of 183 cases of cervical cord injuries with permanent disability. High school players accounted for 144 injuries, college players for 33, and 6 others. The later decades in Graph 8.5 only include the data collected by the NCCSIR.

The 1980s show a dramatic reduction of catastrophic cervical cord injuries to 100: 82 high school, 13 college, 3 sandlot, and 2 professional. The same reasons for the decrease in direct fatalities were also responsible for the decrease in catastrophic cervical cord injuries: the 1976 rule change concerning head contact in blocking and tackling, the NOCSAE helmet standard, better coaching, and improved medical care. The 1990s continued the decrease initiated in the 1980s with the number of cervical cord injuries being reduced to 69, including 55 high school, 9 college, 1 sandlot, and 5 professional. A concern for the return to head-first and helmet-to-helmet contact in the first eight years of the 2001–10 decade is illustrated in Graph 8.5 with an increase to 76 cervical cord injuries. With two more years of data collection in this decade, there may be an increase of 10 to 20 injuries.

The data from the NCCSIR does show that the rate of cervical cord injuries per 100,000 participants is less than one for both high school and college play-

Graph 8.5 Cervical Cord Injuries

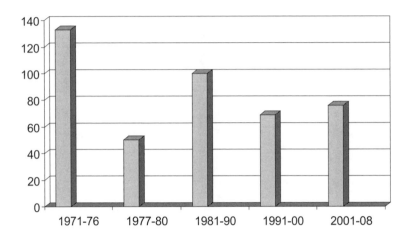

ers. The data also demonstrate that of the 295 cervical cord injuries from the NCCSIR, 205 of the injured players were playing defense at the time of the injury—67% were tackling, and 35% were defensive backs. Nine percent of the injured players were involved in either tackling, being tackled, blocking, or being blocked on a kickoff.

In 1984, the NCCSIR began an effort to collect data on cerebral injuries for all levels of football. As shown in Graph 8.6, there were 28 cerebral injuries (head and brain) with permanent disability from 1984 through 1990. Twenty-five of the injuries were at the high school level and three were in college football. In the 1990s there were 50 disability cerebral injuries, with 46 in high school and 4 in college. In the first eight years of the 2001–10 decade, there was a total of 43 cerebral injuries with disability and 37 were in high school players, 4 were in college players, and 2 were in sandlot/recreational play. For the 25-year period from 1984 through 2008, there was a total of 121 catastrophic cerebral injuries with permanent disability: 108 in high school, 11 in college, and 2 in sandlot/recreational players. For that same period of time, if both catastrophic cerebral and cervical spine injuries were combined, there would be a total of 416 catastrophic injuries to football players at all levels. Three-hundred-fifty-one were high school players, 44 were college players, 13 were professionals, and 8 were sandlot/recreational players. It was impossible to compare these numbers with earlier years due to the fact that catastrophic injuries with disability were not collected.

In 1987, the NCCSIR initiated data collection for serious catastrophic injuries (fractured cervical vertebra, fractured skull, brain injury) in football

Graph 8.6 Permanent Brain Injuries

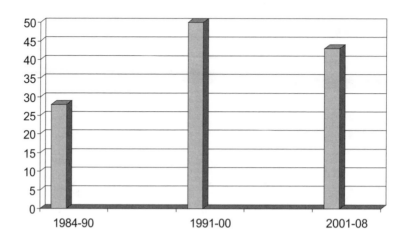

where the individual had complete recovery from the injury. The authors of the research did not feel confident in these numbers due to the fact that it was much more difficult collecting information on these injuries. There were 343 serious head or neck injuries with complete recovery during this time period. These injuries could have very well ended in death or disability, but the player received the proper medical care and recovered.

As stated in earlier chapters, rule changes and equipment research both played a major role in the reduction of football fatalities and catastrophic injuries. Following is a listing of significant rules and protective equipment advances that have made the game of football a safer activity for the participants:

1932: All players required to wear soft knee pads.
　　　　Flying block and tackle (made with both feet off the ground) was given five-yard penalty.
1933: Recommendations introduced for all college players to wear head protectors or helmets.
　　　　Three recommendations: 1) teach better techniques for blocking and tackling, 2) complete medical exams for players, 3) physician present at all games and practices.
1935: Helmets required for high school players.
1936: First plea to train sports physicians.
1937: Too many players allowed to continue play after a concussion and this practice must be eliminated.

1939: Helmets made mandatory for college players.

1940: Continued concern placed on helmets, and reduction of head injuries could only be achieved by a scientifically designed helmet. Research needed in best materials used in constructing helmets.

1946: Four time-outs given instead of three.

1947: Striking with forearm on any part of the opponent's body prohibited.

1950: Kicker and holder given equal protection.
Flying block and tackle prohibitions deleted from rules.
Fair catch reinstated and redefined.

1951: Any face mask was prohibited unless made of nonbreakable, molded plastic with rounded edges or rubber-covered wire.

1952: Clipping redefined as blocking an opponent, other than the runner, from behind.
Mandatory suspension given for striking with forearm, elbow, or locked hands.
Mandatory suspension given for flagrantly rough play.

1953: Two-platoon football abolished and players allowed to enter game only once in each quarter.

1957: It was determined illegal for a defensive player to grab face mask.

1959: One player permitted to substitute when the clock was stopped.
Recommendation in 1950s to inspect head suspensions of all helmets before every game and to discard helmets where suspension could not keep head from contact with crown of helmet.

1960: One player may enter game anytime between successive downs.

1962: Recommended that all players wear properly fitted mouth protectors.

1963: An offensive player outside the legal clipping area, in motion toward the ball when snapped, was not permitted to clip in the legal clipping area.

1964: No player could deliberately and maliciously use the helmet or head to butt or ram an opponent, and flagrant offenders were disqualified.

1965: No player allowed to deliberately and maliciously use the helmet or head to unnecessarily butt or ram an opponent, and flagrant offenders were disqualified.

1968: Metal face masks having surfaces with material as resilient as rubber allowed.

1970: Spearing was defined as the deliberate and malicious use of the head and helmet in an attempt to punish a runner after his momentum has stopped.

1972: All players required to wear mouth protectors beginning with 1973 season.

1973: All players required to wear head protectors with a secured chin strap.
All players required to wear mouth protectors.

1974: All players required to wear shoulder pads, and beginning in 1975, recommended that all institutions purchase head protectors that meet NOCSAE test standards.

1975: Four-point chin strap to be made mandatory in 1976.

1976: All players required to wear hip pads and thigh guards.

1976: Spearing redefined as the deliberate use of the helmet in an attempt to punish an opponent.

1980: All players required to wear a jersey with sleeves that completely cover the shoulder pads.

1980: No player permitted to tackle or run into a receiver when a forward pass was obviously over- or under-thrown.

1982: Face mask penalty divided between incidental and twisting, turning, or pulling face mask.

1983: All players required to wear an intraoral mouthpiece that covered all upper jaw teeth (changed from two-piece mouthpiece).

1984: Legal clipping zone was changed from four to five yards laterally in each direction.

1989: Continuous contact with the head was a defensive foul.

1990: Yellow or other readily visible colors made mandatory for mouthpieces.

1991: An unconscious or apparently unconscious player, as determined by the officials, was not permitted to return to the game without written authorization from a physician.

1991: Rib and back pads required to be covered by the jersey.

1992: A block in the back made illegal.

1992: NOCSAE seal required on the face mask and removable shoe cleats were no longer approved.
Mandatory equipment was listed as a face mask with NOCSASE seal, a helmet with NOCSAE seal and secured by a properly fastened chinstrap, hip pads with a tailbone protector, a jersey, knee pads, pants which cover the knees and knee pads, shoes, shoulder pads fully covered by the jersey, thigh guards, and a tooth/mouth protector.

1993: Player who was bleeding, had an open wound, or had excessive blood on his uniform required to leave the game for at least one down.

1994: Officials had the right to call an official's timeout for heat and humidity conditions.

1996: Illegal helmet contact was a Point of Emphasis, including spearing, butt blocking, and face tackling.

1997: Dead ball declared when the player's helmet comes off during play. Prohibited use of eye shields which prevented visual examination of an injured player's eyes.

1998: No defensive player could use the hands(s) to slap a player's head.

1999: Clarified rule that prohibited the use of eye shields with less than 100% allowable light transmission.

2000: New rule with two penalties for player who grasps an opponent's face mask: 5-yard penalty for a glancing blow and 15-yard penalty for intentional.

2001: Players legally blocking below the waist required to be on the line of scrimmage and in the free blocking zone at the snap of the ball. Point of Emphasis in 2001 included heat and hydration due to the increase in heat stroke deaths.

2002: Redefined clipping rule to state that clipping is a block against an opponent when the initial contact is from behind, at or below the waist, and is not against a player who is a runner or pretending to be a runner.

Points of Emphasis included late hits and illegal contact (spearing, face tackling, butt blocking) and fluid replacement and hydration.

2003: Point of Emphasis on helmet contact.

2004: Point of Emphasis on the warning statement on helmets by NOCSAE.

2005: In 2006 it will be mandatory that all helmets be secured with a four-point chin strap.

2006: Four-point chin strap mandatory, and mouth guards required to be of any readily visible color other than white or clear.

Major change was the elimination of the word "intentional" from the spearing rule. The rule now stated that "spearing is the use of the helmet in an attempt to punish an opponent."

Point of Emphasis included the proper procedure for handling apparent concussions—an action plan if player is suspected of having a concussion—and a section on signs observed by the coach and symptoms reported by the player.

2007: Rule book placed all illegal helmet contact under one section which stated that illegal helmet contact is an act of initiating contact with the helmet against an opponent.

Point of Emphasis mentioned mandatory and illegal equipment.

2008: Clarified mandatory equipment that must not be altered, including hip pads, tailbone protector, knee pads, and thigh pads.

Points of Emphasis were communicable skin diseases and their prevention and treatment.

A second Point of Emphasis was (MRSA), a serious problem with potentially serious consequences.

These rules have played a major role in reducing the number of fatalities and catastrophic injuries in football during the past 78 years; coaches, administrators, rule committee members, and others should be applauded for their time and effort in making the game of football what it is today.

References

1. American Football Coaches Association: Proceedings of the Seventy-Ninth Annual Meeting of the American Football Coaches Association, January 2002, San Antonio, TX.

2. American Football Coaches Association: Proceedings of the Eightieth Annual Meeting of the American Football Coaches Association, January 2003, New Orleans, LA.

3. American Football Coaches Association: Proceedings of the Eighty-First Annual Meeting of the American Football Coaches Association, January 2004, Orlando, FL.

4. American Football Coaches Association: Proceedings of the Eighty-Second Annual Meeting of the American Football Coaches Association, January 2005, Louisville, KY.

5. American Football Coaches Association: Proceedings of the Eighty-Third Annual Meeting of the American Football Coaches Association, January 2006, Dallas, TX.

6. American Football Coaches Association: Proceedings of the Eighty-Fourth Annual Meeting of the American Football Coaches Association, January 2007, San Antonio, TX.

7. American Football Coaches Association: Proceedings of the Eighty-Fifth Annual Meeting of the American Football Coaches Association, January 2008, Anaheim, CA.

8. American Football Coaches Association: Proceedings of the Eighty-Sixth Annual Meeting of the American Football Coaches Association, January 2009, Nashville, TN.

9. Mueller FO, Cantu RC. Annual Survey of Catastrophic Football Injuries 1977–2008, University of North Carolina, Chapel Hill, NC.

10. National Athletic Trainer's Association: Consensus Statement—Sickle cell trait and the Athlete, June 2007, Dallas, TX.

11. National Federation of State High School Associations: Football Rules Books, 2000–2008.

12. Torg JS, et al.: National Football Head and Neck Injury Registry Report on Cervical Quadriplegia, 1971 to 1975, *American Journal of Sports Medicine*, Vol. 7, No. 2, 1979.

Chapter 9

Medical Aspects of Football Brain and Spine Injuries

Since 1931, football fatalities due to brain and spinal cord injury and indirect fatalities primarily due to heart arrhythmia and heat stroke have been recorded. The first extensive recording of the various catastrophic brain and spinal injuries, as well as descriptions of the mechanism of injury and underlying pathophysiology, occurred in the hallmark book *Head and Neck Injuries in Football* written by Dr. Richard Schneider and published in 1973. He classified the various craniocerebral and spinal lesions seen in football. His data was compiled from a survey he conducted from members of the American Association of Neurological Surgeons and Congress of Neurological Surgeons (CNS) and most of his more than 350 acknowledgments were those physicians.

In this chapter I discuss the brain and spinal injuries Schneider recorded as well as those found more recently. I cite a number of firsts that Dr. Schneider brought to our attention such as the *acute anterior spinal cord injury syndrome,* for which urgent surgery is indicated, and the more common *acute central spinal cord injury,* for which emergent surgery is usually not indicated, with recovery occurring using conservative immobilization treatment. I will also cite more recent insights into these injuries and others, such as the second impact syndrome and chronic traumatic encephalopathy. I will conclude this chapter with a section on an injury recognized by Dr. Schneider but felt unimportant in his day. Today it is commanding enormous research efforts and attracting media attention; namely, the cerebral concussion and, when cumulative enough, chronic traumatic encephalopathy (CTE).

Before discussing the types of brain and spinal cord injuries resulting from football, it is sobering to reflect that the head and spine are unique in that their contents are incapable of regeneration. The brain and spinal cord cannot regrow lost cells, as can other organs of the body; thus injury to these structures takes on a singular importance. Whereas today virtually every major joint (ankle, knee, hip, elbow, shoulder) and most major organs can be replaced, either by artificial hardware or transplanted parts, the head and spine cannot be replaced: their contents cannot be transplanted. The most complex and vital area of the body, the central nervous system, housed in the skull and spine, can recover from injury to cells, but once cells have died, no replacement is possible.

Etiology of Brain Injury

An understanding of the forces that produce skull and brain injuries requires an understanding of the following principles:

1. A forceful blow to the resting movable head usually produces maximum brain injury beneath the point of cranial impact (*coup injury*).
2. A moving head impacting against an unyielding object usually produces maximum brain injury opposite the site of cranial impact (*contrecoup injury*). Such lesions are most common at the tips and the undersurfaces of the frontal and temporal lobes.
3. If a skull fracture is present, the first two dictums do not pertain because the bone itself, displaced either transiently (linear skull fracture) or permanently (depressed skull fracture) at the moment of impact, may directly injure brain tissue.

With brain and spinal cord injuries, it is also essential to recognize that three types of stresses can be generated by an applied force: *compressive, tensile,* (the opposite of compressive, sometimes called negative pressure), and *shearing* (a force applied parallel to a surface). Neural tissue can tolerate uniform tensile and compressive stresses fairly well, but it tolerates shearing stresses very poorly.

The cerebrospinal fluid (CSF) acts as a shock absorber, cushioning and protecting the brain by converting focally applied external stresses to a more uniform compressive stress. Despite the presence of CSF, however, shearing stresses may still be imparted to the brain. If rotational forces are applied to the head, shearing forces will occur at those sites where rotational gliding is hindered. These areas are characterized by:

1. rough, irregular surface contacts between the brain and skull, hindering smooth movement;
2. dissipation of the cerebrospinal fluid between the brain and skull; and
3. dura mater brain attachments impeding brain motion.

The first condition is most prominent in the frontal and temporal regions and explains why major brain contusions occur at these sites. The second condition explains the coup and contrecoup injuries. When the head is accelerated prior to impact, the brain lags toward the trailing surface, thus squeezing away protective CSF and allowing for the shearing forces to be maximal at this site. This brain lag actually thickens the layer of CSF under the point of impact, which explains the lack of coup injury in a moving head injury. On the other hand, when the head is stationary prior to impact, there is neither brain lag nor disproportionate distribution of CSF, accounting for the absence of contre-coup injury and the presence of coup injury.

The scalp also has energy-absorbing properties. It requires 10 times more force to produce a skull fracture in a cadaveric head with the scalp in place than in one with the scalp removed. In addition, Newton's law (force equals mass times acceleration) pertains in this situation. An athlete's head can sustain far greater force without brain injury if the neck muscles are tensed at the moment of impact. In the relaxed state, the mass of the head is essentially its own weight. However, with the neck rigidly tensed, the mass of the head approximates the mass of the body.

Etiology of Cervical Spine Injury

The cervical spine is composed of seven vertebrae joined by multiple ligaments, intervening cartilage, and muscles. In the lateral view, it is curved, convex forward (*lordosis*). The ligaments, consisting of elastin and collagen, provide the primary stabilizing component of the cervical spine. Elastin fibers arranged in a parallel manner longitudinally allow the ligaments to stretch up to twice their normal length and yet return to their original size. The main ligaments are the anterior and posterior longitudinal, intertransverse and capsular, interspinal and supraspinal, and ligamentum flavum.

The muscle groups posterior to the spinal column are significantly greater than those anterior to it. Coupled with the fact that neck movement in flexion is limited by chin contact with the sternum (whereas extension is possible until the head strikes the posterior chest wall), this muscle disparity makes extension injuries potentially more serious than flexion injuries, given an equivalent amount of force. Thus, the spine is more resistant to flexion injury than extension injury.

External forces can flex, extend, rotate, or compress the spine. In flexion injury (see Figure 9.1), the anterior elements are compressed, causing anterior wedging, vertebral body fracture, chip fracture, and occasionally anterior dislocations. The posterior elements are injured, which results in a rupture of the posterior longitudinal, interspinal, and supraspinal ligaments and the ligamentum flavum. Occasionally, rupture of the posterior half of the disc is seen.

Figure 9.1 Flexion Injury to the Spine

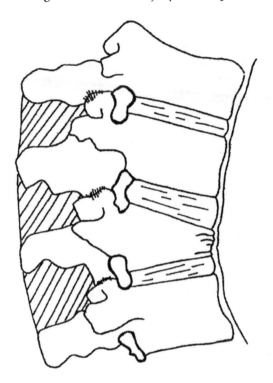

With an extension spine injury (whiplash) (see Figure 9.2), the anterior elements are disrupted and the posterior elements are compressed. This leads to rupture of the anterior longitudinal ligament and anterior disc, with posterior bony injury to the spinous processes, facets, and the neural arch.

A compressive, or burst injury (see Figure 9.3), occurs with the vertical loading of the spine, such as from a blow to the vertex with the neck flexed. This leads to vertebral end-plate fractures before the disc injury. At higher forces, the entire vertebra and the disc may explode into the spinal canal. Analysis has shown this to be the major mechanism of cervical fracture or dislocation and quadriplegia, not only in football (e.g., spearing, butt blocking) but also in diving injuries and, increasingly, in (Canadian) ice hockey neck injuries (Tator and Edmonds 1984; Torg 1985).

With the normal head-up posture, the cervical spine has a gentle lordotic curve, and forces transmitted to the head are largely dissipated in the cervical muscles. When the neck is flexed, however, the cervical spine becomes straight,

Figure 9.2 Extension Injury to the Spine

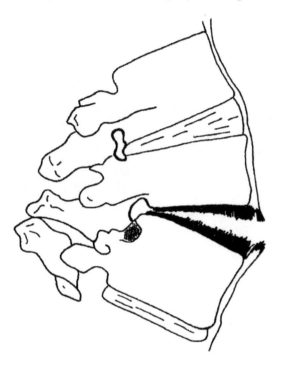

with the vertebral bodies lined up under one another. The forces of impact to the vertex of the head are directly transmitted from one vertebra to the next. This allows for minimal dissipation of the impact forces in the neck muscles. If the impact force exceeds the strength of the bone, it compacts it at one or more levels. This results in a compression fracture. If the fractured vertebra malaligns and is driven back into the spinal cord, quadriplegia may result.

A combined flexion-rotation injury (see Figure 9.4) is most likely to result not only in a flexion injury, but also in anterior subluxation. Subluxation is usually found only in the presence of rotation and is more easily produced in flexion than in extension.

Most cervical spine flexion, extension, and rotation injuries occur with head trauma, but it is important to realize that such injuries can result from other causes as well. Extension injury can occur with sudden acceleration forward, that is, a block or tackle from the rear. Flexion injury can occur with sudden deceleration, that is, when the force is delivered from the front. Neck fractures also may occur with sudden cranial acceleration of the lower torso or buttocks

Figure 9.3 Compression Injury to the Spine

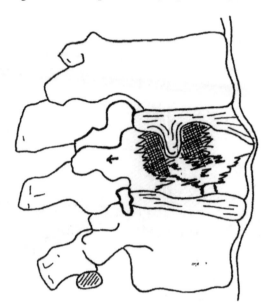

Figure 9.4 Flexion-rotation Injury to the Spine

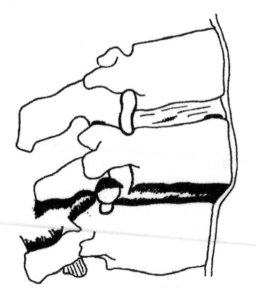

(as with a fall broken by landing on one's buttocks or by direct impact to the posterior cervical region by blunt trauma).

Types of Brain Injury

The types of brain injury seen in football include intracranial hemorrhage, second impact, malignant brain edema or dysautoregulation syndrome, cerebral concussion, postconcussion syndrome, and chronic traumatic encephalopathy.

Intracranial Hemorrhage

The leading cause of direct death from the skills of the sport in football is intracranial hemorrhage (Cantu and Mueller 1999). There are four types of hemorrhage to which the examining trainer or physician must be alert in every instance of head injury: (1) epidural hematoma, (2) subdural hematoma, (3) intracerebral hematoma, and (4) subarachnoid hemorrhage. Because all four types of intracranial hemorrhage may be fatal, rapid and accurate initial assessment as well as appropriate follow-up is mandatory after an athletic head injury.

Epidural Hematoma

An epidural (or extradural) hematoma is usually the most rapidly progressing intracranial hemorrhage. It may reach a fatal size in 30–60 minutes. It is frequently associated with a fracture of the temporal bone and results from a tear of the artery supplying the covering (dura) of the brain. This hematoma accumulates inside the skull but outside the covering of the brain. The athlete may have a lucid interval, initially remaining conscious or regaining consciousness after the head trauma, before starting to experience increasing headache and progressive deterioration in the level of consciousness as the clot accumulates and the intracranial pressure increases.

This lesion will almost always declare itself within one to two hours from the time of injury. Usually the brain substance is free from direct injury; thus, if the clot is promptly removed surgically, full recovery is to be expected. Because this lesion is rapidly and universally fatal if missed, however, all athletes receiving a major head injury must be observed very closely during the ensuing several hours, and preferably the next 24 hours. Ideally, this observation should be done at or near a facility where full neurosurgical services are immediately available.

Prior to the hard polycarbonate outer shelled helmet, deaths due to skull fracture and intracranial bleeding, including the epidural hematoma, were seen. Schneider reported five cases in the five year study reported in his book (Schneider 1973). However, since the National Operating Committee on Standards for Athletic Equipment (NOCSAE) standards were put in place in 1978 in colleges, and in 1980 in high schools, there have been neither skull fractures nor epidural hematomas in football, according to the National Center for Catastrophic Sports Injury Research statistics (NCCSIR). This is an outstanding success story for the National Federation of State High School Associations (NFHS), National College Athletic Association (NCAA), and NOCSAE.

Subdural Hematoma

The most common fatal football head injury, accounting for 75% of deaths, is a subdural hematoma, which occurs between the brain surface and the dura (Cantu and Mueller 1999, 2000; Cantu 2003). It is thus located under the dura and directly on the brain. It often results from a torn vein running from the surface of the brain to the dura, but may also result from a torn venous sinus or even a small artery on the surface of the brain. With this injury, there is often associated injury to the brain tissue. If a subdural hematoma necessitates surgery in the first 24 hours, and the mortality rate is high, due not to the clot itself but to the associated brain damage. With a subdural hematoma that progresses rapidly, the need for immediate neurosurgical evaluation and evacuation is obvious.

Occasionally, the brain itself will not be injured, and a subdural hematoma may develop slowly over a period of days to weeks. This chronic subdural hematoma, although often associated with headache, may initially cause a variety of very mild, almost imperceptible mental, motor, or sensory symptoms. Because its recognition and removal will lead to full recovery, it must always be suspected in an athlete who has previously sustained a head injury and who, days or weeks later, is "not quite right." A computerized axial tomography (CT) scan of the head will definitely show such a lesion as will the even more sensitive brain magnetic resonance imaging (MRI) scan.

The acute subdural hematoma was the most common cause of death 50 years ago (Schneider 1973) as well as today (Boden et al. 2007; Cantu 2003; Cantu and Mueller 1999, 2000). Since NOCSAE standards have been in place, the overall number of acute subdural hematomas has been reduced by nearly 80% (Cantu and Mueller 2000).

Subarachnoid Hemorrhage

Subarachnoid hemorrhages are confined to the surface of the brain. Following head trauma, such bleeding is the result of disruption of the tiny sur-

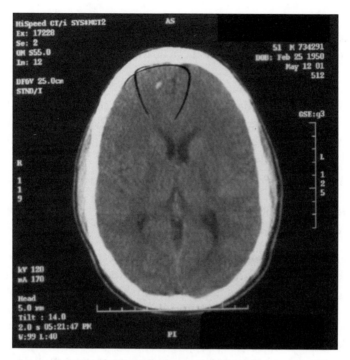

**Image 9.1 Head CT with abnormal white matter deposit
in right frontal lobe.**
Photo courtesy of R. Cantu.

face brain vessels and is analogous to a bruise. As with the intracerebral hematoma, there is often brain swelling, and such a hemorrhage can also result from a ruptured cerebral aneurysm or arteriovenous malformation. Because bleeding is superficial, surgery is not usually required unless a congenital vascular anomaly is present.

Such a contusion of the brain usually causes headache and, not infrequently, an associated neurologic deficit, depending on the area of the brain involved. Once again, since NOCSAE standards have been in place, this lesion in football is also rare.

The irritative properties of the blood may also precipitate a seizure. If a seizure occurs in a head-injured athlete, it is important to roll the patient onto his or her side so that any blood or saliva will roll out of the mouth or nose and the tongue cannot fall back, obstructing the airway. If one has a padded tongue depressor or oral airway, it can be inserted between the teeth. Under no circumstances should one insert one's fingers into the mouth of an athlete who is having a seizure, as the athlete could easily bite them off under the force of convulsions. Usually such a traumatic seizure will last only for a minute or two. The athlete will then relax and can be transported to the nearest medical facility.

Following any of the four types of intracranial hemorrhage, prophylactic anticonvulsant therapy with phenytoin (trade name Dilantin) is usually given for one year. Because the chance of posttraumatic epilepsy is under 10% with a concussion or contusion, anticonvulsant therapy is given in these conditions only if late epilepsy actually occurs (Gruber et al. 1985).

Second Impact Malignant Brain Edema, or Dysautoregulation Syndrome

Second impact syndrome (SIS), or rapid brain swelling (actually vascular engorgement) and herniation following a second head injury, is more common than previous reports in the medical literature have suggested (Cantu 1992; Cantu et al. 1995; Kelly et al. 1991; Saunders and Harbaugh 1984). Between 1980 and 1993, the NCCSIR in Chapel Hill, North Carolina, identified 35 probable cases among football players alone. Autopsy or surgery and MRI findings confirmed 17 of these cases. An additional 18 cases probably are SIS, though they have not been conclusively documented with autopsy findings. Careful scrutiny excluded this diagnosis in 22 of 57 cases originally suspected.

In a more recent publication from NCCSIR, additional cases of (SIS) or severe dysautoregulation were identified (Boden et al. 2007). Schwarz, in a 2007(b) *New York Times* article recognized cases that might fit this syndrome.

SIS is not confined to football players, however. Reports of head injury among athletes in other sports almost certainly represent the syndrome but do not label it as such. Prior to Saunders and Harbaugh's article, Fekete (1986), for example, described a 16-year-old high school hockey player who fell during a game, striking the back of his head on the ice. The boy lost consciousness and afterward complained of unsteadiness and headaches. While playing the next game four days later, he was checked forcibly and again fell, striking his left temple on the ice. His pupils rapidly became fixed and dilated, and he died within two hours while in transit to a neurosurgical facility.

The autopsy report revealed occipital contusion of several days' duration, an edematous brain with a thin layer of subdural and subarachnoid hemorrhage, and bilateral herniation of the cerebellar tonsils into the foramen magnum. Though Fekete did not use the label SIS, the clinical course and autopsy findings in this case are consistent with the syndrome.

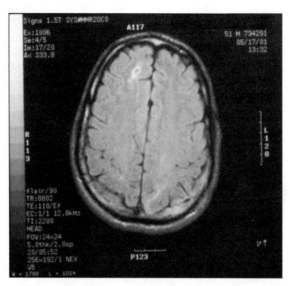

Image 9.2 Head MRI with abnormal white matter changes in right frontal lobe consistent with old trauma.

Photo courtesy of R. Cantu.

Such cases indicate that the brain is vulnerable to accelerative forces in a variety of contact and collision sports. Therefore, physicians who cover athletic events, especially those in which head trauma is likely, must understand SIS and be prepared to initiate emergency treatment.

Recognizing the Syndrome

What Saunders and Harbaugh (1984) called the second impact syndrome of catastrophic head injury in 1984 was first described by Schneider in 1973. The syndrome occurs when an athlete who sustains a head injury—often a concussion or worse injury, such as cerebral contusion—sustains a second head injury before symptoms associated with the first have cleared. Typically, the athlete suffers postconcussion symptoms after the first head injury. These may include visual, motor, or sensory changes and difficulty with thought and memory processes. Before symptoms resolve—which may take days or weeks—the athlete returns to competition and receives a second blow to the head. The second blow may be remarkably minor, perhaps involving a blow to the chest, side, or back that merely snaps the athlete's head and indirectly imparts accelerative forces to the brain. The athlete usually remains standing for 15 seconds to 1 minute or so, and indeed, often completes the play or walks off the field. But the athlete seems dazed, similar to someone suffering from a Grade I concussion.

What happens in the next 15 seconds to several minutes sets this syndrome apart from a concussion or even a subdural hematoma. The athlete, conscious though stunned, quite precipitously collapses to the ground, semicomatose, with rapidly dilating pupils, loss of eye movement, and evidence of respiratory failure.

The pathophysiology of SIS is thought to involve loss of autoregulation of the brain's blood supply. This loss of autoregulation leads to vascular engorgement within the cranium, which in turn markedly increases the intracranial pressure and leads to herniation, either of the medial surface (uncus) of the temporal lobe or lobes below the tentorium, or herniation of the cerebellar tonsils through the foramen magnum. The time from second impact to neurological compromise is usually just a few minutes with coma, fixed dilated pupils, and respiratory failure precipitously. This demise occurs far more rapidly than that usually seen with an epidural hematoma.

Prevention Is Primary

For a catastrophic condition that has a mortality rate approaching 50% and a morbidity rate nearing 100%, prevention takes on the utmost importance. An athlete who is symptomatic from a head injury *must not* participate in contact or collision sports until all cerebral symptoms have subsided, and preferably for at least one week. Whether it takes days, weeks, or months to reach the asymptomatic state, the athlete must *never* be allowed to practice or compete while exhibiting postconcussion symptoms.

Players and parents, as well as the physician and medical team, must understand this. Files of the NCCSIR include cases of young athletes who did not report their cerebral symptoms. Fearing they would not be allowed to compete and not knowing they were jeopardizing their lives, they played with postconcussion symptoms and developed SIS.

Types of Spine Injuries

The same traumatic lesions that affect the brain—concussion, contusion, and the various types of hemorrhage—may also affect the cervical spinal cord.

Fracture, Concussion, Contusion, Hemorrhage

Unlike the head, where the subdural hematoma is the most common lethal type of hemorrhage, the subdural hematoma is uncommon in the spine. Since I have been associated with NCCSIR, there have been no spinal subdural hematomas. Instead, the intraspinal (within the cord) type is the most common and epidural is the next most common type of hemorrhage. In addition, all spinal hemorrhages have been in the cervical region, and none have been seen in the thoracic or lumbar region.

The major concern with a cervical spinal injury is the possibility of an unstable fracture that may produce quadriplegia. In the NCCSIR registry, all the cases of quadriplegia in the absence of spinal stenosis resulted from a fracture dislocation of the cervical spine. At the time of injury on the athletic field, there is no way to determine the presence of an unstable fracture. This requires appropriate X-rays to be taken.

There also is no way of differentiating between a fully recoverable and a permanent case of quadriplegia. If the patient is fully conscious, a cervical fracture or cervical cord injury is usually accompanied by rigid cervical muscle spasm and pain that immediately alerts the athlete and physician to the presence of such an injury. It is the unconscious athlete, unable to state that the neck hurts and whose neck muscles are not in protective spasm, who is susceptible to potential cord severing if one does not always think of the possibility of an unstable cervical spine fracture.

With an unconscious or obviously neck-injured athlete, it is imperative that no neck manipulation be carried out on the field. Definitive treatment must await appropriate X-rays at a medical facility, to which the athlete must be transported with the head and neck immobilized. There, a detailed neurologic examination is carried out, including motor, sensory, or reflex abnormalities, anal sphincter tone, and sensation of the perineal and sacral areas.

If the neurologic examination is normal, the next step is a lateral cervical spine X-ray. If this is also normal, a complete cervical spine series of anterior, posterior, lateral, oblique, and flexion-extension views should be obtained. This last step is important, because up to 20% of unstable cervical spine injuries may be missed when the cross-table lateral cervical spine X-ray is used alone (Herzog et al. 1991b). It is also important to remember that in the adolescent, displacement of the second cervical vertebrae over the third occurs because of the hypermobility of those segments. Failure to recognize this normal 1–2 mm subluxation variation may lead to unnecessary treatment of this pseudosubluxation.

When a spinal cord injury is documented on the neurologic examination, a lateral cervical spine X-ray is taken on the still neck-immobilized patient. In this instance, oblique and flexion-extension views are not taken for fear of further injuring the spinal cord. Instead, one proceeds to a CT of the cervical spine to further define the extent of the trauma and presence of spinal cord compression by bone, disc, or hematoma. A contrast positive cervical CT is often more sensitive in showing spinal cord compression. An MRI scanner best defines intraspinal soft tissue pathology, disc and spinal cord, while the CT best images the osseous injury. Therefore, with a cervical injury with neurologic deficit, both a cervical CT and MRI are needed.

Most quadriplegia in football, as first pointed out by Schneider (1973), involves the acute anterior cervical spinal cord injury syndrome where there is immediate acute paralysis of all four limbs with loss of pain and temperature to the level of the lesion but preservation of posterior column sensation of position, vibration, and light touch (Schneider 1951, 1955). Typically there is no progression of neurological signs. In Schneider's era, surgery was indicated as one could not distinguish between anterior spinal cord compression and irreparable cord destruction. Today, with much more sophisticated MRI and CT imaging available, such distinctions can often be made and surgery deferred if stabilization of an otherwise complete spinal cord injury is the objective.

In the NCCSIR registry, the incidence of quadriplegia per 100,000 was more than 1.5 times higher in college as compared to high school athletes. Professional athletes were over 10 times more likely to suffer quadriplegia as compared to high school. We believe the higher rate of injuries to professional and college athletes may be explained by faster, bigger, and stronger athletes, resulting in higher collision forces. Since 1990, there have been no acute fatalities identified in our quadriplegia of upper cervical spine injured athletes. We believe this reflects the significant advancement of on-the-field medical management of such injuries.

The quadriplegia data concur with the findings of Torg et al. (1990, 1991, 2002), that the predominant mechanism of injury reported was spearing. When the neck is in a neutral position, the cervical vertebrae are in a lordotic alignment. It has been documented that during spearing, the neck is flexed to 30 degrees, placing the cervical spine into a straight column. When an axial force is applied to the vertex, the paravertebral muscles are no longer effective at dissipating the forces, and the vertebral column fails in flexion mode, often leading to fracture, subluxation, or facet dislocation (Torg et al. 1994).

It should be pointed out that Schneider first noted this in his 1973 book. He stated the worst injuries to the cervical spine occur when the football player tends to lower his head and makes acute contact with his opponent with his neck in flexion, a position in which he can withstand a blow less well than if the head and cervical spine are in some degree of hyperextension. The muscles involved

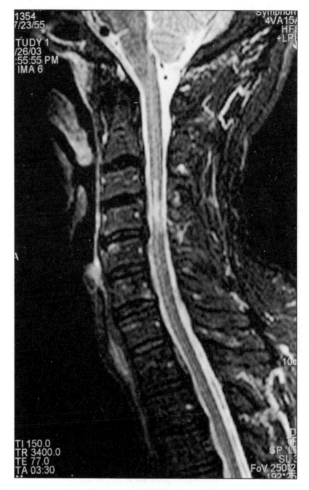

Image 9.3 Spinal stenosis with abnormal white signal in
cord indicative of cord damage.
Photo courtesy of R. Cantu.

in maintaining the latter stance are stronger by far and better able to withstand
the impact.

Thus, while Torg has been appropriately credited with coining the term
"spearing" and axial load to the cervical spine, it was Schneider who first described this mechanism of quadriplegia in football.

Similar to other studies on football injuries resulting in quadriplegia, we
also found that most of these injuries occurred at a subaxial level (Cantu and
Mueller 2000), likely due to the relative narrowing of the spinal canal at these

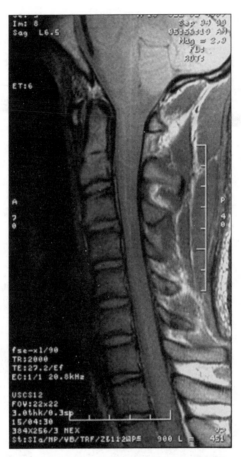

Image 9.4 Normal T1 image of spinal cord (cervical).
Photo courtesy of R. Cantu.

levels (Park 1988). Our study also concurs with previous studies that most injuries occur to defensive players (63%) who are making a tackle (80%) (Cantu 2003; Cantu and Mueller 1999, 2000). In addition, considering the small percentage of time involved, we showed that a disproportionate number of injuries occurred to players on special teams (18%), likely owing to the high speed of collisions during special teams plays (Cantu and Mueller 1999, 2000).

In 1976, the NCAA banned spearing, or the intentional striking of an opponent with the crown of the helmet. Shortly thereafter, spearing was made illegal at the high school level. These rule changes resulted in a dramatic reduction of quadriplegia injuries in football. In 1976, there were 34 reported cases of quadriplegia at the high school and college levels, with high school and college rates of 2.24 and 10.66 per 100,000 players, respectively (Torg et al. 1979). In 1977, the high school and college rates decreased to 1.3 and 2.66 per 100,000 players, respectively (Cantu and Mueller 2000). The mean number of quadriplegia injuries at the high school and college levels in the 1980s (1980–81 to 1989–90 academic years) was 10 incidents per year, compared with 6 incidents per year in the 1990s (1990–91 to 1999–2000 academic years) (Cantu and Mueller 2000). Because the participation numbers steadily increased at the high school level, but remained constant at the college level, the incidence of quadriplegia decreased more than that shown by the absolute numbers of these injuries (NFHS 2002). The rate of injuries resulting in quadriplegia remained fairly steady in the 1990s and early 2000s at 5.19 per 1 million participants, or 1 injury per 192,000 participants (Boden 2006).

In an effort to reduce the number of quadriplegia injuries, the NCAA strengthened its spearing rule, effective for the 2005–06 academic year. The revision removes the word "intentional" from the rule, which makes it easier for the referees to call spearing penalties. Under the previous rule, intent was difficult for referees to assess on the field, and the penalty was rarely called. As part of that organization's efforts to publicize its spearing rule change, it has produced a poster for locker rooms, a PowerPoint presentation, and a video on the risks, mechanism of injury, the concept of axial loading, and injury prevention through the adoption of safe techniques (NCAA 2005).

In an attempt to assist referees in calling the spearing penalty, in 2008 at their February meeting the NCAA Football Rules Committee directed game officials to strictly penalize head-down contact as well as players that target defenseless opponents when making contact above the shoulders.

Future epidemiological data will reveal if this new rule and strong message to officials to call it will further reduce the incidence of quadriplegia in football.

Cervical Cord Neurapraxia or Transient Quadriplegia

Transient quadriplegia, or what Schneider refers to as a spinal cord concussion, is defined as an acute, transient neurologic episode associated with sensory changes in more than one extremity with or without motor changes of weakness or complete paralysis. The cervical area is often pain-free at the time of injury with full painless range of motion.

The proposed mechanism of injury of cervical cord neurapraxia is hyperextension or hyperflexion of the cervical spine, which causes compression of the spinal cord between the anterior and posterior structures of the spinal canal (Torg et al. 1997). In NCCSIR data, the mechanism of injury varied, with the hyperextension, hyperflexion, axial forces, and a combination of these forces being reported (Boden et al. 2006). In an animal study evaluating the effect of a compression injury to the vertex of the head, Gosch et al. (1972) found central hemorrhagic necrosis at the cervical spinal level. The authors postulated that the transmission of shear strain along the axis of acceleration produces central spinal cord hemorrhages when the elastic deformation of the cervical spinal cord is exceeded (Gosch et al. 1970). Our clinical data provide further support that axial forces without spinal column disruption can result in central cord injury. Injury to the spinal cord is likely secondary to shear forces from continued momentum of the body on the fixed head segment.

With transient quadriplegia, by definition there is complete neurological recovery so the forces imparted usually do not result in hemorrhage that can be seen on CT or MRI. If hemorrhage is seen, the lesion is a contusion of the cord and recovery is usually not complete. With transient quadriplegia, one usually sees a central cord syndrome where the neurological deficit is more profound in the arms, especially the hands, than the legs and clears from the legs before the arms. In its most mild form, it involves paresthesia in the hands and has been called "burning hands syndrome" by Maroon (1977). It was Schneider (1954) who first pointed out that this syndrome can usually be treated without surgery.

Central Cord Syndrome

In our experience with NCCSIR data, in some athletes, spinal stenosis may be a contributing factor for transient quadriplegia. Though radiographic bone measurements can suggest that spinal stenosis may be present, physicians are cautioned against making the diagnosis of spinal stenosis with this technique alone (Cantu 1993, 1993; Herzog et al. 1991a). Instead, diagnostic technologies that view the spinal cord itself, for example, MRI, CT, or myelography, should be employed. These imaging methods can determine if the spinal cord has a normal functional reserve: the space largely filled with a protective cushion of cerebrospinal fluid between the cord and the spinal canal's interior walls lined by bone, disk, and ligament. In addition, these techniques also determine whether the nerve tissue is deformed by an abnormality such as a disc protrusion, bony osteophyte, or posterior buckling of the ligamentum flavum.

Controversy persists as to whether cervical stenosis increases the risk of spinal cord injury. I believe very strongly that those who have had spinal cord symptoms from sport-related injuries and are shown to have true spinal stenosis on MRI should not be allowed to return to contact sports.

Though this is still debated in the sports medicine literature, there is a body of literature, primarily in neurosurgery and radiology, that indicates spinal

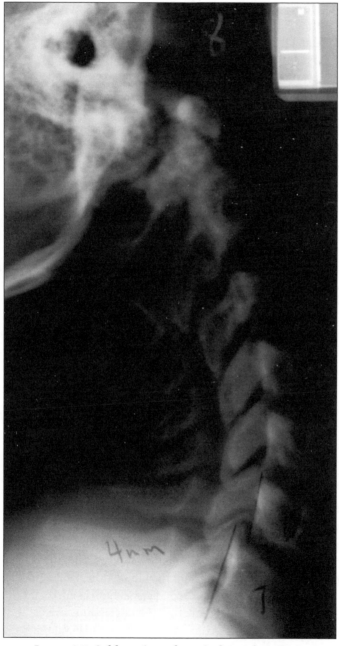

Image 9.5 Subluxation of cervical vertebra C6-7.
Photo courtesy of R. Cantu.

stenosis predisposes a patient to spinal cord injury (Alexander et al. 1958; Eismont et al. 1984; Matsuura et al. 1989; Mayfield 1955; Nugent 1959; Penning 1962; Wolfe et al. 1956). Matsuura and his group (1989), for example, compared the spinal dimension of 100 controls with those of 42 patients who had spinal cord injuries. They found that the control group had significantly larger sagittal spinal canal diameters than did the patients who had spinal cord injuries. Furthermore, the NCCSIR has seen no instance of complete neurologic recovery in spinal stenotic athletes with fracture dislocation of the cervical spine, while there are a number of such complete recoveries in athletes with normal size spinal canals. There are also several instances of permanent quadriplegia in athletes with tight spinal stenosis without fracture or demonstrated instability. For these reasons, we are adamant that, following spinal cord symptoms, athletes exhibiting "functional spinal stenosis" should no longer participate in contact collision sports.

Increased attention is being focused on this question, however, as several National Football League (NFL) teams now require detailed investigations of the cervical spine (including MRIs) as a prerequisite to the draft process. Presently, there is no consensus as to how to manage an athlete with a narrow asymptomatic cervical spinal canal. Thus, when such an abnormality is encountered, management must be individualized according to the patient's symptoms, the degree of canal stenosis, and the perceived risk of permanent neurologic injury.

Stingers

Stingers or *burners* are colloquial terms used by athletes and trainers to describe a set of symptoms that involve pain, burning, or tingling down an arm, occasionally accompanied by localized weakness. Typically, these symptoms abate within seconds or minutes, rarely persisting for days or longer. It has been estimated that a stinger will occur at least once during the career of over 50% of football athletes (Feldick 1976).

There are two typical mechanisms by which stingers may occur, traction on the brachial plexus, or nerve root impingement within the cervical neural foramen. The majority of high school level injuries are of the brachial plexus type, whereas most at the college level and virtually all in the professional ranks result from a pinch phenomenon within the neural foramen.

The brachial plexus stinger commonly involves a forceful blow to the head from the side. However, it can also result from head extension or shoulder depression while the head and neck are fixed. Nerve root impingement usually occurs when the athlete's head is driven toward the shoulder pad. The dorsal spinal nerve root ganglion, which lies close to the posterior intervertebral facet joints, is pinched when the neural foramen is compressed.

With either type of stinger, the athlete experiences a shock-like sensation of pain and numbness radiating into the arm and hand. The symptoms are typically purely sensory in nature and most commonly involve the C5 and C6 dermatomes. On occasion, weakness may also be present. The most common muscles involved include the deltoid, biceps, supraspinatus, and infraspinatus.

Stingers are always unilateral and virtually never involve the lower extremities. Thus, if symptoms are bilateral or involve the legs, a spinal cord injury with all its implications must be assumed and assessed with imaging studies, including a cervical MRI.

If there is no neck pain or limitation of neck movement, and if all unilateral sensory and present motor symptoms clear within a second to minutes, the athlete may safely return to competition. This is especially true if the athlete has previously experienced similar symptoms. If there are any residual symptoms or complaints of neck pain, return should be deferred pending further workup.

On rare occasions, a stinger may result in prolonged sensory complaints or weakness. In such a situation, an MRI of the cervical spine should be considered to look for a herniated disc or other compressive pathology. If symptoms persist for more than two weeks, electromyography should be considered for an accurate assessment of the degree and extent of injury.

Some athletes seem predisposed to develop a series of recurrent stingers. It has been suggested that repeated stinger injuries over many years may lead to a proximal arm weakness and constant pain. Thus, if an athlete suffers two or more stingers, particularly in rapid succession, consideration should be given to the use of high shoulder pads supplemented by a soft cervical roll that should limit lateral neck movement. Examining and possibly changing the athlete's blocking and tackling techniques or changing the player's position may also be helpful in preventing recurrences. If, despite these interventions, the stingers repeatedly recur, the athlete may need to stop participating in contact sports.

Vascular Injury

A final uncommon, but very serious, neck injury involves the carotid and vertebral arteries. By either extremes of lateral flexion or extension, or a forceful blow by a relatively fixed, narrow object, such as a stiffened forearm, the inner layer (intima) of the carotid artery may be torn. This can lead to dissection, clot formation at the site of injury, which results in emboli to the brain

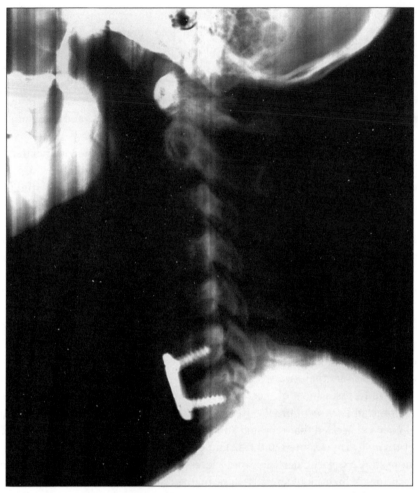

Image 9.6 Cervical plate and screws at C6-C7 anterior spinal fusion.
Photo courtesy of R. Cantu.

or, more commonly, a complete occlusion of the artery, causing a major stroke. Especially with a cervical spine fracture dislocation, injury to the vertebral artery may occur, leading to a brainstem stroke.

Concussion

I want to conclude this chapter with a discussion of the most common football brain injury, one that today's helmet cannot prevent. Today, it commands more research effort and dollars than any one athletic head or spine injury. While usually only a metabolic injury and thus reversible, when repeated it can have profound consequences.

What are the definitions and grades of severity of concussion? Consensus on the definition of concussion does not exist, making evaluation of the epidemiologic data extremely difficult. The Committee on Head Injury Nomenclature of the CNS (1966) has put forth a working definition of concussion that has gained general acceptance: "a clinical syndrome characterized by immediate and transient posttraumatic impairment of neural function, such as alteration of consciousness, disturbance of vision, equilibrium, etc. due to brainstem involvement."

Maroon et al. (1980), in attempting to simplify the clinical problem, divided concussion into three grades based on duration of unconsciousness: mild (no loss of consciousness), moderate (loss of consciousness under five minutes with retrograde amnesia), and severe (unconsciousness longer than five minutes) (Cantu and Mueller 1999). Others have classified concussion according to duration of posttraumatic amnesia (Jennet 1971). As a team physician, I have seen many concussions. Most were mild, and posttraumatic amnesia, which helped me make the diagnosis, was usually present. Combining elements of the various definitions of concussion has afforded me an easy practical on-the-field grading scheme first proposed in 1986 (Cantu 1986) and updated in 2001 (Cantu 2001) (see Table 9.1). Today there are a number of consensus statements regarding concussion (Aubrey et al. 2002; Guskiewicz et al. 2004a, 2004b; Herring et al. 2006; McCrory et al. 2005), but much is yet to be learned.

Grade I (Mild) Concussion

The mild concussion is the most difficult to recognize and judge. The patient does not lose consciousness but suffers from impaired intellectual function, especially in remembering recent events and in assimilating and interpreting new information. Grade I concussion occurs most frequently (more than 90% of concussions) and often escapes medical attention (Yarnell and Lynch 1983). Players are commonly "dinged" or have their "bell rung" and continue playing. Dave Meggyesy, a professional football player-turned-author, described this condition: "Your memory's affected, although you can still walk around and sometimes continue playing. If you don't feel pain, the only way others know that you have been 'dinged' is when they realize you can't remember the plays" (1970).

Initial treatment of a mild concussion requires the player to be removed from the game and observed on the bench. After a sufficient period of time

Table 9.1 Cantu Concussion Grading Guidelines

Grade I	(mild)	No LOC*; PTA† 30 minutes
Grade II	(moderate)	LOC < 5 min or PTA > 30 min
Grade III	(severe)	LOC ≥ 5 min or PTA ≥ 24 hours

* Loss of consciousness
† Posttraumatic amnesia
Source: Cantu RC: Guidelines to return to contact sport after cerebral concussion. *PhysSportsmed* 14: 76, 1986 with permission.

Table 9.2 Data-Driven Cantu Revised Concussion Grading Guidelines

Grade I	(mild)	No LOC* PTA†/PCSS‡ < 30 min
Grade II	(moderate)	LOC < 1 min or PTA > 30 min < 24 hrs. other PCSS > 30 min < 7days
Grade III	(severe)	LOC ≥ 1 min or PTA ≥ 24 hrs. PCSS > 7 days

* Loss of consciousness
† Posttraumatic amnesia (antrograde/retrograde)
‡ Postconcussion sign/symptoms
Source: Cantu RC: Post-traumatic (retrograde and anterograde) amnesia: pathophysiology and implications in grading and safe return to play. *J Athletic Training* 36(3)244–248, 2001.

(which may be as short as 15–30 minutes), if the athlete has no headache, dizziness, or impaired concentration (including orientation to person, place, and time, as well as full recall of events that occurred just before the injury), return to the game may be considered (Aubrey 2002; Cantu 2001). Before such players are allowed to return, however, they should be asymptomatic not only at rest but also after demonstrating that they can move with their usual dexterity and speed during exertion. If an athlete has any symptoms during either rest or exertion, continued neurologic observation is essential.

Grade II (Moderate) Concussion

With moderate concussion (unconsciousness lasting less than five minutes), initial management should be the same as for Grade III. The athlete should be removed from the game and evaluated by a neurologist at a medical facility. Here, though, clinical judgment may dictate that if the period of unconsciousness is brief and the athlete has no neck problems after regaining consciousness, removal on a fracture board may not be necessary.

Grade III (Severe) Concussion

It is not difficult to recognize a severe concussion (unconsciousness lasting five minutes or more). Initial treatment should be the same as the treatment for a suspected cervical spine fracture. The athlete should be transported on a fracture board, with head and neck immobilized, to a hospital with neurosurgical treatment facilities. All severe concussions should be admitted to check for possible intracranial bleeding (Hugenholtz and Richard 1982; Lindsay et al. 1980).

Postconcussion Syndrome

This syndrome consists of headache (especially with exertion), labyrinthine disturbance, fatigue, irritability, and impaired memory and concentration (Murphey and Simmons 1959). Its true incidence is not known; however, it has been uncommon (in my experience) for it to last longer than a week or two. Persistence of symptoms reflects altered neurotransmitter function (Murphey and Simmons 1959), usually correlates well with duration of posttraumatic amnesia (Guthkelch 1980), and suggests that the athlete should be evaluated with a CT scan and neuropsychiatric testing. The athlete's return to competition should be deferred until all symptoms have abated and diagnostic studies are normal.

Chronic Traumatic Encephalopathy (CTE)

CTE, or dementia pugilistica, was first described by Harrison S. Martland in his landmark *Journal of the American Medical Association* article published in 1928 as being characteristic of boxers "who take considerable head punishment seeking only to land a knockout blow." It was also "common in second rate fighters used for training purposes." The early symptoms he described were a "slight mental confusion, a general slowing in muscular movement, hesitancy in speech, and tremors of the hands." Later, marked truncal ataxia, Parkinsonian syndrome, and marked mental deterioration may set in, "necessitating commitment to an asylum."

Although Martland first described the clinical syndrome of CTE and Roberts (1960) echoed the dangers of chronic brain damage in boxers in 1969, it was Corsellis et al. (1976) who first identified the neuropathology of this syndrome in the brains of 15 deceased boxers, 8 of whom were either world or national champions.

Table 9.3 summarizes his findings of the four main components of this entity, areas of the brain damaged, and resultant signs and symptoms. It is critical to understand that although Corsellis pointed out four different areas of the brain and the resultant signs and symptoms, he did not state that all four

Table 9.3 Four Main Components of Chronic
Brain Damage in Dementia Pugilistica

Area Damaged	Clinical Symptoms/Signs
Septum pellucidum, adjacent	Altered affect
Periventricular grey matter, frontal and temporal lobes	(euphoria, emotional ability) and memory
Degeneration of the substantia nigra	Parkinson's syndrome of tremor, rigidity, and bradykinesia
Cerebellar scarring and nerve cell loss	Slurred speech, loss of balance and coordination
Diffuse neuronal loss	Loss of intellect, Alzheimer's syndrome

areas needed to be involved for the diagnosis to be made. In fact, only 8 out of 15 brains studied had all four areas of pathology present (Corsellis 1976).

It was Corsellis who also reported CTE not only in boxers but other sports with a high risk of head injury, including in declining frequency jockeys (especially steeplechasers), professional wrestlers, parachutists, and even a case of battered wife syndrome.

When Andre Waters, a hard-hitting NFL safety from 1984 to 1995, made the front page of the *New York Times* on January 18, 2007, he became the third NFL player known to have died as a result of CTE, attributed to the multiple concussions he experienced while playing in the NFL (Schwarz 2007a). Subsequent to Waters, Justin Strzelczyk became the fourth NFL case (Schwarz 2007c). Preceding the 44-year-old Andre, were Mike Webster, age 50, the Hall of Fame Pittsburgh Steelers center who died homeless, and Terry Long, age 42, who, like Waters, took his own life (Omalu et al. 2005; Omalu et al. 2006).

All of these athletes were known as iron men, hard hitters who never came out of the game, continuing to play through countless injuries, including concussions. All of these athletes, as well as Ted Johnson, whose front page story was widely circulated on February 2, 2007 in the *New York Times* and *Boston Globe*, shared symptoms of sharply deteriorated cognitive function, especially recent memory loss and psychiatric symptoms such as paranoia, panic attacks, and major depression after multiple concussions experienced in the NFL (Schwarz 2007b).

The brains of these deceased athletes were examined by multiple neuropathologists who concluded that they shared common features of CTE, including neurofibrillary tangles, neutrophil threads, and cell dropout.

Certainly, the Waters finding was no surprise to Julian Bailes, M.D., Medical Director, and Kevin Guskiewicz, Ph.D., Director of the Study for Retired

Athletes at the University of North Carolina, Chapel Hill. Their study of retired NFL players published in the journal *Neurosurgery* found that those who sustained three or more concussions were three times more likely to experience "significant memory problems" and five times more likely to develop earlier onset of Alzheimer's disease (Guskiewicz et al. 2007). A study published in 2007 by the same authors found a similar relationship between three or more concussions and clinical depression (Dungy 2007).

According to a book by Super Bowl-winning Indianapolis Colts coach Tony Dungy and colleagues (2007):

- Sixty-five percent of NFL players leave the game with permanent injuries.
- Twenty-five percent of NFL players report financial difficulties within the first year of retirement.
- Fifty percent of failed NFL marriages occur in the first year after retirement.
- Seventy-eight percent of NFL players are unemployed, bankrupt, or divorced within two years of retirement.
- The suicide rate for retired NFL players is six times greater than the national average.

I have personally examined a number of retired NFL players with postconcussion/CTE symptoms, and the sources of depression and suicide are often more than CTE. Only a thorough prospective study of NFL players, however, will determine the true incidence of this problem. Although this study could be funded by the NFL charities, I would hope that the NFL would refrain from introducing potential bias by not soliciting the team of neurosurgeons, neurologists, neuropsychiatrists, and neuropathologists with athletic head injury expertise to carry out the study.

Finally, it is clear that not all players with long concussion histories have met premature and horrific ends to their lives. However, as the list of NFL players who retire as a result of postconcussion syndrome (e.g., Harry Carson, Al Toon, Merrill Hodge, Troy Aikman, Steve Young, Ted Johnson, Wayne Chrebet) grows and as the number of documented CTE cases increases, I believe the time for independent study of the problem is now. Fortunately there are no known or reported cases of CTE to my knowledge at the high school or college level, though this does not preclude their existence.

Bibliography

1. Alexander MD, Davis CH, Field CH: Hyperextension injuries of the cervical spine. *Arch Neurol & Psyciat.* 1958; 79: 146–150.

2. Aubry M, Cantu R, Devorak J, et al: Summary and agreement statement of the first international conference on concussion in sport, Vienna 2001, *Physician and Sportsmedicine.* 2002; 30(2): 57–63.

3. Boden B, Tachetti R, Cantu R, Knowles S, Mueller F: Catastrophic cervical injuries in high school and college football players, *AJSM* 2006; 34(8): 1223–1232.

4. Boden B, Tacchetti R, Cantu R, Knowles S. Muller F: Catastrophic head injuries in high school and college football players. *AJSM.* 2007; 35: 1–7.

5. Cantu RC. Functional cervical spinal stenosis: a contraindication to participation in contact sports. Med Sci Sports Exer 1993; 25: 1082–1083.

6. Cantu RC: Guideline to return to contact sport after cerebral concussion. *Phys Sportsmed.* 1986; 14: 76.

7. Cantu RC: Second impact syndrome: immediate management. *Physician and Sportsmedicine.* 1992; 20(9): 55–66.

8. Cantu RC. Cervical spinal stenosis: challenging an established detection method. *Phys Sportsmed.* 1993; 21: 57–63.

9. Cantu RC: Post-traumatic (retrograde and anterograde) amnesia: pathophysiology and implications in grading and safe return to play. *J Athletic Training.* 2001; 36(3): 244–248.

10. Cantu RC: Invited commentary: athletic head injury. *Current Sports Medicine Reports.* 2003; 2(3): 117–119.

11. Cantu RC, Mueller FO: Fatalities and catastrophic injuries in high school and college sports, 1982–1997. *Physician and Sportsmedicine.* 1999; 27: 35–48.

12. Cantu RC, Mueller FO: Catastrophic football injuries. *Neurosurgery* 2000; 47: 673–677.

13. Cantu RC, Voy RO: Second impact syndrome: a risk in any contact sport. *Physician and Sportsmedicine.* 1995; 23(6): 27–34.

14. Committee on Head Injury Nomenclature of the Congress of Neurological Surgeons: Glossary of head injury including some definitions of injury to the cervical spine. *Clin Neurosurg.* 1966; 12: 386.

15. Corsellis JA: Brain damage in sport. *Lancet.* 1976; 1: 401–402.

16. Corsellis JA, Bruton CJ, Freeman-Browne D: The aftermath of boxing. *Psychol Med.* 1974; 3: 270–303.

17. Dungy T, Whitaker N, Washington D:*Quiet Strength: The Principles, Pratices & Priorities of a Winning Life.* Washington Group Publishing 2007.

18. Eismont FJ, Clifford S, Goldberg M, et al: Cervical sagittal spinal canal size in spine injury. *Spine.* 1984; 9(7): 663–666.

19. Fekete JF: Severe brain injury and death following minor hockey accidents. *Can Med Assoc J.* 1986; 99: 1234–1239.

20. Feldick HG, Albright JP: Football survey reveals "missed" neck injuries. *Phys Sportsmed.* 1976; 4: 77–81.

21. Gosch HH, Gooding E, Schneider RC: Cervical spinal cord hemorrhages in experimental head injuries. *J Neurosurg.* 1970; 33: 640–645.

22. Gosch HH, Gooding E, Schneider RC: An experimental study of cervical spine and cord injuries. *J Trauma.* 1972; 12: 570–576.

23. Gruber R, Bubl R, Fruttiger V: Anticonvulsant therapy after juvenile cranio-cerebral injuries: a retrospective evaluation. *Z Kinderchir.* 1985; 40: 199–202.

24. Guskiewicz K, Bruce S, Cantu R, Ferrara M, Kelly J, McCrea M, Putukian M, McLeod T: National Athletic Trainer's Association position statement: management of sport-related concussion. *J Athletic Training.* 2004a; 39(3): 280–295.

25. Guskiewicz KM, Bruce S, Cantu R, Ferrara M, Kelly J, McCrea M, Putukian M, Valovich T: Recommendations on management of sport-related concussion: summary of the National Athletic Trainer's Association position statement. *Neurosurgery.* 2004b; 55(4): 891–896.

26. Guskiewicz KM, Marshall SW, Bailes J, McCrea M, Cantu RC, Randolph C, Jordan BD: Association between recurrent concussion and late-life cognitive impairment in retired professional football players. *Neurosurgery.* 2005; 57: 719–726.

27. Guskiewicz KM, Marshall SW, Bailes J, McCrea M, Harding HP, Matthews A, Mihalik JR, Cantu RC: Recurrent concussions and risk of depression in retired professional football players. *Med Sci Sports Exerc.* 2007; 39: 903–909.

28. Guthkelch AN: Posttraumatic amnesia, postconcussional symptoms and accident neurosis. *Euro Neurol.* 1980; 19: 91–102.

29. Herring S, Cantu R, et al.: ACSM team physician concussion consensus statement. *Med Sci Sports Exerc.* 2006; 38(2): 395–399.

30. Herzog RJ, Weins JJ, Dillingham MF, et al.: Normal cervical spine morphometry and cervical spinal stenosis in asymptomatic professional football players. *Spine* 1991a; 15: 178–186.

31. Herzog RJ, Weins JJ, Dillingham MF, et al.: Normal cervical spine morphometry and cervical spinal stenosis in asymptomatic professional football players: plain film radiography, multiplanar computed tomography, and magnetic resonance imaging. *Spine.* 1991b; 16(6 suppl): S178–S186.

32. Hugenholtz H, Richard MT: Return to athletic competition following concussion. *Can Med Assoc J.* 1982; 127: 827.

33. Jennet B: Late effects of head injuries. In: Critchley M, O'Leary JL, Jennet B (eds): *Scientific Foundations of Neurology.* Philadelphia. FA Davis; 1971: 441.

34. Kelly JP, Nichols JS, Filley CM, et al.: Concussion in sports: guidelines for the prevention of catastrophic outcome. *JAMA.* 1991; 266(20): 2867–2869.

35. Lindsay KW, McLatchie G, Jennet B: Serious head injury in sport. *Br Med J.* 1980; 281: 789.
36. Maroon JC: Burning hands in football spinal cord injuries. *JAMA* 1977; 238: 2003–2049.
37. Maroon JC, Steele PB, Berlin R: Football head and neck injuries: an update. *Clin Neurosurg.* 1980; 27: 414.
38. Martland HS: Punch drunk. *JAMA.* 1928; 91: 1103–1107.
39. Matsuura P, Waters RL, Atkins RH, et al.: Comparison of computerized tomography parameters of the cervical spine in normal control subjects and spinal cord-injured patients. *J Bone Joint Surg (AM).* 1989; 71(2): 183–188.
40. Mayfield FH: Neurosurgical aspects of cervical trauma. *Clinical Neurosurgery.* Baltimore: Williams & Wilkins; 1955: vol. 2.
41. McCrory P, Johnston K, et al.: Summary and agreement statement of the Second International Conference on Concussion in Sport, Prague 2004. *Physician and Sportsmedicine.* 2005; 33(4): 29–44.
42. Meggyesy D: *Out of their league.* Berkley, CA: Ramparts; 1970:125.
43. Murphey F, Simmons JC: Initial management of athletic injuries to the head and neck. *Am J Surg.* 1959; 98: 379–383.
44. National Collegiate Athletic Association. National Collegiate Athletic Association Web site. Available at http://www.ncaa.org/library/research/participation_rates. Accessed October 3, 2005.
45. National Federation of State High School Associations. *Participation Survey.* Indianapolis, IN: National Federation of State High School Associations; 1989–2002.
46. Nugent GR: Clinicopathologic correlations in cervical spondylosis. *Neurology.* 1959; 9: 273–281.
47. Omalu BI, DeKosky ST, Hamilton RI, Minster RL, Kamboh MI, Shakir AM, Wecht CH: Chronic traumatic encephalopathy in a National Football League player: part II. *Neurosurgery.* 2006; 59: 1086–1092.
48. Omalu BI, DeKosky ST, Minster RL, Kamboh MI, Hamilton RI, Wecht CH: Chronic traumatic encephalopathy in a National Football League player. *Neurosurgery.* 2005; 57: 128–134.
49. Parke WW: Correlative anatomy of cervical spondylotic myelopathy. *Spine.* 1988; 13: 831–837.
50. Penning L: Some aspects of plain radiography of the cervical spine in chronic myelopathy. *Neurology.* 1962; 12: 513–519.
51. Roberts AH: *Brain Damage in Boxers.* London, Pitman Medical & Scientific Publishing; 1969; 61–99.
52. Saunders RL, Harbaugh RE: The second impact in catastrophic contact sports head trauma. *JAMA.* 1984; 252(4): 538–539.

53. Schneider RC: A syndrome in acute cervical injuries for which early operation is indicated. *J Neurosurg.* 1951; 8: 360.

54. Schneider RC: The syndrome of acute anterior cervical spinal cord injury. *J Neurosurg.* 1955; 12: 95.

55. Schneider RC: *Head and Neck Injuries in Football: Mechanisms, Treatment and Prevention.* Baltimore: Williams & Wilkins; 1973.

56. Schneider RC, Cherry G, Pantek H: The syndrome of acute central cervical spinal cord injury. *J Neurosurg.* 1954; 11: 546.

57. Schwarz A: Expert ties ex-players suicide to brain damage. *New York Times,* Jan. 18, 2007a.

58. Schwarz A: Ted Johnson.Dark Days Following Hard Hitting Career in NFL *New York Times,* February 2, 2007b.

59. Schwarz A: Lineman, dead at 36, exposes brain injuries. *New York Times,* June 15, 2007c.

60. Schwarz A: Slience on concussions raises risk of injury. *New York Times.* Sept. 15, 2007d.

61. Tator CH, Edmonds JE: National survey of spinal injuries in hockey players. *Can Med Assoc.* 1984; 130: 875.

62. Torg JS: Epidemiology, pathomechanics, and prevention of athletic injuries to the cervical spine. *Med Sci Sports Exer.* 1985; 17: 295.

63. Torg JS, Corcoran TA, Thibault LE, et al.: Cervical cord neuropraxia: classification, pathomechanics, morbidity, and management guidelines. *J Neurosurg.* 1997; 87: 843–850.

64. Torg JS, Gennarelli TA: Head and cervical spine injuries. In: DeLee JC, Drez D Jr (eds) *Orthopaedic Sports Medicine: Principles and Prqctice.* Philadelphia, PA: WB Saunders; 1994: 417–462.

65. Torg JS, Guille, JT, Jaffe S: Injuries to the cervical spine in American football players. *J Bone Joint Surg Am.* 2002; 84: 112–122.

66. Torg JS, Quedenfeld TC, Burstein A, et al.: National football head and neck injury registry: report on cervical quadriplegia, 1971to 1975. *Am J Sports Med.* 1979; 7(2): 127–132.

67. Torg JS, Sennett B, Vegso JJ, Pavlov H: Axial loading injuries to the middle cervical spine segment: an analysis and classification of twenty-five cases. *Am J Sports Med.* 1991; 19: 6–20.

68. Torg JS, Vegso JJ, O'Neill MJ, Sennett B: The epidemiologic, pathologic, biomechanical, and cinematographic analysis of football-induced cervical spine trauma. *Am J Sports Med.* 1990; 18: 50–57.

69. Wolfe BS, Khilnani M, Malis L: The sagittal diameter of the bony cervical spinal canal and its significance in cervical spondylosis. *J Mt Sinai Hosp.* 1956; 23: 283–292.

70. Yarnell PR, Lynch S: The "ding" amnestic states in football trauma. *Neurology*. 1983; 23: 196.

Chapter 10

History of the National Operating Committee on Standards for Athletic Equipment, 1969–2008

As presented in previous chapters, the 1960s was associated with the greatest number of direct football fatalities (244) since the American Football Coaches Association (AFCA) initiated the First Annual Survey of Football Fatalities in 1931. Included in the 244 fatalities were 179 head injuries and 40 neck injuries. When combined, the head and neck injuries accounted for 219, or 89.8% of the 244 fatalities. In 1968, there were 36 fatal injuries with 30 being head injuries and 6 being neck injuries. In addition to this major increase in football fatalities, Schneider (1973) reported 56 injuries to the cervical spine from 1959 through 1963, and 30 of these injuries involved permanent quadriplegia. Torg et al. (1979) continued collecting catastrophic injury data in the early 1970s and recorded 259 cervical spine and spinal cord injuries from 1971 to 1975, of which 99 involved permanent quadriplegia. As one can imagine, the football community was greatly concerned with the rising number of fatal injuries and the new concern of paralyzing cervical cord injuries. Football was once again in a crisis period and something had to be done to reverse the increasing number of fatalities and catastrophic injuries.

This rise in fatal and paralyzing head and neck injuries prompted the football community—led by Walter Byers, Executive Director of the National Collegiate Athletic Association (NCAA) and G. E. Morgan, President of Riddell Helmets and representing the Sporting Goods Manufacturing Association—to form the National Operating Committee on Standards for Athletic Equipment (NOCSAE) in 1969. There were a number of informal meetings held by this group of concerned individuals, but the first formal planning meeting was held on April 8, 1970, in Kansas City, Missouri. Individuals attending the meeting were as follows:

- W. A. Bird, Rawlings Sporting Goods Co.
- Jack Harvey, Wilson Sporting Goods Co.
- W. L. Eken, MacGregor Sporting Goods Co.
- Walter Dufresne, Spaulding Sporting Goods Co.
- G. E. Morgan, Riddell Sporting Goods Co.
- Homa S. Thomas, National Junior College Athletic Association
- William Tuten, National Junior College Athletic Association
- Clifford Fagan, National Federation of State High Schools Association
- Ray Ball, National Federation of State High School Associations
- Elmer Morrow, National Federation of State High School Associations
- Jack Miles, National Federation of State High School Associations
- Donald Cooper, Oklahoma State University
- John Waldorf, Big Eight Conference
- Jim Wilkinson, National Collegiate Athletic Association
- Walter Byers, National Collegiate Athletic Association
- Jack Rockwell, National Athletic Trainers Association

Walter Byers, executive director of the NCAA, presided over the meeting and in his opening statement said the purpose of the meeting was to provide necessary steps to establish standards for athletic equipment, to provide a sound and valid organization necessary to carry out these functions, and to provide a permanent structure for the NOCSAE committee. It was the general consensus of the group that any resulting equipment standards should be implemented through the rules of each sport for better enforcement. It was agreed that it would be the responsibility of this committee to accept and study valid research before making recommendations to the Rules Committees, and the final selection of equipment is to be left to this committee.

The NOCSAE committee unanimously agreed on the following conclusions and recommendations that were sent to the members and dated April 10, 1970:

1. It is in the best interests of interscholastic and intercollegiate athletics to create a permanent structure which will be responsible for evaluating present research and authorizing and/or conducting additional research to the end of establishing minimum standards for competitive athletic equipment, and for arranging a testing and certification program to determine that such equipment meets the established standard.

2. The permanent committee should be tentatively identified as NOCSAE.

3. The committee should be composed of the following voting representatives: Sporting Goods Manufacturers (2 votes), National Junior

College Athletic Association (2 votes), National Federation of State High School Athletic Associations (2 votes), National Collegiate Athletic Association (2 votes), National Athletic Trainers Association (1 vote), American Medical Association (1 vote), American College Health Association (one vote).

4. The committee's interests should be limited to those activities which are recognized as competitive sports by one or more of the high school–college sports governing bodies. Equipment that should be given attention includes football head gear, baseball batting helmets, football shoulder pads, ice hockey masks, tooth guards, fiberglass vaulting poles, and trampolines.

5. The immediate concern should be in the areas of equipment designed to protect the head and neck. Steps should be undertaken to create, if possible, minimum required standards.

6. The National Operating Committee is urged to take immediate steps to collect all valid and meaningful scientific information from responsible sources on the subject in paragraph five. These steps should be taken to determine whether there is sufficient evidence on hand to make initial judgments for standards, and if not, to initiate promptly whatever additional scientific studies seem appropriate.

7. The participating organizations should consider the legal responsibilities of setting standards and certifying adherence.

8. The National Operating Committee should promptly request the rules committees of the participating organizations to forward all available information they may have regarding equipment that the rules committees believe should be considered by the committee.

9. The National Operating Committee should establish liaison with any other responsible organizations (or individuals) which have an interest in this area and urge them to forward pertinent information for evaluation.

10. Each participating organization shall name its delegates by April 15, 1970, and the first meeting of the National Operating Committee shall be held April 28–29, 1970, in Kansas City, Missouri. The National Operating Committee shall be responsible for organizing itself by electing its own officers and establishing other procedures.

11. This planning meeting urges each participating organization to consider financial allocations to the National Operating Committee so as to facilitate its work and enable it to hire staff if the committee deems it necessary.

On August 15, 1970, a news release announced that the NOCSAE established a fundraising program to secure a minimum of $100,000 for research on head and neck injuries in football. The committee also endorsed a recommendation by the NCAA Competitive Safeguards and Medical Aspects of Sports Committee to abolish spearing and butt blocking from all football through changes in rules and officiating enforcement.

In 1970, work began to establish a football helmet standard under the direction of V. R. Hodgson at the Gurdjian-Lissner Biomechanics Laboratory at Wayne State University. Three years later in September 1973, the NOCSAE Football Helmet Impact Standard was published. Although the standard was not mandated by the NFHS Rules Committee until the 1980 season, improved and redesigned helmets began to appear as early as 1970, with popular head sizes shifting to a larger shell and liner material changes.

The standard test required a helmet to withstand numerous simulations of game experience high-energy impacts to six locations without exceeding the 1500 Severity Index level on the humanoid head form to which the helmet was attached. It was concluded that if the helmets in the field could absorb enough energy to reduce the second of two such repetitive impacts to a linear head acceleration level below a skull fracture threshold for the average player experiencing an equivalent jolt, that such helmets would also reduce the numbers of hemorrhagic injuries by lowering the tangential and angular accelerations thought to cause most subdural hematomas.

An essential part of the standard was the development of a humanoid head model to accurately measure the impact forces generated from lab tests. The head model was constructed to conform as closely as possible to the average human head in shape, weight, mass distribution, and impact response. Later, two additional head form sizes were added in order to have three models to test the three shell sizes common among helmet manufacturers. Certification of new helmets according to the NOCSAE football helmet standard began in 1974, when all new helmets were submitted to Wayne State University (which then had the only standard test facility) for certification. Helmet manufacturers later installed the drop test system to maintain standard performance quality in their models. Every new helmet manufactured after the standard was approved had a permanent seal on the outside back of the helmet which stated "Meets NOCSAE Standard." In later years, in an effort to warn players of the risk of injury, the NOCSAE Board of Directors developed a warning statement which was put on all football, baseball/softball batting, and lacrosse helmets. The warning label and content were added as a part of each standard and are intended to warn participants of the possibility of severe head or neck injury despite the fact that a certified helmet is being worn. The helmet is designed to help protect the head, and neither football, baseball/softball batting, or lacrosse helmets can protect the neck.

Colleges and high schools were given a grace period to replace their supply of helmets with new ones meeting the NOCSAE standard. The NCAA did not mandate use of NOCSAE-certified helmets until the 1978 season, and the high schools gave their member schools until the fall of 1980 to comply.

In the fall of 1974, Don Gleisner, president of the All-American Recondi-tioning Company, installed a standard test system in a reconditioning plant to screen and improve the performance of used helmets. With the use of this new tool, Gleisner reported 15% of the helmets were only cleaned, 25% were re-jected due to not meeting the NOCSAE standard, 36% (suspension helmets) were reduced in size to provide more stand-off from head to shell, and 25% were renewed with parts made by the reconditioner to bring them up to meet the standard. In 1976, 13 reconditioners banded together to form the National Athletic Equipment Re-conditioners Association (NAERA), which has had two representatives on the NOCSAE board since that time. All NAERA members have the capability of selectively evaluating the impact protective qualities of used helmets on the NOCSAE drop test system. The goal of this process is to ensure, with a high degree of confidence, that all reconditioned helmets are returned to their original certified condition.

A recertification section was added to the NOCSAE standard in 1977 to take advantage of the NAERA network and maintain helmet standard protective quality as much as possible. The NOCSAE standard for new helmets has played a major role in the reduction of football head injury related fatalities, but the maintenance of certified performance in reconditioned helmets by NAERA has also been essential to head injury reduction.

Interesting high school data from both before and after implementation of the NOCSAE standard show that from 1965 to 1970 (pre-NOCSAE), the high school head death injury rate per 100,000 participants was 1.92. The data from 1971 to 1976 (post-NOCSAE) show the high school head death injury rate per 100,000 participants to be 0.87.

It should be emphasized that NOCSAE was not financially sound during the first 10 to 15 years of its existence, and in many cases was not able to fund the research that Voigt Hodgson was performing at Wayne State University. Despite the lack of funding, Hodgson kept the football helmet research on track and deserves much of the credit for the NOCSAE Standard. He not only carried on the research but worked simultaneously for NOCSAE and the man-ufacturers to keep them all on the same page.

Dr. Hodgson also had a plan to start a foundation to reduce the high num-ber of lawsuits related to football's paralyzing injuries. His plan was to create a Catastrophic Injury Foundation to be funded by a surcharge on every football ticket sold at high school, college, and professional games. In addition, the foundation would receive a fair share contribution from broadcasting companies and other media who receive huge income from football. The realistic goal was to raise $20 million annually to help pay medical and other costs for paralyzed football players. Voigt was hoping to raise a war chest of $100 million to accomplish his goals. This idea was never realized, however, and football lawsuits based on paralyzing neck injuries helped put a majority of the football helmet manufacturers out of business. It has been made clear in a number of publications, and reinforced in the NOCSAE mandated warning label, that helmets do not protect the neck. There have been a number of attempts to design football helmets to protect the neck, but as of 2008, none have been successful.

The mission of NOCSAE was and is to commission research on and, where feasible, establish standards for athletic equipment. NOCSAE also acts as an information organization to create, organize, and disseminate knowledge about athletic safety equipment within the breadth and scope of its research and standards. Since the creation of the football helmet standard in the 1970s, NOCSAE has been involved in a number of other athletic equipment standards. The NOCSAE Baseball Batting Helmet Standard was published in 1981, and in 1983 was designated as the baseball/softball batting helmet standard. Manufacturers began making helmets that met the baseball/softball standard, and the NCAA and the NFHS baseball rules, youth baseball organizations, USA Baseball, American Softball Association, and others required the use of NOCSAE-standard baseball/softball batting helmets beginning in 1985. The NOCSAE seal, "Meets NOCSAE Standard," is also permanently stamped on the rear portion of each helmet. A standard for the lacrosse helmet and face mask was published by NOCSAE in 1986. There is also a NOCSAE standard for ice hockey helmets and face masks, polo helmets and helmet-mounted eye protection, and, starting in 2008, soccer shin guards. One of the latest NOCSAE standards specifies the performance limits of football players' gloves. All NOCSAE standards, proposed standards, and laboratory guides can be downloaded in PDF format on the NOCSAE web site, www.nocsae.org.

New or revised NOCSAE standards follow a two-phase process: (1) proposed status and (2) final status. A new or revised standard in proposed status is a formalized document with board approval for the purpose of obtaining written comments from manufacturers, governing bodies, and other interested parties. Each standard is held in proposed status for a minimum of one year. While in this status, the NOCSAE board encourages interested parties to provide comments related to the proposed standard. A standard is elevated

Image 10.1 Lacrosse Face-off
Photo courtesy of NC High School Athletic Association.

from proposed status to final status by board approval and becomes effective no sooner than one year after a vote for elevation.

In its effort to commission research, NOCSAE initiated an external funding program in 1994 and solicits grant proposals from all qualified investigators. The scope of the grants considered for funding include basic and/or applied research bearing a rational relationship toward increasing an understanding of sports injury mechanisms. Grants are funded based on scientific merit as ranked by a study section of national experts and on the priorities of the NOCSAE Board. Since the program's inception in 1994, NOCSAE has awarded nearly $4 million in research grants. Information concerning grant proposals and funding can be found on the NOCSAE web site, www.nocsae.org, or by contacting the research director.

The NOCSAE Board of Directors represents a wide variety of professional organizations. Following is a list of the current board members and the organization each represents:

- Kenneth Stephens, M.D., RPh, American College Health Association, NOCSAE President
- John Miller, M.D., American College Health Association
- Robert C. Cantu, M.D., American College of Sports Medicine, NOCSAE Vice President
- John Ryan, M.D., American Orthopaedic Society for Sports Medicine

- Grant Teaff, American Football Coaches Association
- Warren Howe, M.D., American Medical Society for Sports Medicine
- Alan Ansell, Athletic Equipment Managers Association
- Terry Schlatter, Athletic Equipment Managers Association, NOCSAE Treasurer
- Ray Cromwell, NAERA
- Ed Fisher, NAERA
- Randy Owsley, ATC, LAT, National Athletic Trainers Association, NOCSAE Secretary
- Michael Sims, AT, National Athletic Trainers Association
- Greg Hartley, Sporting Goods Manufacturers Association International
- Art Chow, Sporting Goods Manufacturers Association International
- Don Gleisner, Member at Large
- Donald Cooper, M.D., Member at Large

NOCSAE administrative personnel are as follows:

- Mike Oliver, Executive Director/Legal Counsel; Mike.Oliver@NOCSAE.org
- Frederick O. Mueller, Research Director; mueller@email.unc.edu
- David Halstead, Technical Director; daveh@soimpact.com

Additional information about NOCSAE can be found on its web site, www.NOCSAE.org.

References

1. Schneider RC: *Head and Neck Injuries in Football.* Baltimore, William and Wilkins, 1973.
2. Torg JS, Truex R, Quedenfeld TC, Burstein A, Spealman A, Nichols C: The National Football Head and Neck Injury Registry. *JAMA*, Vol. 241, No. 14, April 6, 1979.

Chapter 11

Risk Management Strategies for Football

On November 11, 1941 (Armistice Day), Weequahic High School played its inner-city rival, South Side High School in football. Both teams were located in Newark, New Jersey, and all of their home games were played in Newark's City Stadium. A large crowd attended the rivalry game, and several unexpected things happened that made the game memorable to all who were present. First, South Side came on the field, to the surprise of everyone, with brand-new plastic helmets. Weequahic's players were shocked and intimidated by the shiny, gold helmets because all teams were wearing leather helmets at the time, and no one expected what they saw that day. Second, and most important, Walter Eisele, an outstanding defensive halfback, received a hard blow to the head as he tackled a Weequahic runner and was knocked unconscious. He was taken by ambulance to a nearby hospital and died three days later from a cerebral hemorrhage. Eisele's death stunned the football players across the state of New Jersey. On the day after the fatal injury, a photo in the *Newark Star Ledger* showed Eisele making the tackle with his helmet turned sideways due to an improper fit. At that time, it appeared that coaches and equipment managers did not know how to properly fit the new helmets. Plastic was officially introduced as the major part of helmets in 1944 when West Point Academy (Army), led by running backs Doc Blanchard and Glenn Davis began using them. As a result, plastic helmets began to replace the leather helmet.

During the 1970s, a helmet crisis threatened the existence of football as a number of lawsuits increased against helmet manufacturers. In a book by Appenzeller and Appenzeller (1980), it was reported that there were 100 helmet-related cases with claims of over $200 million pending in the courts. As a result, manufacturers such as Spaulding, Wilson, Rawlings, Kelly, MaxPro, Bike and Hutch, and others decided not to produce football helmets, electing to concentrate on other equipment. In 1976, the first guidelines for helmet safety were adopted and they convinced helmet companies to stop producing football helmets. Twenty companies producing helmets dropped to the three today, Riddell,

Schutt, and Adams. At this critical time for football, the claims against helmet manufacturers suddenly shifted to litigation against the way coaches taught tackling and blocking, and several key court cases affected the coaching profession.

Richard Lester, general counsel for the Riddell Company, noted that defendants in lawsuits involving head injuries were the coaches who were now sued for improper instruction (Appenzeller 1985). Lester reported on the following two lawsuits:

1.   In July, 1981, in Portland, Oregon, a jury retained a verdict against the Oregon School Athletic Association for $1,800,000 in a case filed by a former high school football player who was paralyzed during a practice session.
2.   In February, 1982, a similar court case received national attention, *Thompson v. Seattle School District*, in which a jury found the coach negligent for failing to warn his players of the risk of playing football. The player who was rendered quadriplegic was awarded $6,400,000 for his injuries: the emphasis on helmet safety shifted to the athletic administrator, coach, and school district. No longer were the helmet manufacturers the main defendants in helmet-related injuries.

In 1980, the National Operating Committee on Standards for Athletic Equipment (NOCSAE) adopted warning language and recommended its use by all organizations in football. The warning was placed on a sticker on the back of a helmet, and each player was supposed to read it with coaches emphasizing the words of the warning and discussing the proper way to tackle and block under the rules of the game. The *Thompson* case had a tremendous effect on all who were associated with the sport of football and the proper technique of tackling and blocking to prevent concussions and catastrophic injuries (Appenzeller 1985).

Richard Lester suggested several strategies for all coaches and administrators, including:

•   Demonstrate that the coach is qualified by his education and experience.
•   Demonstrate that he has the knowledge of the football rules and accepted coaching techniques.
•   Demonstrate a continuing desire to keep abreast of rule changes, techniques that have been identified as injury producing.
•   Understand methods of administering emergency treatment to an injured player.

Lester emphasized the need for a coach to attend workshops, conferences, and clinics. He strongly recommended that a coach develop and maintain a library of books, videos, periodicals, and articles that identify current techniques of butt blocking, head tackling, and spearing as the leading causes of serious head and neck injuries in football (Appenzeller 1985).

Studies such as those by Dr. Frederick Mueller in 1976 "outlawed the use of the head as the initial point of contact in blocking and tackling." Because of these changes, the incidence of cervical fracture or dislocation injuries has been reduced by 50 percent (Appenzeller 1985).

Lester pointed out that a school must provide adequate protective equipment and make sure that the equipment fits properly. He noted that:

> Virtually all equipment manufacturers provide fitting and maintenance instructions with their helmets at the time of purchase and will provide additional copies of these instructions on request. Coaches should read and follow those instructions, distribute copies to each player and maintain a copy on file for periodic reference. In order for any helmet to perform its protective function, it must be properly fitted. (Appenzeller 1985)

Finally, Lester cautioned coaches who have a player who sustains a severe head injury to do the following:

- Keep the helmet, label it and isolate it. Never return it to practice.
- Preserve all game (and practice) films.
- Locate and preserve the records of purchase of the helmet, maintenance and reconditioning of the helmet.
- Notify the state association and the National Center for Catastrophic Sports Injury Research of the injury (Appenzeller 1985).

Developed in a time when sport risk management was in its infancy, Lester's strategies are still applicable today (Appenzeller 1985).

To address this crisis, the NOCSAE formulated safety standards for football helmets that became mandatory for colleges in 1978 and for high schools in 1980. The NOCSAE helmet was intended to decrease the number of head injuries in football and, hopefully, reduce the number of helmet-related lawsuits.

Other sport authorities believed that the injury problem could be reduced if coaches teach blocking and tackling using the shoulders instead of the head. One such authority is Dr. Frederick O. Mueller, who wrote: "over the years data regarding the number of football-related injuries has made important contributions to the safety of the participants." The American Football Coaches Association's data collection each year and subsequent evaluation of the injuries reportedly led to the change in the rules, equipment, coaching techniques, and other safety measures. These changes, according to Dr. Mueller, have led to a reduction of injuries from the sport of football. A prominent New York attorney reported that he settled helmet-related injury court cases for substantial amounts. In three cases in which the athletes were permanently crippled, the issue was not the construction or design of the helmet, but the technique of tackling taught by the coach. Kenneth Clarke, a sport safety expert cautions coaches to teach safe blocking and tackling technique if they are to avoid lawsuits. In 1980, Clarke predicted that helmet-related litigation would be predicated on the technique of blocking and tackling rather than the helmet itself. Those who followed helmet-related lawsuits from 1980 to 2009, saw Clarke's prediction come true (Appenzeller 1985).

Risk management entered the sports industry after years of existence in the insurance, business, and medical professions. Today, risk management has become a companion with sport law.

Importance of Risk Management

Defining sport risk management is not an easy task. Many risk management scholars and practitioners admit that its definition is complex, and at times, confusing. According to this writer, the following is a potential definition of sport risk management:

> a process that develops a comprehensive risk management plan designed to eliminate or minimize loss exposure for injuries to participants and spectators and limit or avoid financial loss. Sport risk management strategies need constant reevaluation, compliance with legal duties, and the responsibility to create a safe environment. (Appenzeller et al. 2008)

Dr. Annie Clement (2004), a sport risk management authority, believes liability can be controlled in four ways:

1. Accept the risk and assuming responsibility.
2. Retain the activity and transferring the risk through contracts and insurance.
3. Alter the activity to reduce the risk.
4. Eliminate the risk.

Each program is unique and needs a risk management plan tailored for the organization's individual needs.

Dr. Sarah Young commented on risk management when she wrote, "No longer will risk management be viewed as a necessary evil, rather it will be considered a management priority" (Appenzeller 2005).

Risk Management Strategies for Football

The following recommendations can help prevent situations that may lead to injuries and/or litigation:

- Require a thorough physical examination before the athlete engages in football practice. Consider a test for sickle cell disease for African American athletes.
- Assign someone to make certain that all equipment, especially the headgear, fits properly.
- Assign someone to inspect equipment for defects and the facilities for hazards. Keep an accurate record of each inspection. Check the helmets periodically for cracks and defects. Document the date of the inspection.
- Obtain medical insurance coverage for the athlete and liability insurance for the coaches and other staff members. Consider *per occurrence* insurance for adequate protection.
- Adopt a medical plan for emergency treatment for all athletes involved in physical contact or strenuous exercise.
- Assign drills within the athlete's range of ability and commensurate with size, skill, and physical condition.
- Prepare the athletes gradually for all physical drills and progress from simple to complex drills in strenuous and dangerous drills.
- Warn the athlete of all possible dangers inherent in the sport of football.
- Adopt a policy regarding injuries. Do not attempt to be a medical specialist in judging the physical condition of an athlete under your care.
- Require a physician's permission before permitting seriously injured or ill athletes to return to practice or game.
- Avoid moving the injured athlete until it is safe to do so. Whenever the athlete is moved, make certain he is taken away from potentially dangerous playing areas.
- Conduct periodic medical/legal in-service training for all personnel.
- Encourage all staff members to be certified in cardio pulmonary resuscitation (CPR), first aid, and automated external defibrillators (AED).

Risk management has become a vital part of the overall athletics programs, and football coaches should develop risk management strategies as they relate to their program.

Important risk strategies include the following:

- Avoid using terminology such as suicide drills, death run, and hamburger drills. These terms could come back to haunt you.

- In the event of an injury, always follow up with a call or visit to check on the athletes condition. However, never admit fault or assign blame for the injury.
- Isolate and keep under lock and key equipment involved in a serious injury (helmets, protective pads, etc.).
- Be aware that you can be sued, but don't panic. Be prepared and coach with confidence.

References

1. Appenzeller, H. 1985. *Sport and Law: Contemporary Issues.* Michie Law Publisher, Charlottesville, VA.
2. Appenzeller, H. 2005. *Risk Management in Sport: Issues and Strategies,* 2nd ed. Carolina Academic Press, Durham, NC.
3. Appenzeller, H. and Appenzeller, T. 1980. *Sports and the Courts.* Michie Law Publisher, Charlottesville, VA.
4. Appenzeller, H., Mueller, F., and Appenzeller, E. 2008. *Cheerleading and the Law.* Carolina Academic Press, Durham, NC.
5. Clement, A. 2004. *Law in Sport and Physical Activity,* 3rd ed. Sport and Law Press, Dania, FL.

Chapter 12

The Prevention of Catastrophic Head and Spine Injuries

Chapter 12 will emphasize the prevention of catastrophic football injuries and will make a number of safety recommendations to help reduce these injuries. It will also compare the incidence and rate of football catastrophic injuries to other high school and college sports, and make injury preventive recommendations for each individual sport.

The incidence of catastrophic injuries in sports at the high school and college levels is low, < 0.5 per 100,000 participants, but even one is too many (Mueller and Cantu 2008). Permanent paralysis, brain damage, and death should not be associated with teenagers and young adults participating in high school and college athletics. Catastrophic injury is devastating not only to the injured athlete but also to the athlete's family, school, and community. By utilizing proper data collection, medical care, and safety precautions such as implementing safer rules, proper conditioning, and coaching techniques, many of these injuries can be prevented.

While there are some sports with a higher incidence of catastrophic injury than others, there are also some sports with higher injury rates per 100,000 participants. For example, football has the greatest number of catastrophic injuries, but it also has the greatest number of participants. Gymnastics, ice hockey, and cheerleading each have higher rates per 100,000 participants than football, but fewer participants, and thus fewer total injuries. Table 12.1 gives the participation numbers for high school and college sports from the fall of 1982 through the spring of 2008, and Table 12.2 gives injury rates per 100,000 participants.

Emphasis should be placed on the fact that no matter how low the incidence levels or rates per number of participants, an increased effort should be placed on prevention of catastrophic injuries.

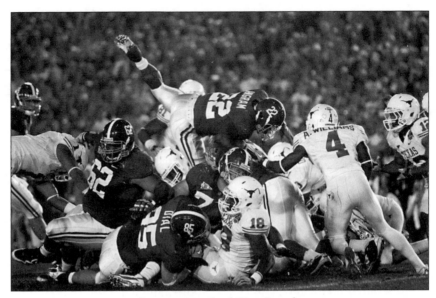

Image 12.1 Goal Line Stand
Photo courtesy of NCAA.

Methods

The collection of football fatality data began in 1931, when the American Football Coaches Association (AFCA) initiated the first Annual Survey of Football Fatalities (Mueller and Diehl 2000). The research has been carried out on a national level every year except for 1942 and has been conducted at the University of North Carolina, Chapel Hill, since 1965. The title of the survey was changed in 1980 to the Annual Survey of Football Injury Research. The primary purpose of the research was, and still is, to make the game of football a safer and, therefore, a more enjoyable sport.

As a result of these surveys, the game of football has realized many benefits with regard to rule changes and improved equipment, medical care, and coaching techniques. The survey was expanded in 1977 to include neck injuries with permanent disability and again in 1984 to include brain injuries with permanent disability. The annual survey is today known as the Annual Survey of Catastrophic Football Injuries (Mueller and Cantu 2000). Data collection was expanded again in 1982 to include all sports at the high school and collegiate levels, and a National Center for Catastrophic Sports Injury Research (NCCSIR) was established. This expansion was related to the lack of catastrophic injury data in sports other than football, the expansion of female sports and female participation due to Title IX, and the dearth of female sport injury data.

The term *catastrophic injury* is defined as any severe injury incurred during participation in a school- or college-sponsored sport. Catastrophic injuries are categorized as follows:

- Fatal
- Nonfatal: permanent, severe, neurological functional disability
- Serious: no permanent functional disability but severe injury, for example, a fractured cervical vertebra without paralysis

Sport-related injuries are also considered direct or indirect.

- Direct: injuries resulting directly from participation in the skills of the sport
- Indirect: injuries caused by systematic failure as a result of exertion while participating in a sport activity or by a complication secondary to a nonfatal injury

Only direct injuries will be discussed in this chapter.

Data were compiled with the assistance of coaches, athletes, trainers, athletic directors, executive officers of state and national athletic organizations, a national newspaper clipping service, and professional associates of the researchers. The National Collegiate Athletic Association (NCAA), National Federation of State High School Associations (NFHS), and AFCA also assisted in data collection. On receiving information concerning a possible catastrophic sports injury, contact by telephone, personal letter, and questionnaire was made with the injured player's coach or athletic director. Data collected included background information on the athlete (age, height, weight, experience, previous injury, etc.), accident information, immediate and postaccident medical care, type of injury, and equipment involved. Autopsy reports were used when available. Data were collected as close to the time of the injury as possible; however as with any surveillance system, some cases were studied much later. Occasionally, a catastrophic injury is not detected until several years after the event. Furthermore, it is impossible to guarantee that every case is identified by the catastrophic surveillance system; infrequently, a case may be missed. However, every effort is made to identify injured athletes. The system is publicized within the sports medicine community and is supported by the NCAA, the NFHS, and the AFCA. The use of a national press clipping service provides a timely and economic mechanism for case identification.

In 1987, a joint endeavor was initiated with the Section on Sports Medicine of the American Association of Neurological Surgeons and its then chairman, Dr. Cantu. The purpose of this collaboration was to enhance the collection of

Table 12.1 Participation Figures 1982–83 Through 2007–08

Sport	High School		College	
	Men	Women	Men	Women
Baseball	10,916,754	23,517	616,947	0
Basketball	13,796,973	11,041,039	374,600	328,237
Cross-country	4,546,218	3,486,467	275,202	235,937
Equestrian	621 (2004–07)	4,322 (2004–07)	1,268 (2003–07)	6,245 (2003–07)
Field Hockey	2,781	1,431,676	0	145,133
Football	35,623,701	17,872	1,929,069	0
Golf	480,989 (2005–08)	199,721 (2005–08)	24,844 (2005–08)	12,197 (2005–08)
Gymnastics	98,169	637,467	15,298	38,775
Ice Hockey	722,874	72,537	99,626	17,309
Lacrosse	858,712	586,973	151,309	106,153
Rowing	16,147 (2001–07)	17,111 (2001–07)	14,107 (2001–07)	47,310 (2001–07)
Skiing	154,979 (1994–2007)	131,660 (1994–2007)	16,923	15,052
Soccer	7,175,341	5,184,875	429,603	321,982
Softball	29,743	8,141,827	0	322,777
Swimming	2,242,814	2,919,225	203,271	231,394
Tennis	3,677,132	3,832,588	199,274	203,695
Track	13,266,497	10,747,774	933,764	728,059
Volleyball	536,747 (1994–2007)	5,364,475 (1994–2007)	15,391 (1994–2007)	182,530 (1994–2007)
Water Polo	220,778	180,126	25,543	10,266 (1998–2007)
Wrestling	6,235,016	46,361	175,353	0
TOTAL	100,602,986	54,067,623	5,501,432	2,953,051

medical data. He has been responsible for contacting physicians involved in each case and collecting the medical data.

Discussion

An analysis of the data from all catastrophic injuries from all sports participated in by males and females at the high school and college level allows for

Table 12.2 Direct Injuries per 100,000 Participants

Sport	High School						College					
	Men			Women			Men			Women		
	F	NF	S	F	NF	S	F	NF	S	F	NF	S
Baseball	0.09	0.16	0.20	0.00	0.00	0.00	0.49	0.65	0.81	0.00	0.00	0.31
Basketball	0.01	0.03	0.07	0.00	0.01	0.03	0.27	0.53	1.60	0.00	0.00	0.00
Cross-country	0.00	0.02	0.00	0.00	0.00	0.00	0.00	0.00	0.00	0.00	0.00	0.00
Equestrian	—	—	—	—	—	—	—	—	—	16.01	0.00	0.00
Field Hockey	—	—	—	0.00	0.21	0.00	0.00	0.00	0.00	0.00	0.69	1.38
Football	0.29	0.75	0.74	0.00	0.00	0.00	0.47	1.81	4.98	0.00	0.00	0.00
Golf	0.00	0.00	0.00	0.00	0.00	0.00	0.00	0.00	0.00	0.00	0.00	0.00
Gymnastics	1.02	2.04	1.02	0.00	0.94	0.47	0.00	19.61	6.54	0.00	5.16	0.00
Ice Hockey	0.28	0.97	1.11	0.00	0.00	2.76	0.00	4.02	7.03	0.00	0.00	5.77
Lacrosse	0.23	0.47	0.58	0.00	0.00	0.17	2.64	1.98	1.32	0.00	1.88	0.00
Rowing	0.00	0.00	0.00	0.00	0.00	0.00	0.00	0.00	0.00	0.00	0.00	0.00
Skiing	—	—	—	—	—	—	0.00	0.00	0.00	6.64	0.00	0.00
Soccer	0.10	0.03	0.08	0.00	0.02	0.02	0.00	0.00	0.00	0.00	0.31	0.00
Softball	—	—	—	0.01	0.03	0.01	—	—	—	0.00	0.00	0.31
Swimming	0.00	0.22	0.13	0.00	0.14	0.03	0.00	0.49	0.00	0.00	0.00	0.00
Tennis	0.00	0.00	0.00	0.00	0.00	0.00	0.00	0.00	0.00	0.00	0.00	0.00
Track	0.15	0.11	0.14	0.01	0.01	0.06	0.32	0.32	0.32	0.00	0.14	0.00
Volleyball	—	—	—	0.00	0.02	0.00	0.00	0.00	0.00	0.00	0.00	0.00
Water Polo	—	—	—	—	—	—	0.00	0.00	0.00	—	—	—
Wrestling	0.03	0.58	0.32	0.00	0.00	0.00	0.00	0.57	0.00	0.00	0.00	0.00

F = Fatal
NF = Nonfatal
S = Serious
— = No Data for That Time Period

both general and sport-specific recommendations for catastrophic sports injury prevention. General recommendations include the following.

Preparticipation Examinations

- Mandatory medical examinations and medical history should be taken before an athlete is allowed to participate. Included should be a detailed history of all prior head or spine injuries on or off the athletic field. Any athlete with residual symptoms or signs of a prior brain or spinal cord injury should be precluded from athletic participation in a collision sport. The NCAA recommends a thorough medical examination when the athlete first enters the college athletic program and an annual health history update with the use of referral exams when warranted (NCAA 2009). This initial evaluation should include a comprehensive health history, immunization history as defined by the current Centers for Disease Control and Prevention guidelines, an a relevant physical exam, part of which should include an orthopedic and neurologic evaluation.

- High schools should follow the recommendations set by their state high school athletic associations. If there are no set recommendations, the NCAA guidelines are appropriate.
- If the physician or coach has any questions about the readiness of an athlete, the athlete should not be allowed to participate.

Proper Conditioning

- All personnel concerned with training athletes should emphasize proper, gradual, and complete physical conditioning. Adequate conditioning includes cardiovascular conditioning and development of muscular strength and flexibility.
- An important area of muscular strength development is the muscles of the neck. Neck muscles should be strengthened and players should be educated concerning risk of neck injuries.

Medical Care

- Medical coverage of both practice and game situations is important. Certified athletic trainers can provide good medical coverage, but a physician should be on call for practices and possibly present at games. More than half of the catastrophic injuries occur in games, and a physician on site would be advantageous. Written emergency procedures should be prepared in advance.
- An athlete who has experienced or shown signs of head trauma (loss of consciousness, visual disturbances, headache, inability to walk correctly, obvious disorientation, memory loss) should receive immediate medical attention and should not be allowed to play without permission from the proper medical authorities.
- Emergency plans in case of a catastrophic injury should be written and distributed to all personnel involved with the program. Personnel will include but not be limited to, the head coach, assistant coaches, managers, athletic trainers, and physicians. Players should also be made aware of emergency procedures. If everyone understands his or her responsibility in the event of a catastrophic injury, the chances of permanent disability may be reduced.

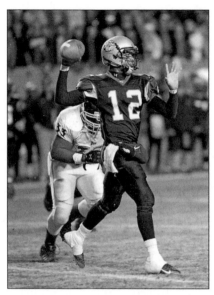

Image 12.2 Head Down Tackle
Photo courtesy of NCAA.

- Each institution should strive to have a team trainer who is a regular member of the faculty and is adequately prepared and qualified. Trainers certified by the National Athletic Trainers Association (NATA) are preferred.
- Coaches should never be involved in making medical decisions concerning athletes, and only medical personnel should decide if and when an athlete returns to play after an injury or illness.
- Cooperation should be maintained by all groups interested in the field of athletic medicine (coaches, trainers, physicians, manufacturers, and administrators).

Proper Training of Coaches

- It is imperative to hire coaches with the ability and expertise to teach the proper fundamental skills of the game.
- Competent coaching in athletics is a major area of concern. High schools are having a difficult time employing coaches who are full time faculty members, and in many cases have to hire part time coaches. This is not a problem if these coaches know the fundamental skills of the sport and have the ability to teach these skills to the participants. Improper teach-

ing of sport skills can be a direct cause of injuries—both catastrophic and others.

- In some sports, coaching certificates are available. Coaches in these sports should be certified. In addition, a small number of states require that their high school coaches have a coaching certification. This is a step in the right direction and should receive increased emphasis.
- There should be emphasis on providing excellent facilities and securing the safest and best equipment possible.

Supporting Referees' Decisions

- There should be strict enforcement of game rules, and administrative regulations should be enforced to protect the health of the athlete. Coaches and school officials must support the game officials in their decisions during sports events. Strict enforcement of the rules of the game by both coaches and officials will help reduce catastrophic injuries.
- Officiating is also important when discussing injury prevention. Quality officials can spot dangerous situations during a game or match, and can stop the activity before it results in a serious or catastrophic injury.

Sport-specific Recommendation

Football

- Rule changes initiated for the 1976 football season that eliminated the use of the head and face as the initial contact area for blocking and tackling are of the utmost importance. Coaches should continue to emphasize and teach the proper fundamentals of blocking and tackling to help reduce catastrophic head and neck injuries. Both present and past data show that poorly executed tackling and blocking are the major causes of cervical spine injuries, not the football helmet. *Shoulder block and tackle with the head up—keep the head out of football.*
- The use of the helmet face mask in making initial contact is illegal, and should be called for a penalty. If more of these penalties are called, there is no doubt that both coaches and players will get the message and discontinue this type of play.
- There should be continued research concerning the safety factor in football (rules, facilities, equipment, etc.).
- Players should be taught to respect the football helmet as a protective device, and that it should not be used as a weapon.
- Coaches, trainers, and physicians should take special care to see that the players' equipment is properly fitted, particularly the helmet.

Image 12.3 Head Tackle from Behind
Photo courtesy of NCAA.

Soccer

The main problems in soccer catastrophic injuries in adults have been head collisions in the act of heading the ball. In youth soccer, it has been goals falling on the participants or children climbing on the goals (K&K Insurance 1993).

- Keep soccer goals supervised and anchored.
- Never permit hanging or climbing on a soccer goal.
- Always stand to the rear or side of the goal when moving it, *never* to the front.
- Stabilize the goal as best suits the playing surface, but in a manner that does not create other hazards to players.
- Develop and follow a plan for periodic inspection and maintenance (e.g., dry rot, joints, and hooks).
- Advise all field maintenance persons to reanchor the goal if moved for mowing the grass or other purposes.
- Remove goals from fields no longer in use for the soccer program as the season progresses.

- Secure goals well against unauthorized access when stored.
- Educate and remind all players and adult supervisors about the past tragedies of soccer goal fatalities.

Basketball

Direct fatalities and catastrophic injuries at both the high school and college levels are minimal. This means that the injuries should continue to be monitored and that the present rules and safety measures should be enforced.

Ice Hockey

Ice hockey injuries are low in number, but the injury rates per 100,000 participants are high when compared with other sports, both at the high school and college levels. Ice hockey catastrophic injuries usually occur when the athlete is struck from behind by an opponent, slides head first into the boards surrounding the rink, and makes contact with the top or crown of the head. Resulting injuries are usually fractured cervical vertebrae with paralysis. Both head and cervical spine injury rates are high per 100,000 participants (Table 12.2) (Wennberg et al. 2008). Research in Canada has revealed high catastrophic injury rates with similar results. After an in-depth study of ice hockey catastrophic injuries in Canada, Dr. Charles Tator et al. (1984) have made the following recommendations concerning prevention:

- Enforce current rules and consider new rules against pushing, or checking from behind.
- Continue epidemiological research in injury data collection, equipment, and rink construction.
- Educate players concerning the risk of neck injuries related to rule violations.

Baseball

Catastrophic injuries in high school and college baseball usually happen in one of the following three ways:

1. The athlete is hit by either a thrown or batted ball, resulting in a serious head injury or a chest impact death.
2. The athlete collides with a teammate while chasing a fly ball, resulting in a serious head or neck injury. Collisions usually involve an infielder and an outfielder or two outfielders chasing the same fly ball.
3. The athlete uses the head first slide and makes contact with the top or crown of the head and the opposing player's lower body or the base.

This type of injury usually results in fractured cervical vertebrae with possible paralysis.

The catastrophic injury rate per 100,000 participants is low for both high school and college baseball programs. Proper preventive measures can be implemented to further reduce the chance of catastrophic injuries in baseball including:

- Coaches should teach the proper skills of the head-first slide if it is going to be used. Players should be warned that, if not properly executed, the head-first slide can result in serious injuries.
- It should be made mandatory for all players to wear batting helmets in practice as well as in game situations. Batting practice pitchers should wear protective helmets. Coaches should not be exempt from this rule. Proper fitting of the helmets should be stressed.
- Student managers and nonplayers should be required to wear protective helmets when on the field.
- Protective screens should be used to protect the batting practice pitchers and other players who may be involved in other activities during batting practice. Coaches should not be exempt from this rule.
- Strategies that can and should be used when two players from the same team are chasing a fly ball should be discussed and taught.

Lacrosse

Lacrosse has not been associated with a great number of catastrophic injuries over the years, but the participation figures are low at both the high school and college levels, which make the injury rate higher in lacrosse when compared with other sports. This is especially true at the college level. To reduce the number of catastrophic injuries the following is recommended:

- Injury research at both the high school and college levels is essential. At the present time there is a lack of good injury research in lacrosse.
- Current rules which make it illegal to use the head in contact should be enforced.
- Research in the type of equipment that is mandatory for lacrosse players should be continued.
- Coaching certification for coaches is important in a sport like lacrosse that involves many skills and body contact.
- Women's lacrosse is changing rapidly and in some instances is influenced by the men's game. Decisions on rule and equipment changes should be based on safety concerns and the results of adequate injury data.

Image 12.4 Dangerous Head Down Contact
Photo courtesy of NFHS.

Gymnastics

It is important to mention that with such a small number of catastrophic injuries in gymnastics, it is difficult to make safety recommendations based on the data. However, as in all sports, there are safety recommendations that should be followed. We support the following recommendations of the U.S. Gymnastics Federation.

- Athletes should be made aware of the risks involved in gymnastics, and that there is a possibility of catastrophic injury, paralysis, and death.
- A gymnast should never participate in gymnastics activity without competent supervision.
- Athletes should dress appropriately, follow accepted warm-up practices, and be mentally prepared to engage in activity.
- Before activity, make sure the equipment is adjusted and secured properly and that adequate matting appropriate to the activity is in the correct position.
- Gymnastics is an activity requiring active concentration. Horseplay or any form of carelessness cannot be tolerated at any time for any reason.
- A safe learning environment includes a correct understanding of the skill being performed and following proper skill progressions.

- Safe learning practices demand mastering basic skills before progressing to new or more difficult skills.
- The readiness and ability level of the athlete, the nature of the task, and the competency of the spotter all must be taken into consideration when attempting a new or difficult skill.
- Safe dismounts, as well as unintentional falls, require proper landing techniques. No amount of matting can be fail-safe. Avoid landing on head or neck at all costs, as serious catastrophic injuries may result (George 1985).

Rugby

In the United States, rugby is a club sport and thus injury statistics are incomplete. From international experience, the incidence of catastrophic injury to especially the cervical spine is high with most injuries occurring in the scrum or in the act of tackling (Brooks and Hemp 2008; Fuller et al. 2007). Fortunately there is some evidence these injuries may be on the decline (Bohu et al. 2009).

Swimming

A recent advertisement from a company that manufactures starting blocks also included a warning notice. This notice stated that since the development of the pike dive, competitive swimmers have sustained serious cervical injuries resulting in quadriplegia. It continues by strongly recommending that starting blocks not be used for deep entry into the water until the pool depth has been determined.

It is apparent that, because all of the catastrophic injuries follow the same etiology, the recommendations for prevention will focus on the racing dive.

- If possible, the starting blocks should be moved to the deep end of the pool.
- The proper fundamental skills needed for a successful dive must be taught if the pike dive is to be used as a racing start.
- Swimmers must be warned concerning the possibility of catastrophic injury when using the pike dive in the shallow end of the pool.
- All involved should be knowledgeable concerning the NFHS rules governing the racing dive and water depth. These rules state that in 4 or more feet of water, the swimmers may use a starting platform up to a maximum of 30 inches above the water. With a water depth of between 3.5 and 4 feet, swimmers may start no higher than 18 inches above the water. With less than 3.5 feet of water, the swimmers must start the race in the pool. These rules are being monitored, and a research project concerning a safe pool depth for the pike dive is in progress.

- A plan should be developed to be prepared for a catastrophic injury situation. All staff members and swimmers should be aware of this plan and of their role in carrying out their duties.

Wrestling

While catastrophic wrestling injuries can occur at higher levels (Kordi et al. 2008), the great preponderance in our experience occur at the high school level. Prevention of wrestling catastrophic injuries includes:

- Proper supervision at both practice and matches is important. Any activity that is potentially dangerous should be stopped immediately.
- Good-quality mats and knowledge of how they are set up for both practices and matches is crucial.
- Competent coaching in a sport like wrestling is a major area of concern. Improper teaching of the skills of wrestling can be the direct cause of catastrophic injuries.
- Quality officials can spot dangerous holds and can stop the activity before it results in a serious or catastrophic injury.
- Most catastrophic neck injuries occur in a take-down in which the downed wrestler's head is pile driven into the mat.

Track and Field

The pole vault has been associated with the majority of catastrophic injuries, while injuries from being hit during the throwing events ranked second. There is no excuse for someone being hit with a shot put, discus, hammer, or javelin. All of these injuries are preventable.

The rule changes that the NFHS Track and Field Rules Committee adopted include:

- Rule 7-4-3 that states the vaulter's weight shall be at or below the manufacturer's pole rating, and that the manufacturer's pole rating shall be visible in a one-inch contrasting color. A vaulter using an illegal pole shall be immediately disqualified from an event.
- Rule 7-4-15 allows the crossbar to be moved a maximum of 30 inches in the direction of the landing surface. The previous rule limited the distance to 24 in. This change will allow the bar to be moved deeper in the landing pad, which will allow vaulters to penetrate further back on the landing mat.
- Rule 7-4-7 recommends that concrete, metal, wood, or asphalt surfaces that extend out from under the landing pad be cut away and removed.

If this is not possible, these hard surfaces should be padded with a minimum of two inches of dense foam or suitable material.

The NFHS also recommends the following safety recommendations for the pole vault:

- Landing pads should be maintained, reconditioned, or replaced if they lose their density or load capabilities.
- Proper supervision should be provided at all times. A vaulter should not be allowed to vault alone.
- By rule, all exposed projections on the base of the standards of uprights must be padded or covered. Adjustment knobs should be located on the outside of the standards.
- By rule, the base of the standards must be anchored to minimize the possibility of a displaced crossbar or released vaulting pole knocking a standard into the landing pit.
- Only a nonmetal, circular crossbar should be used.
- Vaulting poles should be constantly inspected for cracks or dents, which can reduce the original stress level of the pole.
- Special clinics emphasizing safety procedures and appropriate teaching techniques should be offered for coaches who do not have a strong background in vaulting.
- Pole vaulters need a significant amount of diversified conditioning before they are allowed to vault for height.
- Coaches should emphasize how the vaulter arrives at the decision to abort a vault that may or may not get into the landing pad.
- The first rule for terminating an attempt after becoming airborne is to hang onto the pole and look for a safe place to land, then release the pole if over the landing pad, or ride the pole to the safest landing area.
- If smaller or minimum landing pads are in use, caution should be urged where 14-foot poles or less are used.
- The space between the stop board and landing pad should be covered by wrestling mat material or similar padded material.
- Correct alignment and safe pole penetration is urged at all times.
- With a large bend and deep penetration, a stronger pole should be used. With a small bend and deep penetration, a higher grip, not to exceed limitations, should be used. With a large bend and poor penetration, a lower grip should be used. With a small bend and poor penetration, a softer pole, not below the body weight, should be used. (A large bend would be defined as 90° or more.)

Cheerleading

The NCCSIR has been collecting cheerleading catastrophic injury data for the past 26 years, 1982–83 through 2007–08. During this time, cheerleading has changed dramatically and now serves two distinctive purposes: (1) as a service-oriented leader of cheer on the sideline, and (2) as a highly skilled competitive sport. High school cheerleading accounts for 62.5% of all catastrophic injuries to female athletes. Being a flier in cheerleading is the most risky position of catastrophic injury in all sports. A number of schools, both high schools and colleges, across the country, have limited the types of stunts that can be attempted by their cheerleaders. Rules and safety guidelines now apply to both practices and competition. Inexperienced and untrained coaches should not attempt to teach stunts with a higher level of difficulty than their team is capable of achieving or beyond the knowledge and ability they have to teach.

A basic question that has to be asked is, what is the role of the cheerleader? Approximately 20–25 states have a state championship for competitive cheer and it is not clear how many states consider cheerleading a sport. The 2007–08 high school participation survey for competitive spirit squads shows 111,307 females. There were also 2,673 male cheerleaders. The NFHS had a news release on May 21, 2009, that stated there were approximately 400,000 individuals participating in high school cheerleading. The release stated that the 400,000 included freshman, junior varsity, and varsity levels. The release did not distinguish between the numbers of males and females. There are 18,922 high schools in the 51 member associations, and the new participation number translates to an average of 21 cheerleaders per school. Past participation numbers only included competitive cheer groups (113,980 males and females in 2007–08). College participation numbers are hard to find since cheerleading is not an NCAA sport.

We question why it is called "cheerleading" when competitive cheer has nothing to do with leading the crowds at athletic events in cheering for the athletic teams on the playing field. Following are a list of sample guidelines that may help prevent cheerleading injuries:

- Cheerleaders should have medical examinations before they are allowed to participate. Included would be a complete medical history.
- Cheerleaders should be trained by a qualified coach with training in gymnastics and *partner stunting*. This person should also be trained in the proper methods for spotting and other safety factors.
- Cheerleaders should be exposed to proper conditioning programs and trained in proper spotting techniques.
- Cheerleaders should receive proper training before attempting gymnastics and partner-type stunts, and should not attempt stunts they are not

capable of completing. A qualification system demonstrating mastery of stunts is recommended.

- Coaches should supervise all practice sessions in a safe facility.
- Mini-trampolines and flips or falls off of pyramids and shoulders should be prohibited.
- Pyramids over two high should not be performed. Two-high pyramids should not be performed without mats and other safety precautions.
- If it is not possible to have a physician or certified athletic trainer at games and practice sessions, emergency procedures must be provided. The emergency procedure should be in writing and available to all staff and athletes.
- There should be continued research concerning safety in cheerleading.
- When a cheerleader has experienced or shown signs of head trauma (loss of consciousness, visual disturbances, headache, inability to walk correctly, obvious disorientation, memory loss), she/he should receive immediate medical attention and should not be allowed to practice or cheer without permission from the proper medical authorities.
- Cheerleading coaches should have some type of safety certification. The American Association of Cheerleading Coaches and Advisors offers this certification.
- The NFHS should make cheerleading a sport, which will place cheerleading under the same restrictions and safety rules as all other high school sports. The NCAA should follow this same recommendation.

According to the NFHS, a primary purpose of sideline spirit groups (dance, pom, drill, or cheer) is to serve as support groups for the interscholastic athletic programs within the school. A primary purpose for competitive spirit groups is to represent the school in organized competition. In January 1993, 18 rule revisions were adopted for spirit groups. One of the major rules prohibits tumbling over, under, or through anything (people or equipment). All of the other rules were adopted to enhance the safety of the participants. Today, emphasis is placed not only on the stunting athlete but also on the base athlete and the spotter. Proper conditioning and attentiveness will help minimize the risk involved in a competition. Information concerning these new rules and updates are available from the NFHS in Indianapolis,Indiana.

Conclusion

Catastrophic head and spine injuries may never be totally eliminated from sport, but with reliable injury data collection systems and constant attention to prevention measures, the frequency of these injuries can be dramatically reduced. Data from the NCCSIR have played a major role in helping to reduce the incidence of these catastrophic injuries. This chapter identifies the mechanism of these injuries as well as general and sport-specific prevention recommendations to minimize their occurrence.

References

1. Bohu Y, Julia M, Bagate C, Peyrin JC, Colonna JP, Thoreau P, Pascal-Moussellard H. Declining incidence of catastrophic cervical spine injuries in French rugby 1996–2006. *Am J Sports Med* 2009; 37: 319–323.
2. Brooks JH, Kemp SP. Recent trends in rugby union injuries. *Clin J Sports Med* 2008; 27: 51–73.
3. Fuller CW, Brooks JH, Kemp SP. Spinal injuries in professional rugby union: a prospective cohort study. *Clin J Sport Med* 2007; 17: 515–6.
4. George GS. USGF gymnastics safety manual. Indianapolis: USGF Publications Dept.; 1985.
5. K&K Insurance Group. Loss Bulletin, Soccer Injuries. Fort Wayne, IN; 1993.
6. Kordi R, Akbarnejad A, Wallace AW. Catastrophic injuries in the Olympic styles of wrestling in Iran. *Br J Sports Med* 2008; [epub ahead of print].
7. Mueller FO, Cantu RC. Annual Survey of Catastrophic Football Injuries, 1977–1999. Overland Park, KS; National Collegiate Athletic Association; 2000: 1–21.
8. Mueller FO, Cantu RC. Catastrophic Sports Injury Research Twenty-Sixth Annual Report Fall 1982–Spring 2008. www.unc.edu/depts/nccsi.
9. Mueller FO, Diehl JL. Annual Survey of Football Injury Research, 1931–1999. Chapel Hill, NC; American Football Coaches Association, National Collegiate Athletic Association, National Federation of State High School Associations; 2000: 1–27.
10. National Collegiate Athletic Association. 2009–10 NCAA sports medicine handbook. 22nd ed. Overland Park, KS; 2009.
11. Tator CH, et al. National survey of spinal injuries in hockey players. *Can Med Assoc J* April 1, 1984; 30.
12. Wennberg RA, Cohen HB, Walker SR. Neurologic injuries in hockey. *Neurol Clin* 2008; 26: 243–255.

About the Authors

Frederick O. Mueller, Ph.D. is professor emeritus in the Department of Exercise and Sport Science at the University of North Carolina at Chapel Hill. He has been at the University of North Carolina for 44 years. He is also the Director of the National Center for Catastrophic Sports Injury Research—a national data base collecting fatality and catastrophic sports injuries on a national level for the National Federation of State High Schools Association and the National Collegiate Athletic Association. Annual reports cover football fatalities from 1931, catastrophic football injuries from 1977, and all sport fatalities and catastrophic injuries from 1982. All reports are on the web site www.unc.edu/depts/nccsi. He is also Chair of the USA Baseball Medical/Safety Advisory Committee and the Research Director of the National Operating Committee on Standards for Athletic Equipment (NOCSAE).

Robert C. Cantu, M.A., M.D., F.A.C.S., F.A.C.S.M. Currently Dr. Cantu's professional responsibilities include those of Clinical Professor Department of Neurosurgery and Co-Director Center for the Study of Traumatic Encephalopathy, Boston University School of Medicine, Boston, MA; Senior Advisor to the NFL Head, Neck and Spine Committee; second opinion expert on head and spine conditions for the NLFPA; member of the Mackey/White TBI Committee for the NFLPA; Founding member and Chairman Medical Advisory Board Sports Legacy Institute, Waltham, MA; Adjunct Professor Exercise and Sport Science and Medical Director National Center for Catastrophic Sports Injury Research, University of North Carolina, Chapel Hill, an ongoing registry instituted in 1982 for data collection and analysis of spine and head injuries, Chapel Hill, NC; Co-Director, Neurologic Sports Injury Center, Brigham and Women's Hospital, Boston; Chief of Neurosurgery Service, Chairman Department of Surgery, and Director of Sports Medicine at Emerson Hospital in Concord, Massachusetts. He also serves on the Board of Trustees as Vice President of NOCSAE (National Operating Committee on Standards for Athletic Equipment). Dr. Cantu also is Co-Director of the Neurological Sports Injury Center at Brigham and Women's Hospital in Boston, MA. and Neurosurgical Consultant Boston Eagles football team, and Neurosurgical Consultant Boston Cannons professional soccer team. Dr. Cantu also consults with numerous NFL, NHL and NBA teams.

He has authored over 340 scientific publications, including 23 books on neurology and sports medicine, in addition to numerous book chapters, peer-reviewed papers, abstracts and free communications, and educational videos. He has served as associate editor of *Medicine and Science in Sports and Exercise* and *Exercise and Sports Science Review,* and on the editorial board of *The Physician and Sports Medicine, Clinical Journal of Sports Medicine,* and *Journal of Athletic Training.* In 2003 Dr. Cantu became the section head for the Sports Medicine Section of Neurosurgery.

Index

Note: *f* indicates a figure, *g* a graph, *i* an image, and *t* a table.